AF560583

Indian Booker Prize Winners

A Critical Study of Their Works

Volume – I

Edited by
Sunita Sinha

Published by

ATLANTIC

PUBLISHERS & DISTRIBUTORS (P) LTD

7/22, Ansari Road, Darya Ganj,
New Delhi-110002
Phones : +91-11-40775252, 23273880, 23275880, 23280451
Fax : +91-11-23285873
Web : www.atlanticbooks.com
E-mail : orders@atlanticbooks.com

Branch Office
5, Nallathambi Street, Wallajah Road,
Chennai-600002
Phones : +91-44-64611085, 32413319
E-mail : chennai@atlanticbooks.com

© 2010 Sunita Sinha for selection and editorial matter;
the contributors for individual articles

ISBN 978-81-269-1482-1 (Vol. I)
ISBN 978-81-269-1483-8 (Set)

All rights reserved. No part of this publication may be reproduced, stored in a retrieval system, transmitted or utilized in any form or by any means, electronic, mechanical, photocopying, recording or otherwise, without the prior permission of the copyright owner. Application for such permission should be addressed to the publisher.

Printed in India at Nice Printing Press,

Dedicated to my grandfather,
Late Dr. R.K. Sinha M.A. (Pat.), D. Phil (Oxon),
Professor Emeritus, Head,
Department of English,
Patna University

Preface

The Man Booker is, by common consent, the most prestigious and the highest profile prize awarded each year for the best original full-length novel, written in English, by a citizen of the British Commonwealth or the Republic of Ireland. Unlike the Nobel Prize, the booker focuses on a particular novel rather than a particular author, and unlike the Pulitzer Prize, it is associated with England and the Commonwealth rather than with USA.

The Booker holds the key to both commercial and critical success, and is therefore construed as an effective weapon in the book marketer's armoury and as such, it is one of the mighty engines of the 21st-century book trade. Hence, the Booker Prize winner is considered "a signifier of marketplace success, a definition of literary value and a self-reflexive act in which the books Booker chooses actively construct what is meant by Bookers". It seeks to confer literary recognition on novels that are winners and attend to the novel as a form and medium for new voices, styles and cultures.

India has been consistently producing award-winning authors or inspiring others to base their works on Indian colours, themes and identity. As a matter of fact, India's prominence in the brief history of Booker fiction is unquestionable. Just two years after the first ever Booker Prize was conferred in 1969, V.S. Naipaul—the Indian Trinidadian writing about the displaced ethnic Indians—was awarded the Booker for *In a Free State*. As many as three of the winning novels in the next seven years—though authored by non-Indians—were based on Anglo-Indian colonial experience, viz. *The Siege of Krishnapur* by J.G. Farrel (1973); *Heat and Dust* by Ruth Prawer Jhabvala (1975); and *Staying On* by Paul Scott

(1978). In the last 25 years, the prize has been bestowed on four Indians—Salman Rushdie in 1981 for *Midnight's Children*; Arundhati Roy in 1997 for *The God of Small Things*; Kiran Desai in 2006 for *The Inheritance of Loss*; and Aravind Adiga in 2008 for *The White Tiger*. In addition, diasporic Indian authors appear regularly in the shortlist for Booker.

Such achievement of literary distinction has drawn attention of reviewers and critics all over the world to Indian writing in English. In fact, as Aravind Adiga—the latest Indian star in the Booker's horizon—puts it:

> India just teems with untold stories, and no one who is alive to the poetry, the anger and the intelligence of Indian society, will ever run out of stories to write.

Not only has the readership of novels by Indian writers, particularly those experimenting with new ideas, themes and styles, swelled in Europe, India and elsewhere over the years, there is also a new wave of enthusiasm in literary circles for research, critical analysis and academic pursuits pertinent to English literature. The book *Indian Booker Prize Winners,* in two volumes, has been brought to sustain and to add to that fervour so that a ground is prepared for still higher achievements by Indian English writers. It will provide deeper insights into issues, emotions, themes and styles of the celebrated Indian Booker prize-winning novelists as exhibited in their works. It will immensely benefit students and teachers of English literature, particularly Indian English literature and the genre of fiction, and researchers in these fields.

Representing the combined efforts of erudite scholars in the field of English literature, the book is multivocal and inclusive. I am thankful to the legion of contributors who have worked hard to present their articles. I also wish to thank Dr. K.R. Gupta, Honorary Advisor, Atlantic Publishers and Distributors (P) Ltd. for the confidence evinced in me and for seeing the book through the press.

Sunita Sinha

Contents

Introduction

Literary prizes form a fascinating interface between literature and society as not only do these prizes result in an immediate boost in sales for that year's winner but they also result in an almost immediate canonization for a number of writers. The British have a prize-giving culture and they host some of the world's most prestigious prizes offered for writing in English. In 1968, a young editor at Jonathan Cape, Tom Maschler, successfully approached the agricultural and food company Booker Brothers, for sponsorship of an annual award intended to stimulate interest "in serious British fiction as a whole". Called the Booker, this remains by common consent the most prestigious and highest profile prize awarded each year for the best original full-length novel, written in the English language, by a citizen of either the Commonwealth of Nations or Ireland. The prize was initially named Booker McConnell Prize, after the company's full corporate name at the time. In 2002, Booker's new owners, The Icelandic Group, transferred administration of the prize to the Booker Prize Foundation. The Foundation sought out corporate sponsorship and received it from the investment group, Man. Currently, the official name of the prize is Man Booker, though colloquially it is still referred to as Booker Prize.

Unlike the Nobel Prize, the Booker focuses on a particular novel rather than on a particular author, and whereas the Nobel aims at rewarding "an ideal direction", the Booker aims at catching "the imagination of the press" by establishing an explicitly sporting-style atmosphere—a shortlist of authors, a high-profile panel of judges, and an exciting victor. Unlike the Pulitzer Prize, it is associated with England and Commonwealth rather than with the USA. Talking about the

Booker, Richard Todd, in his book, *Consuming Fictions*, aptly remarks, "English fiction has been invigorated by the pluralism that the Booker Prize pre-eminently has encouraged". Todd further celebrates the positive side effects of the otherwise money-generating colonial-inscribed institution of the Booker which has played a vital role in raising consciousness of the global dimensions of English language fiction, "[The] unprecedented exposure of fiction from English speaking countries other than the United Kingdom or the United States led to an increasingly global picture of fiction in Britain during the course of 1980s.... This reflects a new public awareness of Britain as a pluralist society and has transformed the view that prevailed in 1960s that English language fiction from 'abroad' meant fiction from the United States" (Todd 1996:83). Graham Huggan in his book, *The Postcolonial Exotic: Marketing the Margins* makes a relevant comment, "In a global cultural economy controlled by huge multinational companies, the corporate sponsorship of arts has become an indisputable fact. The corporate prize 'like the endowed chair' is a 'gift' that brings publicity to the company while functioning as a symbolic marker of 'authorising power'".

The Booker holds the key to both commercial and critical success and is therefore an effective weapon in the book marketer's armoury and we can easily say that as far as the 'quality' or 'literary' novel is concerned, the Booker is definitely one of the mighty engines of the 21st century book trade. Hence, a Booker Prize winner is "a signifier of marketplace success, a definition of literary value and a self-reflexive act in which the books Booker chooses actively construct what is meant by Booker". It seeks to confer literary recognition on novels that are winners and attend to the novel as a form and medium for new voices, styles and cultures.

Though also criticised for being unpredictable, arbitrary and unreliable, the Man Booker Prize has picked winners who have staying power and will surely endure. The Booker expresses a postcolonial response in which society is characterised by "the attempt to attain independence from the former coloniser and to establish hybridized identities separately from the formerly colonising culture". It can also be seen as "a post imperial response in which Great Britain refashions its own identity in post imperial terms".

Indian writing has traversed a long drawn path of restorative progress and has come of age. The Empire Writes Back—that's what the world said when a host of Indian authors writing in English burst upon the global literary scene more than a decade ago. Now, the Indian literary empire is conquering new territories and the Indian writers have successfully created a niche of their own in English, leaving an indelible mark on the global scene. In little over a decade, four Indians have prevailed over the competition to fetch home the bounty. In the wake of Aravind Adiga's glowing victory for his debut novel, *The White Tiger*, Thomas Abraham, President and CFO of Hachette Book Publishing India remarked, "What we all are very happy about is that we've reached a stage where abroad you are not counted as an 'Indian'...an Indian author is not an oddity that has to be given a quota of awards". If you track the Booker over the last seven years, there has always been an Indian connection—whether it was Yann Martel writing a book based on an Indian story, or Indian authors being shortlisted. Nandita Aggarwal, an editor at HarperCollins India, says, "As the world gets smaller, more and more people are getting interested in Indian writers."

The prominence of India in the brief history of Booker fiction is unquestionable. Two years after the first Booker Prize was conferred in 1969, V.S. Naipaul—the Indian Trinidadian writing about displaced ethnic Indians—was awarded the Booker for *In a Free State*. Though authored by non-Indians, three of the winning novels in the following seven years, were about the Anglo-Indian colonial experience—*The Siege of Krishnapur* by J.G. Farrell (1973), R.P. Jhabvala's *Heat and Dust* (1975), and Paul Scott's *Staying On* (1978). In the past twenty-five years, the prize has been awarded to four Indians—Salman Rushdie in 1981, Arundhati Roy in 1997, Kiran Desai in 2006 and most recently in 2008 to Aravind Adiga. In addition, diasporic Indian authors regularly appear on the shortlist that comes out several months before the prize is actually awarded. There are many more, and they're not "all peddling Indian exotica or the diaspora experience. Indian authors experimenting with new genres are also selling in the European market".

India first made a mark on the global literary map with Salman Rushdie's *Midnight's Children* in 1981. Interestingly, after the Booker picked a forgettable first winner—P.H. Newby's *Something to Answer For*, there was talk of cancelling it altogether during its first few years. The watershed, however, was undoubtedly 1981 when Salman Rushdie, the first India-born writer bagged it for his book, *Midnight's Children*. It was for the first year that the prize had live coverage on television and the first time that a truly controversial winner had emerged. Written in exuberant style, the comic allegory of Indian history revolves around the lives of the narrator Saleem Sinai and the 1000 children born after the Declaration of Independence. The book traces India's development from Independence and partition in 1947, through the secession of Bangladesh to the state of emergency under Indira Gandhi. The history of India is given phantasmagorical form by the novel's protagonist and narrator Saleem Sinai, a Hindu child raised by wealthy Muslims, who comes to believe that his own life is a metaphor for the state of his country. Saleem has decided to tell his life story and the story of India as he is, quite literally, falling apart, "I mean quite simply that I have begun to crack all over like an old jug". The children of the book's title are all born at midnight on the day India's Independence is declared and all of them have a special ability. Saleem's is telepathy and it is this gift which allows him to discover the truth about his own identity and those of the other children. Considered by many to be Rushdie's masterpiece, *Midnight's Children* is extraordinary for its vast historical sweep and the confidence of its archly modernist prose. It recalls Gunter Grass's *Tin Drum* but distinguishes itself by its dazzling pyrotechnic display of style: the dizzying array of puns and alliteration, word play and rhyme is at times breathtaking for its exuberant bravery. Rushdie has stated that Joyce and Grass taught him that anything was possible in literature, that boundaries are arbitrary limits imposed by man, that art with belief in itself can rewrite any set of conventions, however firmly entrenched. *Midnight's Children* has become a part of the literary canon, drawing comparisons to *Arabian Nights* for its multi-layered narrative, to Joyce's *Ulysses* for its literary and linguistic inventiveness, to Marquez's *One Hundred Years of Solitude* for its lush magical-realism, and Gunter Grass's *The Tin Drum* for its ability to capture the history and zeitgeist of a nation. The novel is narrated by Saleem Sinai, a child born at the exact moment India gained Independence in 1947, who discovers he has the telepathic ability to hear the thoughts of the one thousand other children born within the first hour of India's Independence: the other 'midnight's children'. Mixing historical events and figures with witches, prophecy, and magic, the novel acts as an allegory for India's turbulent history, a coming-of-age tale, and an epic family saga. Hailed by *Time* magazine as one of the hundred greatest novels in the English language, *Midnight's Children* won the Booker prize in 1981, The 'Booker of Bookers' in 1993 and also won the 'Best of the Booker' prize in 2008, proving its lasting power. Anglo-Indian novelist, who uses in his works, tales from various genres—fantasy, mythology, religion, oral tradition, etc.—Rushdie's narrative technique has connected his books to magic realism, which includes such English-language authors as Peter Carey, Angela Carter, E.L. Doctorow, John Fowles, Mark Helprin and Emma Tennant.

Arundhati Roy, whose debut novel *The God of Small Things* won the Booker in 1997 and made her "the first non-expatriate Indian author" and the "first Indian woman" to win the prize, is undoubtedly a prominent figure in literary India. She has brought recognition to, and opened up a global market for, Indian writing in English. *The God of Small Things* is a lyrical and poetic novel of post-Independence India. Set in Kerala in the 1960s, it is about two children, the two-egg twins Estha and Rahel, and the shocking consequences of a pivotal event in their young lives, the accidental death-by-drowning of a visiting English cousin. In a magical and poetic language, the novel paints a vivid picture of life in a small rural Indian town, the thoughts and feelings of the two small children, and the complexity and hypocrisy of the adults in their world. It is also a poignant lesson in the destructive power of the caste system and moral and political bigotry in general. The overriding emotional tone of the book is one of sadness and nostalgia punctuated by a fragile sense of redemptive transcendence. Examining India's cultural transformation from colonial and postcolonial period to contemporary era of globalization, the novel represents to us the hybrid elements of Indian culture and the oppressed subordinate "cultural others" that require our deep concern. Roy's narrative deploys a highly intimate and sentimental language. Here, "the post 1960's historicization of post-Independence India, are acted out in microcosm". Talking about her book, Roy says, "I have to say that my book is not about history but biology and transgression. And, the fact is that you can never understand the nature of brutality until you see what has been loved being smashed. And so the book deals with both things—it deals with our ability to be brutal as well as our ability to be so deeply intimate and so deeply loving." Further, "Twisting the language to suit her own storytelling, she managed to make the whole world a stage for Ayemenem and its people. For all we know, she might be a one-book marvel. But irrespective of whether Roy writes another novel or not, she has built a pedestal from which future Indian writers can scan the wide horizon of English literature. Roy triumphed because, unlike the others, she had the guts and the overwhelming talent to invent a new idiom and vocabulary to tell the story of a seemingly remote people. Mammachi, Susie Mol, Estha, Rahel, Ammu and Velutha will stay with us, popping up once in a while to remind us of some eternal truth" (The *India Today* Cover Story, "Princess of Prose", 27 October 1997). "Roy stretches the English language in all directions", Rosemary Dinnage wrote in the *New York Review of Books*. The Booker committee's praise is equally memorable: "With extraordinary linguistic inventiveness, Roy funnels the history of south India through the eyes of seven-year-old twins." Roy sure has an eagle's eye for the beautiful and the tragic, creating great lines for literature like "dissolute bluebottle hum vacuously in the fruity air".

With Kiran Desai the 'fine tradition' of Indian Booker Prize winners continues. At thirty-five, Kiran Desai, not only became the youngest ever woman writer to win the prestigious Man Booker Prize for 2006, but also achieved a victory which had repeatedly eluded her mother. Like her mother Anita, Kiran Desai is a gifted writer who draws from her Anglo-Indian literary inheritance and writes not only about India, but also about Indian communities in the world. A moving representation of the contemporary moment and with many hallmarks of a compelling tale of modern disenchantment, Desai's novel firmly places her in the canon of postcolonial literature. *The Inheritance of Loss* tries to capture what it means to live between East and West and what it means to be an immigrant. It also uncovers the ways in which political, economic, and social systems have been constructed and transformed in societies where cultures have been forcibly meshed by imperialism and colonization. In *The Inheritance of Loss*, two untold South Asian histories emerge—one takes place in Kalimpong, in a colonial-era villa located in the border country between Bangladesh, Bhutan and Nepal where a nationalist movement to establish a land for Gurkhas makes its way into the lives of ordinary people, and the other begins in New York City, but not among the city's middle-class Indians whose immigrant stories have largely formed how the diaspora is seen. In Desai's New York, a "shadow class" of Indian restaurant workers living without legal status find themselves discovering an America less like a land of plentitude than one of unrelenting exclusion. In holding a mirror up to the contemporary scene of globalization and its discontents, Desai introduces us in her novel to the character Biju, the son of an Indian cook sent to the United States to make money for himself and his family. Angry at his father for this burden, Biju realizes his anger would have been doubled had his father not sent him away in the first place. In capturing the conflicting feelings of the immigrant, Desai tells in *INDIA New England* that she relied heavily on her own experiences: "I've seen a lot of cruelties with immigrants to the States with families left completely behind. It's sometimes this desire to just be American and forget". Desai sees the cruelties as two-fold—they affect not only the immigrants, but also their entire families. For both those at home as well as those abroad, there is a persistent feeling of exile from what one holds most dear in the process of assimilation. Desai wonders whether this phenomenon is about "immigrant shame or rather the process of where one finds dignity in life". Though the issues Desai raises are not new, they are, nevertheless, relevant in today's world, "the past informing the present, the present revealing the past". From the fablesque magic and satiric comedy in her celebrated debut, exuding "poetry and joy in language and life", Desai's Man Booker Prize winning novel moves effortlessly to "illuminate the pain of exile, describing the encroaching morass of Westernization and the lingering effects of colonialism", spanning continents, generations, religions and races, with equal felicity and ease. Though Desai's novel holds a mirror up to the world today, looking at the cultural collisions, cultural encounters, postcolonialism and continuing consumerist imperialism, yet what makes her irresistible, is her immense tenderness for the human condition, her understanding of human relationships—*la condition humanitie*—the estate of man, which forms the core of her entire artistic vision. None less than Jorge Luis Borges provides her with the right words, in the Epigraph, for expressing these feelings: "My humanity is in feeling we are all voices of the same poverty. They speak of homeland."

The youngest winner of the Booker prize, Aravind Adiga, joins V.S. Naipaul, Salman Rushdie, Arundhati Roy and Kiran Desai in the Booker Hall of Fame. The awards administrators emphasized, "*The White Tiger* is the ninth winning novel to take its inspiration from India or Indian identity." Adiga's winning novel is described as a "compelling, angry, and darkly humorous" novel about a man's journey from an Indian village to entrepreneurial success. This extraordinary and brilliant first novel takes the form of a series of letters to Wen Jiabao, the Chinese premier, from Balaram Halwai, the Bangalore businessman who is the self-styled "White Tiger" of the title. Balram Halwai narrates his story through letters he writes, but doesn't send, to the Chinese premier, Wen Jiabao. Wen is poised to visit India to learn why it is so good at producing entrepreneurs, so Balram presumes to tell him how to win power and influence people in modern India. Balram's story, though, is a tale of bribery, corruption, skulduggery, toxic traffic jams, theft and murder. Whether communist China can import this business model is questionable. But its unflattering portrait of India as a society racked by corruption and servitude has caused a storm in his homeland. He tells Stuart Jeffries why he wants to expose the country's dark side: "I don't think a novelist should just write about his own experiences. Yes, I am the son of a doctor, yes, I had a rigorous formal education, but for me the challenge of a novelist is to write about people who aren't anything like me." He further remarks that his book was, "an attempt to catch the voice of the men you meet as you travel through India, the voice of the colossal underclass.... This voice was not captured and I wanted to do so without sentimentality or portraying them as mirthless, humorless weaklings as they are usually". Far removed from the glossy images of India—the technology entrepreneurs, Indian stereotypes featuring yoga and spirituality, and glittering Bollywood stars, Adiga's book strips away the sheen of a self-congratulatory nation and reveals instead a country where the social compact is being stretched to the breaking point. *The White Tiger* traverses the familiar territory of class and caste divide, poverty and exploitation and the triumph of the human spirit that one expects in a book that unfolds from a place called 'Darkness', in Bihar and draws its protagonist from an impoverished family of rickshaw pullers who were in the business of making sweetmeats before fate intervened. How this change in family fortune happened is explained succulently by Adiga: "See, this country, in its days of greatness, when it was the richest nation on earth, was like a zoo. A clean, well-kept, orderly zoo. Everyone in his place, everyone happy. Goldsmiths here. Cowherds here. Landlords there. The man called a Halwai made sweets. The man called a cowherd tended cows. The untouchable cleaned faeces.... To sum up—in the old days there were one thousand castes and destinies in India. These days, there are just two castes: Men with Big Bellies, and Men with Small Bellies. And only two destinies: eat or get eaten up." If the aim of literature is to help us understand the world we live in and lead more meaningful lives, then undoubtedly all the three recent Indian books that have won the coveted prize have achieved this admirable objective.

Considering how enormous the book prize industry has become, how ubiquitous its rhetoric of competition, achievement and reward, scholarly literature on the topic is relatively slim. *Indian Booker Prize Winners* unites studies of award winning novels and aims at encapsulating the enormous literary dynamism of the rich tradition of India's noted chroniclers whose books found a permanent place on the shelves, and carved niches in the English literary consciousness. Salman Rushdie, Arundhati Roy, Kiran Desai and Aravind Adiga are the luminaries who have flung open a brave new world to Indian writers and have definitely created a bang in the Booker Hall of Fame. Dealing with these novelists of the Booker fame, *Indian Booker Prize Winners* presents well researched and insightful papers which offer an extensive focus on the emerging role of Indian English fiction in shaping the most significant annual international award in English letters.

In his scholarly paper, "A Postcolonial Bestiary: Metaphors of Power in Aravind Adiga's *The White Tiger*", Esterino Adami discusses Adiga's "use of animal-based imagery to stage what is often overlooked and marginalised, conveying a deep sense of hopelessness, whereas India regresses to a sort of 'primordial' community, dominated and lacerated by the voices of the 'powerful' animals, viz. the Wild Boar, the Buffalo, the Tiger and so on". The paper unveils Adiga's effective use of animal symbolism which "clearly constitutes a stock of imaginative resources, endowed with special values across societies, with animal metaphors, icons or references spanning over cultural, historical and anthropological structures, from biblical episodes to Shakespearean plays as well as postmodern fiction".

In her innovative paper, "Deconstruction in *The White Tiger*", Jackie Haque shows "Adiga's keenness in showing how the economic, political and caste system, all integral to the Indian society, actually mean the opposite of what they appear to mean". The author concludes, "Adiga successfully shows binary opposites that exist in the Indian society and also later on shows that these oppositions are connected to one another before finally showing they mean just the opposite of what they originally meant to show."

In a competent analysis, "*The Inheritance of Loss*: A Portrayal of Myriad Shades of Life", Prof. Meenakshi Raman deftly illustrates how Kiran Desai's novel *The Inheritance of Loss* delineates the myriad shades of life through its major characters, namely the Judge, Sai, Gyan, Biju and the Cook. The paper extensively explores how "a gamut of expressions such as brutality, humour, whimsy, harshness, delicate emotions, passionate commitment, humiliation, racial prejudice, pathos, outrage, etc. echo through their lives".

In the highly perceptive article, "Cyclical Temporality in Salman Rushdie's *The Satanic Verses*", Erin Warde, discusses the trope of cyclical temporality which "promotes the novel's theme of rebirth that results in a breaking away from Western hegemony. In addition, as the point of view shifts from character to character, the reader is reborn into each character; in this way, the reader is reincarnated into the plethora of characters introduced by the text. The reader participates in the power play between the characters, especially those that serve as symbolic conflicts between the East and the West".

In a learned analysis, "National Allegory, Reshaping Memory and Rewriting History: Salman Rushdie's *Midnight's Children* and *Shame*", John Nkemngong Nkengasong and Magdelene Atanga Mafor revealingly state, "To Rushdie the narrative like the nation should move forward and backwards to indicate the influence of the past in the present. The writer narrates historical realities through memory by which means he brings in his thoughts the past and present intermingled with fiction to imagine the nation by which means he tries to negotiate the discourse of the seemingly illusory border between Islam and the West".

In her well researched paper, "Subaltern Voices and Postcolonial Anxiety in Arundhati Roy's *The God of Small Things*", Diviani Chaudhuri offers a brilliant exploration of Roy's narrative strategies and asks the pertinent questions: "Are postcolonial publishing phenomena like Roy, Rushdie, Ghosh and Seth then peddling Macaulay's dream of a class that would act as an intermediary between the colonizer and the vast mass of the colonized, or, the mainstream and the marginalised, as the case may be?, Are they the literary counterparts of Indian *babu*dom, 'never challenging [systems of oppression], never appearing not to?' (Roy 66), and Do activist-writers like Roy provide any means of positive intervention when they choose the private sphere as the medium of political résistance?"

In his comprehensive paper "From Backward to Forward: Self-upgrading in Contemporary India", Prof. Alessandro Monti focuses on the "Other Backwards section defined by Ambedkar and further institutionalised by the Mandal Commission with its splitting between Backwards and Forwards". Prof. Monti sees Adiga's *The White Tiger* not as "a novel about casteism but rather concerns the backdrop of failed shared belonging in post-Independence India and of his politics of equality. As such, the novel moves on the mimicking edge of parody, since it transposes the rush of economical globalisation into less sedate terms of unchecked leaps of social upgrading".

In a scholarly analysis, "The Subaltern as Hero in Aravind Adiga's *The White Tiger*", Dr. Anita Myles offers an in-depth study of the subaltern in the light of the contemporary Indian social structure which is beset with class struggle, caste wars, religious intolerance and ethnic alienation. As Dr. Myles elaborates, "Aravind Adiga, in his maiden attempt at fiction writing seems favourably inclined and sympathetic towards the neglected classes of India. The narrative throws ample light on the plight of the poor in India whom Adiga considers as 'subalterns'. Economically exploited, socially condemned, medically neglected and educationally ignored, these vanquished sons of the soil struggle to keep body and soul together while people in power make merry at their expense. Most villagers are like bonded labourers of the landlords who take undue advantage of their poverty and ignorance. They are subalterns in the true sense of the word."

Nishi Pulugurtha, in her competent paper, "Dislocation and Identity in *The Inheritance of Loss*" explores the theme of displacement that the characters undergo in the course of their lives. "Almost every character in the novel", says Dr. Pulugurtha, "is unhappy in the environ he/she inhabits. Their displacement creates problems of assimilation, a sense of alienation and a crisis of identity. This paper is an examination of the dislocation and cultural alienation that each of the characters undergo."

In her exhaustive study, "Worlds within Words: A Study of Rushdie's Use of Allusions in the *Midnight's Children*", Dr. Garima Gupta offers a competent analysis of Rushdie's use of allusions in *Midnight's Children*, which contains a wide variety of different types of allusions, each having a role and purpose in the text. As Dr. Gupta states, Rushdie's "literary allusions are more than mere embellishments and also add to their referentiality".

Dr. Prakash Chandra Pradhan's "Democracy and Dictatorship in Salman Rushdie's *Midnight's Children*" is an inclusive analysis of "the political aspects of pre-Independence [1915-1947] and post-Independence [1947-1977] periods of the Indian subcontinent as portrayed in Salman Rushdie's novel *Midnight's Children*". The paper tries to examine "how these aspects have affected life and society of its people to a considerable degree because of violation of democratic norms by the colonial as well as postcolonial rulers".

In her well researched paper, "The Unsafe Edge: Ammu's Agency in *The God of Small Things*", Christina Bertrand Firebaugh discusses the question of female agency in *The God of Small Things* which "is complex not only because of the myriad of social factors that its female characters must negotiate but also because each female character in the novel understands her own position differently". "Agency", says Firebaugh, "is intrinsically tied to one's awareness of her position; she then uses this awareness as motivation for rebellion against both her own position and the sociopolitical structures that cause subalternity in the first place."

In her innovative paper, "The Regional Novel and Aravind Adiga's *The White Tiger*", Arpa Ghosh raises a pertinent question: "Why novelists like Anand and Adiga should not write in an Indian regional language?" Dr. Ghosh further remarks, "In fact, compared to the meticulous and exhaustive representation of the regional novelist's subject (a subject that has enveloped him from childhood, and of which he has a thorough knowledge), the Indo-Anglian writer's grappling with the same subject is often viewed as watery, facile and less grounded."

In the highly perceptive article, "The Subaltern Speaks: A Critical Reading of *The White Tiger*", Dr. Vandana Datta has a truly revealing observation: "It was a landmark novel in that it drew the Indian English novel from the middle class drawing rooms out into the slums. And since then this trend has caught on. With the movie *Slumdog Millionaire* winning the Oscar it has been resounded unequivocally that the era of the underdog has arrived. And the Booker going to Arvind Adiga's *The White Tiger* makes it clear that the subaltern not only speaks, he acts as well, holding the reins in his hands."

The Inheritance of Loss tries to capture what it means to live between East and West and what it means to be an immigrant. It also uncovers the ways in which political, economic, and social systems have been constructed and transformed in societies where cultures have been forcibly meshed by imperialism and colonization. In an insightful paper, "Colliding Scapes of Cultures: A Reading of *The Inheritance of Loss*", Purnendu Chatterjee seeks to "explore the interface of Western and Indian cultures—brought out through the convergence of the tormented colonial past and an indeterminately positioned multicultural/multiethnic, globalized present—and the impact of cultural collisions on the characters in the novel".

In his comprehensive paper, "Narrating History, Rethinking Nation: A Re-reading of Rushdie's *Midnight's Children*", Arindam Das proposes "to show the ways through which Rushdie achieves such subversions and appropriations, stripping bare the hitherto unchallenged conventions and traditions in his *Midnight's Children*". As Das himself remarks, "Rushdie in his *Midnight's Children* (1981) dismantles the structures of universal truths and 'grand narratives' such as History and Nation and in the process shows the slipperiness and gaps of such absolute identities."

Dr. Reena Mitra in her scholarly paper, "Possibilities of the Metaphorical in Salman Rushdie's *Midnight's Children*", offers a brilliant exploration of Rushdie's narrative technique and remarks, "For Rushdie, the fantastic and the metaphorical alone can provide a compelling mode of communication whereby fiction emerges as a mode of reality, the reality of the author's self, caught in a complex interplay with historical reality".

Dr. Joyashri Choudhury's competent paper, "Ecofeminism in Arundhati Roy's *The God of Small Things*, and the Meenachal River as an Encyclopedia of Race, Class and Culture in the Novel" is an interesting exploration of the Meenachal as the novel's major symbol. "The Meenachal River" says Dr. Choudhury, "assumes gigantic proportions in the book, moulding and shaping the lives of almost all the characters in the book." Roy herself has said, "To me, I couldn't think of a better location for a book about human beings." Furthermore, she concludes, "And long after we had finished reading the novel this river-sense pervades through our senses and the Meenachal gets firmly etched in our consciousness as an encyclopedia of race, class and culture in *The God of Small Things*."

In an exhaustive analysis, "'Re-Vision'—Creating a New Stream of Novel Writing: Arundhati Roy's *The God of Small Things*", Dr. Ishmeet Kaur Chaudhry focuses on various different subjects, both simple and complex: love, madness, sex, revolt, anguish, joy and social, cultural, political and psychological human concerns. The depth and high seriousness with which Roy treats these issues and emotions makes them important concerns for life. The element of satire, a little humour and a touch of innocence adds to the rhythmic poetical language and quality of narrative. She not only portrays the ways of the world but also attacks and challenges the hypocrisy of society. Roy is known to be one of those who dares to break the rules.

Representing the combined efforts of scholars, the book is multivocal and inclusive, which would not have come to fruition without the help of many people. Needless to say, *Indian Booker Prize Winners* would not have existed but for the efforts of the legion of contributors who conscientiously and patiently wrote and sometimes rewrote their articles at my request. The book will provide deeper insights into the works of our gallery of Booker Prize winners, and prove immensely useful to the students and teachers of Indian English literature and researchers in this field.

Sunita Sinha

1

A Postcolonial Bestiary: Metaphors of Power in Aravind Adiga's *The White Tiger*

Esterino Adami

> All animals are equal, but some animals are more equal than others.
>
> George Orwell, *Animal Farm*

> There is first of all the problem of the opening, namely, how to get us from where we are, which is, as yet, nowhere, to the far bank. It is a simple bridging problem, a problem of knocking together a bridge. People solve such problems every day. They solve them, and having solved them, push on.
>
> J.M. Coetzee, *Elizabeth Costello*

In *The White Tiger* (2008), Aravind Adiga tackles the question of the representability of contemporary society, namely how it is possible to offer a portrait of fast-developing India in the postmodern era. Constructed as a sort of epistolary novel, based on a series of long letters addressed to the Chinese Prime Minister with the intent to explain the multilayered meaning of India, it modulates the voice of the autodiegetic narrator as inner confessions in the exploration of the black heart of shining India: in particular, what lies at the heart of the novel is an articulated discourse on the idea of power, expressed in binary terms through metaphors of animals. Not only does Adiga denounce and break the modern myth of positive globalization, but he also uncovers the perpetuation of evils and the search for all forms of power, a loaded theme in Postcolonial Studies.

Apparently the author adopts a Manichean vision of power and weakness, against the backdrop of unforgotten historical materialism, by creating opposing classes or forces: the rich and the poor, the urban elite and the rural peasants, the educated entrepreneurs and the rough workers, the people who own luxury cars and the people who drive these vehicles. However, his storytelling increasingly acquires darker tones and goes beyond the superficiality of social injustices and neglected human rights insofar as it tries to penetrate the cultural interstices of postcolonial (neo-colonial may be) India, in particular concentrating on the perpetuation of societal constructions, often disguised under the catchy keywords of democracy, welfare and modernity. In his wickedly acid prose, Adiga uses animal-based imagery to stage what is often overlooked and marginalised, conveying a deep sense of hopelessness, whereas India regresses to a sort of "primordial" community, dominated and lacerated by the voices of the "powerful" animals, viz. the Wild Boar, the Buffalo, the Tiger and so on.

Yet, before focusing on the relevance of the different zoomorphic metaphors, it is worth noticing that the novelist conceives the idea of power within a wider scope of meaning, in the intertwined notions of globalization and postmodernity. Whether the world media try to discursively "build" India as a hi-tech nation, providing IT services to the global community via the implementation of outsourcing, the protagonist Balram Halwai irreverently reconsiders the celebration of the cyber industry in terms of social and economic rise in the East to the detriment of the decaying West, as if foreseeing a dystopian vision of the powerful and the powerless in the times to come: "Out of respect for the love of liberty shown by the Chinese people, and also in the belief that the future of the world lies with the yellow man and the brow man now that our erstwhile master, the white-skinned man, has wasted himself though, buggery, mobile phone usage, and drug abuse, I offer to tell you, free of charge, the truth about Bangalore" (2008: 5-6). The triumph of computer-mediated globalization brings to the fore the modalities of power by turning upside down the old imperial clichés: the strategy of the (former) colonized is aimed at taking over, whilst the (former) colonizer goes through the experiences of decline and fall. To a certain extent, this pattern of rise and fall also mirrors the pathway of Balram, a humble servant who becomes a self-made entrepreneur, shifting from wretched village to the enthralling metropolis.

The double mechanism of powerfulness and powerlessness is pictured at work not only on the global scene by hinting at the multinational economies, but also in the local contexts. It is especially with the animal metaphors that the writer acts to expose the endemic evils of traditional India, since his postcolonial bestiary synthesises the time-honoured corruption and immorality that devour villages and communities. The recourse to metaphorical animals may be vague and imprecise, but given the central role of the animal archetypology, persistently shaping or affecting human perception, it substantiates and frames a system of clear identification into the collective consciousness. The landowning notables of Laxmangarh, Balram's native village, are described as anthropomorphised, "monstrous" animals that dominate with terror and violence the whole region:

> The Stork was a fat man with a fat moustache, thick and curved and pointy at the tips. He owned the river that flowed outside the village, and he took a cut of every catch of fish caught by every fisherman in the river, and a toll from every boatman who crossed the river to come to our village.
>
> His brother was called the Wild Boar. This fellow owned all the good agricultural land around Laxmangarh. If you wanted to work on those lands, you had to bow down to his feet, and touch the dust under his slippers, and agree to swallow his day wages [...].
>
> The Raven owned the worst land, which was the dry, rocky hillside around the fort, and took a cut from

> the goatherds who went up there to graze with their flocks [...].
>
> The Buffalo was greediest of the lot. He had eaten up the rickshaws the roads. So if you ran a rickshaw, or used the road, you had to pay him his feed—one-third of whatever you earned, no less. (2008: 24-25)

In their sophisticated ways to distinguish from the *profanum vulgus*, further reinforced by the hypocritical efforts to uphold religious customs and praise the numerous deities of the Indian Hindu pantheon, the Animals in reality maintain certain forms of colonial order, whereby an oligarchic class controls society by imposing a totalitarian authority via a rooted system of intimidation and corruption. The primordial and bestial force of these characters is evoked in their brutal acts as a heavy legacy burdening the post-1947 condition of life, a "brand" that even the contemporary economic and social development seems to be unable to eradicate. To a certain extent, the meanness, falsehood and greediness of the masters remind the reader of the protagonists of a classic Russian novel *The Golovlyov Family*, by Mikhail Saltykov-Shchedrin (1875), an author who does not explicitly use animal imagery, but whose witty language is clearly influenced by Aesopic fables and tales in its finest satirical tones.

In Adiga's text, even the eponymous narrator himself is assigned an animal role and the image of the white tiger is recurrent in Balram's story from the very *incipit*. A school inspector, positively impressed by Balram's indoctrinated faith in the Great Socialist, the Mafia puppeteer of the over-corrupted Indian political class par excellence, defines the boy a "white tiger", which is described as "the rarest of animals—the creature that comes along only once in a generation" (2008: 35). This apparently banal episode becomes a kind of epiphany and convinces the boy that such semantically pregnant appellative will turn out to be a token of his innermost identity: as a "tiger", metaphorically Balram will have to attack and tear to pieces his enemies, cunningly searching the surrounding environment. Furthermore, the tiger is not just a literary echo, an image of self-imposed strength, but it really appears when the protagonist brings Dharam, a young relative he is looking after, to the National Zoo in New Delhi, in the sixth part of the novel. Here the silent meeting between the man and the beast encapsulates the uncertainty of power relation as the ferocious animal, a symbol of bravery, is kept behind the bamboo bars, whereas the person is safely located in a voyeuristic (and mesmerised) position. But this construction of roles, and its possible inversion, secretly mirrors Balram's viewpoint: "the tiger's eyes met my eyes, like my master's eyes have met mine so often in the mirror of the car" (2008: 277), with its load of fears, expectations, and subjugations. It is too intense a sight, however, and the man's fainting perhaps is a kind of harbinger and, at the same time, forlornly suggests the impossibility of change, or at least the sense of conflict, in Indian society.

The animal symbolism clearly constitutes a stock of imaginative resources, endowed with special values across societies, with animal metaphors, icons or references spanning over cultural, historical and anthropological structures, from biblical episodes to Shakespearean plays as well as postmodern fiction (for a rich catalogue of symbolical and allegorical meanings of animals in western arts and folklore, see Rowland 1973). Of course, I am aware that it is not appropriate to interpret Indian culture via western categories, but the relevance of essential animal symbolism concerns all societies since the theriomorphic aspect of imagination concerns a psychological view of the subject experiencing reality and projecting anxieties or elaborating memories. In *The White Tiger*, the author is not merely interested in engraving a progression of bizarre characters, but as he runs over the same matter subject, he aims at exploring the boundaries and shapes of power relations, in particular within the dichotomy "master-servant", a deep-seated issue in many postcolonial countries. His writing therefore clings not so much to a sociological interpretation of the modern ways in which the dominant groups fully exploit the lower classes through hegemonic policies, but rather it highlights the pathological conditions of maltreatment and marginality accepted as an unalterable system of society organization. Adiga puts across the point of the psychological dimension that the master creates by aptly measuring out fear and reward, so as to completely subjugate the subaltern, imposing on them a pre-fabricated identity, drawing on the tacit consent of family traditions and caste divisions.

As a matter of fact, the complex relationship built between Balram and Mr. Ashok, his employer, is stratified as an accumulation of cultural, social and historical layers of meanings, and what saliently emerges is the oscillation between devotion and hate that the driver feels for his boss, a "common sentiment", we may argue, amongst servants, split between resistance and acceptance. Nonetheless, a simplistic opposition of fixed roles (master versus servant) is not sufficient to comprehend the socio-cultural landscape of India since alchemy of attitudes, responses and emotions jointly informs individuals, classes and behaviours. In his pungent analysis, Balram claims that "masters trust their servants with diamonds in this country!" (2008: 176), and this principle stems from a time-honoured sense of acceptance of dire life conditions that regulates the various social levels and their combinations: "A handful of men in this country have trained the remaining 99.9 per cent—as strong, as talented, as intelligent in every way—to exist in perpetuated servitude; a servitude so strong that you can put the key of his emancipation in a man's hands and he will throw it back at you with a curse" (2008: 175-76).

Moreover, Adiga, via the impudent narratorial voice of the White Tiger, investigates the different connotations of power in India and exposes its nastiest aspects within the architecture of social relationships. Through his metaphor-making vision, he imagines people from poor or derelict backgrounds, which constitute the majority of Indian population, as paralysed as chickens in their coops, apparently free to move and live but, in truth, chained to their assigned positions and crushed by the cogs of society. Beyond the pietistic ritual of upholding traditional respect and deference to the higher classes, here what strikes the reader concerns the "sadistic" dimension, constantly perpetuating forms of suppression, when servants not only have to prostate themselves before their masters but they are also left to their mercy. The author's harsh condemnation invests *in toto* the central constituency of the traditional Indian society, viz. the household, as the main site of identity restrictions, with its numerous ramifications: "the pride and glory of our nation, the repository of all our love and sacrifice, the subject of no doubt considerable space in the pamphlet that the prime minister will hand over to you, *the Indian family*, is the reason we are trapped and tied" (2008: 176; Author's emphasis). To further underscore the hopelessness of the servants' condition, he does not hesitate to openly reveal the gloomiest sides of the annihilating power management that looms as an inscrutable legacy over the lower disadvantaged classes: "only a man who is prepared to see his family destroyed—hunted, beaten, and burned alive by the masters, can break out of the coop. That would take no normal human being, but a freak, a pervert of nature" (2008: 176).

In the light of such tangled emotional milieu, it is not easy to decipher the innermost mood that drives Balram whilst he is perpetrating his secret plans: his desire for vengeance and economic advance takes the form of the appealing mirage of entrepreneurship, but the young man turns into a cynical social climber when he flees into southern India and sets his own business, a private taxi company, boasting the pompous name "The White Tiger" in Bangalore. "Do we loathe our masters behind a facade of love—or do we love them behind a facade of loathing" (2008: 187) wonders the protagonist, unable to break up the mixture of repulsion and attraction that binds him to Mr. Ashok or, after the death of the man, his ghost. However, the maelstrom that surrounds the young driver climaxes with the murder of his boss, rendering the novel a particular type of thriller close to the visions of postmodern pessimism, in which the literary persona fades away being overwhelmed by disastrous actions. And yet, once again, the bloody event belongs to a more complex net of episodes, causes, and consequences: "I could gloat that I am not just any murderer, but one who killed his own employer (who is a kind of second father), and also contributed to the probable death of his family members. A virtual mass murder" (2008: 45). Balram's ill-fated trust in entrepreneurship is not aimed at working within the rising capitalist system of India, but rather it is grounded on the idea of manipulation and plotting as a way out of servitude.

The rhetorical design elaborated by Adiga bisects the vision of modern India, a mosaic made up of traditional castes, emerging bourgeoisie, attracting malls, fetid slums and the steady obliteration of human rights. Within this vision, the country is split into two antithetical cultural terrains or imagined communities: "Please understand, Your Excellency, that India is two countries in one: an India of Light, and an India of Darkness" (2008: 14). After his gory murder, the protagonist claims that he is "in the Light now," (2008: 313) marking the fact that he has managed to break the chains of subjugation through his spiteful and criminal acting. Like a postcolonial Raskolnikov, however, he meditates over his ambiguous choices, in particular whether the end justifies the means: "Am I not part of all that is changing this country? Haven't I succeeded in the struggle that every poor man here should be making—the struggle not to take the lashes your father took, not to end up in a mound of indistinguishable bodies that will rot in the black mud of Mother Ganga? True, there was the matter of murder—which is a wrong thing to do, no question about it. It has darkened my soul. All the skin-whitening creams sold in the markets of India won't clean my hands again" (2008: 318). Apart from a distant echo of Lady Macbeth's ignoble schemes, nearly a didactic decoration in the text, the sharpness of Adiga's writing emerges through the lack of morality and the profusion of doubts of disillusioned Balram, whose satirical storytelling whips the evils of society. To a certain degree, in the drilling reference to the Darkness we could identify a hint of the dreamlike atmosphere that permeates a recent story by Suhayl Saadi, in which the omniscient narrator gains a god-like position: "there is no cruelty and no mercy in me. I am the moment when the dreamer realises it is a dream" ("Darkness", now collected in

Saadi 2001: 196). However, the two works are very different. Adiga's novel is dexterously rendered also in its psychological dimension (for instance with the nightmares and thoughts that haunt the "split" murderous chauffer), but the writer's main preoccupation addresses a "realistic" view of India, combining a documentary viewpoint about rural and metropolitan life with a fictional story of crime, ambition and reprisal, constantly provoking and challenging the readers.

Another aspect of the discourse on power that the author puts on his agenda concerns the socio-cultural and socio-educational dimensions of language, in particular within a wider prospective of English studies in India. First of all, the "White Tiger" metaphor is coined in a school but, more importantly, language mastery represents a particular form of power, especially in a country divided between a huge illiterate population and an English-educated tiny minority. Balram himself is frequently mocked by Pinky Madam, Mr. Ashok's American wife, because of his mispronunciation with words like "pizza" and "malls", fashionable terms defining the new commodities that the Indian upper classes voraciously demand for, following the crazes that consumerism globally impresses, but the novel strives to tackle the educational context too, in particular by means of the "liquor simile". After settling in New Delhi, the young protagonist and his colleague, another driver of Mr. Ashok, take up visiting liquor shops, where the availability of alcoholic drinks mirrors once more the double condition of Indian society, in which the well-off greedily consume the best items and services whilst the much more numerous underprivileged cannot satisfy their basic needs. The narrator illustrates this point by affirming that "in this country we have two kinds of men: 'Indian' liquor men and 'English' liquor men. 'Indian' liquor was for village boys like me—toddy, arrack, country hooch. 'English' liquor naturally is for the rich. Rum, whisky, beer, gin—anything the English left behind" (2008: 72-73). In the postmodern process that attempts to globalize India, alcohol, a morally forbidden item, is still reiterated through colonial and postcolonial echoes and tacitly accepted in the everyday practices of life as a discriminating token of welfare.

Indeed, the "liquor" metaphor can be suggestive of more complex implications, especially within the arena of education and culture. In their close analysis of education accessibility for Indian people, N. Krishnaswamy and Archana S. Burde argue about the current interweaving of several social and cultural elements affecting the spread of literacy, with the controversial position of English in multilingual India against the use of vernaculars. I will quote at length:

> Those who can afford, get imported whisky and the best English education; at the next lower level, people go in for 'Indian-Made-Foreign-Liquor' (IMFL) and better English education; at the lower levels, most people will have to be satisfied with the government-approved locally brewed liquor sold in 'toddy shops' and government-run-English medium-schools, and still lower are those who consume the illicit arrack, the least expensive but the deadliest, while their children learn how to say 'Daddy and Mummy' in some 'teaching shops' which pretend to be 'English medium schools'. The basic rule is the same—one for the Master who can afford it, and one for the poor boy/girl who lives down the lane! (Krishnaswamy and Burde 1998: 72)

The alarming vision of the two linguists envisages Indian society as a hierarchical construction, in which social change and democratic decision do not seem to bring out practical results in the educational context. Aravind assumes this pattern of discrimination and foregrounds the rise and fall of would-be entrepreneurs.

But the exploration of language power also regards the artificiality of political rhetoric, especially in the verbose constructions of slogans, supporting parties and leaders. The language, with an exhibition of pompous words and catchphrases, is used to convey ideological meanings so as to praise power, and reinforce a certain world order. Balram is caustic in commenting the use (and misuse) of language as an ideological weapon to shape public opinion and homologate personal beliefs: "one fact about India is that you can take almost anything you hear about the country from the prime minister and turn it upside down and then you will have the truth about that thing" (2008: 15). Such emptiness of verbal communication blurs the representation of 21st century India as a modern, expanding country on the verge of global transformations, but perhaps we could also talk about the pernicious skill of the powerful to manoeuvre and exploit language in order to enslave the powerless. In considering the functions of official or state discourse as a vehicle regulating cultural and civil practices, Poddar holds that "the claim to truth with regard to culture masks significant continuities in colonial and postcolonial official discourses. Their shared epistemic assumptions, for instance, constitute a veritable silence on structural social inequalities and marginalised identities" (2002: 95). What Adiga condemns, indeed, is the "manipulability" of language when the authorities subtly build up an oligarchic frame of societal organization, restoring forms of colonial rule in spite of the booming celebration of independence and equality. *En passant*, we should also note that, in the varieties of English spoken across the Indian subcontinent, the lexicon pertaining to "terms of gratification", viz. different forms of bribery, corruption and extortion, tends to be particularly articulated and rich, describing an extremely spread socio-cultural phenomenon.

The animal imagery, as a particular realization of language coinage at work, abounds throughout the text, and defines the conditions of the common people, the wealthy and the narrator himself. Condemned to a perennial subaltern confinement, the needy are pictured as the "roosters" kept in coops, and so unable to flee away, paralysed in their limited sphere of identity. The author's bizarre creativity draws on the plentiful bestiary of human imagination, updating and enhancing old icons: for example, the Stork's son, by the evocative power of metaphor, becomes the Mongoose, who "was small, and dark, and ugly, and very shrewd" (2008: 75). Furthermore, we should not forget that apart from the impressive appellative of white tiger, Balram is also connected with a much less glorious animal symbol, being called "country-mouse" by a colleague, a more experienced driver he befriends in New Delhi. Thus, it is evident that animal symbolism in its various epiphanies informs the textual backbone of Adiga's work and provides a pregnant terrain of cultural references. Animals, which play a fundamental role in Indian mythology, from elephant-headed Ganesha to many other deities and creatures, are also instrumental in mediating inner human forces and predispositions, namely they express certain features of identity and replace proper names. In Indian culture, onomastics is derived from caste belonging, and the family name of the central character (Halwai) indicates a class of sweet makers, but it is the first name that really matter here. As a matter of fact, the novelist aptly subverts the ancient principle of *nomen omen*, according to which the name is a sign of destiny, bearing the future of a person, by starting a slow metamorphosis. On the very first school day, the protagonist appals his teacher because of his quite ordinary name ("Munna", meaning "boy") so much that the adult at once rechristens him Balram, "the sidekick of the god Krishna" (2008: 14). Changing names therefore becomes a cathartic strategy of identity transformation that Balram will exploit widely, in his distressed climb across dehumanized Indian society.

As Aravind Adiga paints a poignant portrait of the inequality, the injustice and poverty that disintegrate the surface of bourgeois and democratic India and unfolds the ambiguous story of the White Tiger, in the end what shocks the reader's interpretation is the cynicism that characterizes the deft prose of Balram, rather than the weight of his roguery. Nearly in a postmodern fashion, in which expectations collapse and give way to uncertainty, the skilful writer through the sharp tongue of the narrator casts more doubts than hopes. Dharam emblematically stands out like the "new" child of future India, having gained access to formal education and consequently better chances of social improvement: "He goes to a good school now here in Bangalore—an English school. Now he pronounces English like a rich man's son [...]. All these things I never learned" (2008: 316). But the relationship with his putative father is clouded by sinister implications and suspects—"Oh, he's got it all figured out, I tell you. Little blackmailing thug. He's going to keep quiet as long as I keep feeding him," (2008: 316) as if to suggest that sleaze and bribery are endemic evils in Indian society, vices that corrupt all, regardless the differences dividing social classes or the strength of human relations. It is a mechanism for maintaining fixed roles and functions in a paralyzed society since the dishonest behaviour of the wicked plotter is adopted as a model by the younger generation, with an inversion of roles as Balram criticizes the craftiness of the youth: "the new generation, I tell you, is growing up with no morals at all" (2008: 316).

In closing, I would like to briefly expand my focus on zoomorphic metaphors, by stressing that their potentiality is widely recognized by postcolonial authors, especially in African literature, as a suitable tool of resistance and opposition against the monolithic authority of unprincipled "new" masters. In *Waiting for the Vote of the Wild Animals* (2001), for example, the Ivorian novelist Ahmadou Kourouma collocates in an imaginary country—highly reminiscent of Togo—a postcolonial bestiary, constituted by the wild animals of the bush that are asked to support the despot, after the blind slaughtering of the villagers, and such allegory with its suggestive intensity underscores the inner, oblique contradictions of an entire society. The rituals of power succession cut across the often unstable contexts of postcolonial countries and come forward as unchanging sites of cultural structure: the jackal, the panther, the vulture, the hyena, and the leopard express the myth-based response against the imposition of autocrat governments and the perverse exploiters of the communal archive of traditions: "for you know, you are sure, that if by chance men refuse to vote for you, the animals will come out of the bush, seize ballots, and vote for you" (Kourouma 2001: 258). Aravind Adiga, on the other hand, deploys a different, more sublet technique to deal with the gulf between the illusion of democracy and equality that modernity and globalization have brought into India and the harsh conditions of life throughout the huge country: his "animals" are the ghosts that haunt individuals, striving for power or against corruption, and, through the core of analogy, they eventually become two types of animals, or rather "two castes: Men with Big Bellies, and Men with Small Bellies. And only two destinies: eat—or get eaten up" (2008: 65). *Imago animalium*: the regress to animal instinct is now complete.

References

Adiga, Aravind (2008). *The White Tiger*. London: Atlantic Books.

Kourouma, Ahmadou (2001). *Waiting for the Vote of the Wild Animals*. Translated and with an Afterword by Carrol F. Coates, Charlottesville and London: University Press of Virginia [1998].

Krishnaswamy, N. and Archana S. Burde (1998). *The Politics of Indians' English*. New Delhi: Oxford University Press.

Poddar, Prem (2002). *Violent Civilities*. Aarhus: Aarhus University Press.

Rowland, Beryl (1973). *Animals with Human Faces*. Knoxville: The University of Tennessee Press.

Saadi, Suhayl (2001). "Darkness" in *The Burning Mirror*. Edinburgh: Polygon.

2

Deconstruction in *The White Tiger*

Jackie Haque

Abstract

Deconstruction in literary theory shows how a text is made up of binary oppositions and how these oppositions are related. One of these oppositions becomes central while the other becomes the marginal and hence ignored. Next what deconstruction does is temporarily undoes, subverts and decenters the hierarchy to make the text mean the opposite of what it originally appeared to mean. Then both the terms are deconstructed, they are seen dancing in a free play of non-hierarchical, unstable world with no fixed meanings. Aravind Adiga in his much acclaimed work *The White Tiger* shows the hierarchy of the social system being subverted. The title of the book has a binary opposition, white symbolizing pure and truthfulness and tiger that of fierce strength. And together a white tiger is a rarity. Adiga is keen to show how the economic, political and caste system all integral to the Indian society actually mean the opposite of what they appear to mean. In this essay I would like to show just how Adiga brings in the binary oppositions and subverts the main idea while marginising the other. Thus suggest just the opposite of what it originally supposed to mean.

The White Tiger, the Booker winning Novel by Aravind Adiga is a story about a young driver in India who makes his way up from a dark village of Laxmangarh. Munna alias Balram was born into a family of Halwai caste, the sweet makers. Accordingly he would be hired in teashops or sweet shops. The best that he could do, would be get out of the village and become a rickshaw puller like his father. Balram's father, being rebellious to the system wanted to get out of the vicious cycle of poverty that ruled his life. It's not easy when one is moving along with the centripetal force. The force that pulls one to a life, which absorbs everything, leaves him dry and barren. Balram's father's body succumbed to tuberculosis from over working. But Balram had always aspired to get out of the pothole and make a different life for himself; he wanted to go out of the darkness which engulfed his father. His father instilled this feeling in him when he was very young. So he was sent to school to get education even though it meant hardship for the poverty-stricken family. When his parents died Balram asked his grandmother to lend him money for getting driving lessons. As the elderly lady agreed to finance him he was made to promise on all the Gods in heaven that he would send all the money to her when he earned. Balram becoming a chauffeur of one of the richest person in the village and his subsequent migration to the city made him accustomed to a way of life his village folks could never dream of. He was one of the commoners who would serve his master faithfully. Until he was made to sign a paper saying he ran over a child in the middle of the night. A crime he had nothing to do with. Meanwhile a fellow driver informed him that his class could never be able to make it to be rich. He informed Balram:

> A driver is good till he's fifty or fifty-five. Then the eyes go bad and they kick you out, right? That's thirty years from now, country mouse. If you save from today, you'll make it enough to buy a small home in some slum. If you've been a bit smarter and made a little extra on the side, then you'll have enough to put your son in a good school. He can learn English, he can go to university. That's the best scenario. A house in a slum, a kid in college.

This got him into desperation. He started cheating on his employer and stole his money. One night when Mr. Ashok came out with seven hundred thousand rupees with the intention of giving it to someone, Balram smashed his unsuspecting master's head with a broken whisky bottle. He carried out the heinous act on a lonely highway with a lot of preplanning. He ran away with the bag full of money and started a new life in another part of India where no one recognized him.

The rhetoric of the novel is given by Balram Halwai in forms of letters to the Chinese Premier who was coming to a visit in India. He wanted Mr. Jiabao to get a first-hand knowledge about entrepreneurship in India. He narrated his rebellion against fate, poverty and the tale about reaching the pinnacle of the society in Bangalore. We see the comparison of light and darkness prevailing in the novel. Adiga also confronts the two emerging powers India and China. In this article I would like to point out how the darkness of Balram's life is illuminated with the bright Chandeliers that he so admired. While doing so I'd in fact deconstruct the text as Derrida would put it. Thus, the novel shows opposite of what it originally means to show. In *The White Tiger* Adiga brings the people of darkness into the light and thus change their lives.

While describing Deconstruction; the poststructuralists assert how words say more than what they say. They claimed that language conveyed more than one meaning that it can mean many different things simultaneously rather than giving one authoritarian message. Jacques Derrida gave a lecture at Johns Hopkins University in 1966 "Structure, Sign and Play in the Discourse of the Human Sciences," which caused many previous philosophers to be reassessed. It was something of a disharmonious chord, for his strength was a subversive mode of reading authoritarian texts or any texts. This style of reading came to be known as deconstruction which took America by storm. Deconstruction deals with a way of reading that concerns with decentering, with unmasking the problematic nature of all centers. According to Derrida all western thought is based on the idea of a center, an origin, a truth, an ideal form, a fixed point, an immovable mover, an essence, a god, a presence which is usually capitalized, and which guarantees all meaning. An example is that for 200 years, much of western culture has been centered on the idea of Christianity and Christ. Other cultures had their own symbols. The problem with centers is that they attempt to exclude. In doing so they ignore, repress or marginise the others. Those who become the other are repressed, ignored pushed to the margin.

In Balram's world he is the other, the marginalized. Ashok's life was the center and everything Balram did revolved around Mr. Ashok and Pinky Madam. Stork, Ashok's father was in the coal business and had his palace in Laxmangarh where all the other houses were mud huts except for the four landlords. The Stork, the Buffalo, the Wild Boar and The Raven.

> Each of them got his name from the peculiarities of appetite that had been detected in them.

All the landowners had high walled mansions outside Laxmangarh known as the "The landlord's quarters. They had their own temples inside their mansions, and their own wells and ponds, and did not need to come out into the village except to feed. The children of the four would drive around the village until the Buffalo's son was kidnapped by the Naxals."

All four fed on the village till there was nothing more to feed on. So the villagers left Laxmangarh in search of food, livelihood. But the landlords kept the money flowing one way or the other. Squeezing life out of the poor village folks who did back breaking jobs to keep themselves alive. The villagers were not allowed to sit on chairs rather they had to crouch at the back, in haunch over positions, squatting posture common to servants all over India. Balram's father never crouched he'd rather stand.

> Each year, all the men in the village waited in big group outside the teashop. When the buses came, they got on packing the inside, hanging from the railings, climbing onto the roofs and went to Gaya. (26)

From Gaya they would catch the trains in the same manner to go to Delhi, Calcutta and Dhanbad to find work. As all the landowners manipulated all the resources in the village, nobody could escape from them. The river that flowed outside the village was owned by Stork and he would take a cut from every catch of fish caught by the fishermen and toll from every boatman. Stork's brother, the Wild Boar owned the best land in Laxmangarh and if anyone wanted to work on those lands, they had to bow down to his feet, and touch the dust under his slippers and agree to swallow his daily wages. The Raven had the worst land, dry and rocky. He took a cut from all of them who went to graze their flocks there. The buffalo took share in every rickshaw puller who used the road; one third of whatever you earned was his. They were very cruel too. When one of the sons of Buffalo was kidnapped by the Naxals whose servant was killed along with all his existing family members. Even though the servant had nothing to do with the kidnapping.

Balram was named by one of his teachers as he studied in the village school. Upon enquiry on his first day at school he told the teacher that his name was Munna. The teacher said that it couldn't be his real name and thus gave him a name Balram. To him the school was like a paradise.

> If an Indian village is a Paradise, then the school is a paradise within paradise. (32)

Balram with his heart full of aspiration and a lot of reverence for his father who wanted to be someone different from the commoner of the village. He always wanted to go to the top of the Black Fort. It was ominous to go there and Balram's grandma always warned him against that. Metaphorically he wanted to reach the top and his grandma dissuaded him by saying that a great lizard lived on the fort. Balram was a great admirer of Rumi who says:

> They remain slaves because they can't see what is beautiful in the world.

And so Balram wanted to seek all there was to seek and fulfil his desire. He wrote in one of his letters to the Premier:

> Even as a boy I could see what was beautiful in the world: I was destined not to stay a slave. (41)

Light and darkness pair is one of the many binary oppositions used by the author. Others being Master and slave, fetus and corpse. In Balram's view:

> The Light and the Darkness both flow into Delhi. Gurgaon, where Mr. Ashok lived, is bright, modern end of the city, and this place, Old Delhi, is the other end. Full of things that the modern world forgot all about-rickshaws, old stone buildings, and Muslims.

In any pub in Bangalore what you hear is "can't get enough call-center workers, can't get enough software engineers, and can't get enough sales managers. There are twenty, twenty-five pages of job advertisements in newspaper every week.

Things are different in the Darkness. There every morning, tens of thousands of young men sit in the tea shops, reading the newspaper, or lie on a charpoy humming a tune, or sit in their rooms talking to a photo of a film actress. They have no job to do today. They know they won't get any job today. They have given up the fight. They are the smart ones."

The ones that are the less privileged are known as the people from darkness. So a continuous parallel between light and darkness prevails in Adiga's work. This veiled allegory of light and darkness is what gives *The White Tiger* its distinctiveness.

According to Derrida Deconstruction involves a way of reading that concerns itself with decentering, with unmasking the problematic nature of all centers. In male-dominated societies woman are marginalized, repressed and pushed to the margin. In Laxmangarh the landlords are the center who push all the other villagers into a margin; pushed to the outside. So the longing for a center spawns binary opposites, with one term of the oppositional central, and the other, marginal. Centers want to fix, or freeze, the play of binary opposites. Where one member of the pair is privileged freezing the play of the system, and marginalizing the other member of the pair.

In his letter to the Chinese Premier Balram mentions:

> Please understand your Excellency, that India is two countries in one; an India of the Light and an India of Darkness. The ocean brings light to my country. Every place on the map of India near the ocean is well-off. But the river brings darkness to India—the black river.

The question of why Balram was who he was haunted him.

> Why did I grow up breaking coals and wiping tables, instead of eating gulab jamun and sweet pastries when and where I chose to? Why was I lean and dark and cunning, and not fat and creamy skinned and smiling, like a boy raised on sweets should be?
>
> See, this country, in its days of greatness, when it was the richest nation on earth, was like a zoo. A clean well kept orderly zoo. Everyone in his place, everyone happy. Goldsmiths here. Cowherds here, landlords there. The man called Halwai made sweets.
>
> These days, there are just two castes: men with Big Bellies, and Men with Small Bellies.
>
> And only two destinies: eat—or get eaten up.

Deconstruction is a tactic of decentering, a way of reading, which first reminds us of the centrality of the central term like Adiga made in his work money and power of which Mr. Ashok is the owner so his driver Balram and his family becomes the 'other'. Then what deconstruction does is subverts the central term so that the marginalized term can become central. The marginalized then temporarily overthrows the hierarchy. Balram is accused of running over a child and is made to sign a paper saying he committed the crime. Balram was always treated like a slave by his masters. Even then Ashok and Pinky Madam treat him with a little empathy. Balram was both a cook and a driver and a cleaner all in one. He even acted as a councillor to his employer when Pinky Madam left him and he took heavily to drinking. He became the ruling power in Ashok's life. Temporarily subverting the hierarchy.

But as Derrida points out that one must not pass over and neutralize the phase of subversion too quickly. For this phase of subversion is needed in order to subvert the original hierarchy. The new hierarchy is equally unstable and surrender to the complete free-play of binary opposition in a non-hierarchical way.

Finally Balram takes his master to a deserted lonely highway road where he kills him brutally. He takes the red bag with three hundred thousand rupees. His greed obliterates his sense of kinship. He leaves Delhi for Bangalore a southern vibrant techno city in India which comes alive at night. Balram noticed with his keen entrepreneur vision that the city had everything but taxi service. A service by which young girls could reach home safely. So he invests in that. At the beginning he worked as a driver; as his business goes up he had to hire men to do the driving for him.

The Balram of the darkness becomes an owner of a thriving transport business and lights his house in the center of city with a number of Chandeliers. He read in the newspaper that a family of 16 in Laxmangarh was found dead one morning. He had to be oblivious to the fact that it could be his family in his native village. The dark and thin boy from the village of Laxmangarh had transformed himself into a plump potbellied entrepreneur in the Silicon Valley of India.

A fugitive, a murderer on run lives in a house with Chandeliers; the only house with a chandelier in the toilet and the police couldn't locate him. The police searched for him in the darkness and he hid himself in the light.

> Sometimes, in my apartment, I turn on both chandeliers, and then I lie down amid all that light, and I just start laughing. A man in hiding, and yet he is surrounded by chandeliers! (118)

This is how the novel first decenters the rich and wealthy family in Laxmangarh so Mr. Ashok becomes the marginalized and is removed from the scene as the poor driver-cum-cook becomes the owner of the riches of Ashok. The binary opposition of light and darkness is in play throughout Adiga's work.

In his series of letters Balram informs Mr. Jiabao that India is a country of Democracy. Which again means just the opposite of what it should mean. Democracy according to Wikipedia "is a form of government in which power is held by people under a free electoral system".

The Great Socialist was the leader of the Darkness for a decade, winning one election after another. He had a total of ninety-three cases pending against him; cases of murder, rape, grand larceny, gun-smuggling, and many other offences. He still was a democratically elected representative of his community. The horror of democracy is what Adiga presents by depicting the character of the 'Great Socialist'. The coal miners have to give crores to the high officials to keep their business functioning. Even though the socialist was elected by the four most powerful men in his village at one time they withdrew their support.

> For years there was a deal between the landlords and the Great Socialist—everyone in the village knew about this—but this year something had gone wrong with the deal, so the four animals had joined together and started a party of their own.

The landlords vowed to bring the Great Socialist down this time. They formed a party of their own: named 'All India Social Progressive Front (Leninist Faction)'. They promised the villagers the supply of clean water, roads and hospitals if elected. They waged a tug of war in the village to pull voters on their sides. Later when their feud ended as the great socialist agreed to cut a deal with the landlords. A rickshaw puller was beaten to death by Vijay, a worker of the Great Socialist and the police. The rickshaw puller's crime was that he wanted to cast his own vote, show the landlords the power of democracy. Instead he encountered premature death in the hands of those who swear in the name of democracy. The word 'democracy' had the opposite meaning. So keep himself safe, Balram had never visited the inside of a voting booth though he knew his vote was cast every year since he was eighteen. This he learnt from his father who had also not seen the inside of a booth ever.

Ashok tells Pinky that "there is one thing wrong with this place—we have this fucked-up system called parliamentary democracy".

Then it is shown by Adiga how Ashok and his brother were harassed by the officials because their father was trying to 'distance himself from the Great Socialist'. So when Ashok told his brother to get a tax lawyer and tell all the newspaper that they were ripped apart by the politicians his brother replied:

> you just got back from America. Even this man driving our car knows more about India than you do right now. We need a fixer. He'll get us the interview we need the minister that we need. (121)

As Ashok and Mongoose, his brother's pet name drive past the statue of Mahatma Gandhi the fake democracy laughed on their face.

> We're driving past Gandhi, after just having given a bribe to a minister. It's a fucking joke, isn't it?

Another example of Deconstruction by Adiga is portrayed by driver Ram Persad who was in fact a Muslim but had to pretend to be a Hindu in order to keep his job at a Hindu Landowners residence. Ram Persad woke up at night to have his supper in the month of Ramadan and refrained from having any food during the day. Balram was keen to follow him one evening while Ram Persad went to break his fast in the nearby mosque. Balram unveiled the truth of him being a Muslim thus manipulating the Nepali caretaker into giving him the position of main driver of the house.

The poststructuralist thinkers Gilles Deleuze and Felix Guattari from France oppose the way of knowing which is vertical in nature. This can be traced back to Plato whose vertical, tree like philosophy proclaimed a material world of manifestations stemming from the 'trunk' of a realm of ideal forms or essence. They also criticize the tree like structure of Oedipus complex. It is a tree like structure because all the various psychic processes can be traced back to an original traumatic event in which the child is separated from the mother. This lack of the mother is the basis of the desire, and is compensated for only by the child's entry in the symbolic order. The order of law and name of the father. Both Deleuze and Guattari reject the idea of the Oedipus triangle, of the father principle and of desire based on lack. Desire for them is created horizontally by social interconnections. The interconnection between the infant and his surrounding society are always in movement, flowing, taking lines of flight, like a stringer of a crabgrass in other words like a rhizome. In Adiga's novel *The White Tiger* the protagonist has connections; many of them with different characters from the Darkness but these relationship do not have any meaning neither are they conclusive. Balram's family at Laxmangarh live in darkness like most of Indian villages. And all the family members huddle together in their poverty-stricken hut.

> At night they sleep together, their legs falling one over the other, like one creature, a millipede.

Balram continues to talk about his family but he puts them in the predicament when he kills his master and flees with his money. As a result the village landlord erases out the family of the Halwai in revenge. Then the slum of the aristocratic area is described by Balram as he could relate to the people living there.

> Thousands of people live on the sides of the road of Delhi. They have come from the darkness too—you can tell by their thin bodies, filthy faces, by animal—like way they live under the huge bridges and overpasses, making fires and washing and taking lice of their hair while cars roar past them.

Then there was a fellow driver vitiligo lips that helped him settle down and endeared him by calling by the name of 'Country Mouse'. He befriended Vitiligo lips as they were neighbours. So when Balram tells him where his master lived he says:

> My master lives there too! We're neighbours!

Even though they lived in the most prestigious area of Delhi their way of life was not what they'd hope for. Balram had to live in a room full of cockroaches. And every morning he used the same toilet everyone shared.

> In the morning, after waiting my turn at the common toilet, and then my turn at the common sink, and then my turn at the common bathroom.

Balram and his fellow drivers would wait outside the mall while their masters shopped inside. When one man screamed out to the guard so hard that spit burst from his mouth.

> Am I not a human being too?

All the other drivers felt proud that at least one person among them has stood out revolting against the injustice done towards them.

> "That fellow has balls," one of the drivers said. "If all of us were like that, we'd rule India, and they would be polishing our boots."

Balram felt close to the people who worked in the city for they were from the Darkness too. As he walked past a slum he saw some people whom he could relate to.

> These people were building homes for the rich, but they lived in tents covered with blue tarpaulin sheets, and partitioned into lanes by lines of sewage. It was even worse than Laxmangarh. I picked up my way around the broken glass, wires and shattered tube lights.

These relationships are like Crabgrass with no central root but zillions of them. Each of which interconnects in random, unregulated networks in which any node can interconnect with other nodes. The central root would seek to establish itself but the rhizome is always rearranging interconnections. Balram can be seen doing so throughout the novel.

By various examples Aravind Adiga successfully shows binary opposites that exist in the Indian society and also later on shows that these oppositions are connected to one another before finally showing they mean just the opposite of what they originally meant to show.

Work Cited

Aravind Adiga. *The White Tiger*. India: HarperCollins, 2008.

Powell Jim. *Post Modernism for Beginners*. India: Orient Longman, 2001.

http://en.wikipedia.org/wiki/Democracy 20/2/09.

3

The Inheritance of Loss: A Portrayal of Myriad Shades of Life

Meenakshi Raman

Introduction

The Inheritance of Loss echoes several issues in which human life is entangled—redemption, globalization, colonialism, racism, multiculturalism, justice, economic and social inequality, fundamentalism, immigrant life and alienation (www.nytimes.com). All these themes are discussed through the experiences the characters undergo during the course of their lives. Kiran Desai presents to us an elegant and thoughtful picture of families, the losses each member must confront alone, and lies each tells to make memories of the past more palatable. Sprawling across two continents, the novel is set in India of 1980s and sketches characters, namely, Jemubhai Patel, a former judge; Sai, his granddaughter; his cook and his son Biju; Noni and Lola, his neighbours; and Gyan, Sai's Nepalese maths tutor. These characters are set against the political turmoil of the Himalayan region wherein the Gorkha National Liberation Front (GNLF), a Nepalese independence movement takes a violent turn wherein neighbours turn against neighbours (www.damaris.org).

Kalimpong in the Eastern Himalayas is home to Sai, an orphaned teenager who lives with her grandfather Jemubhai Patel, a retired judge, their poor cook whose son Biju is in New York, and Mutt, the judge's pet dog and his sole source of joy. Their house is broken into by young rebels from the GNLF; an actual political party seeking to empower West Bengal's ethnic Nepalis and once led a separatist uprising. The rebels threaten and humiliate the family and steal the judge's rusty rifles and meagre liquor supply. The Front also draws in Gyan, Sai's maths tutor and lover, who is frustrated by his future as a marginalized Nepali in India and he betrays Sai because of her Westernized ways. In fact, it was he who suggested that the judge's house could be a target for burglary. Kalimpong is in chaos: bands of insurgents invade the town and the police respond by deporting foreigners, confiscating books and detaining and torturing the innocent. Kiran Desai artfully unravels the personal and political strands that have brought her characters to their present life in Kalimpong. She beautifully delineates how little failures are passed down from generation to generation and how each of the character's pasts affect their present circumstances, what losses they have inherited and how they are attempting towards redemption. She portrays with consummate artistic skills the variegated lives of her characters.

The discussion that follows illustrates with examples the multifarious experiences encountered by some major characters of Kiran Desai's *The Inheritance of Loss* during the course of their lives.

Jemubhai, The Embittered Judge

Jemubhai Patel's life reflects memoirs of his past and his hope for redemption in the present. Jemubhai is one of the two main characters Desai's novel revolves around. An embittered, ogre-like judge who seems to prefer living in the past, Jemubhai spends his cramped, angry, old age caring for the 16-year old Sai, his orphaned granddaughter in hope of some redemption for his past. The judge is Cambridge-educated Anglophile and one of those ridiculous Indians who couldn't rid themselves of what they had broken their souls to learn and whose Anglophilia can only turn into self-hatred. These Indians are also an unwanted anachronism in postcolonial India where long-suppressed peoples have begun to awaken their dereliction, to express their anger and despair.

Born in a small village in Gujarat in a middle class Patel family the judge goes to Victorian England in 1939 and subsequently returns as an ICS officer serving the British. He had first left his home at the age of twenty, with a black tin trunk. From there he had journeyed to the Bombay dock, Liverpool and to Cambridge. We can feel his callousness towards his mother through Desai's words:

> Jemu picked up the package, fled to the deck, and threw it over board. Didn't his mother think of the inappropriateness of her gesture? Undignified love, Indian love, stinking, anaesthetic love—the monsters of the ocean could have what she had so bravely packed getting up in that predawn mush. (38)

The judge found it difficult to adapt himself to the English setting. Feeling lost, and scorned for his skin, colour, smell and with full of self-hate as well as hate for his family, community and anyone for not being British which includes his wife, the judge settles in Kalimpong in a crumbling old relic of a mansion from the colonial era. This journey has had the most profound effect and his experiences in England, the humiliations—whether real or perceived—have seared into his soul, changing him forever. So, as Jemubhai climbs the ladder of material success, his soul sinks into new depths. Ashamed of his own skin and arrogant in the extreme, he embraces these Western manners and turns back on his family and his society, placing himself above them. But in no way he has been accepted by the society he aspires to be a part of. The more he is aware of the irony, the more he fills himself with hatred.

> Thus Jemubhai's mind has begun to warp; he grew stranger to himself than he was to those around him, found his own skin odd-coloured, his own accent peculiar. He forgot how to laugh, could barely manage to lift his lips in a smile, and if he ever did, he held his hand over his mouth, because he couldn't bear anyone to see his gums, his teeth. They seemed too private. In fact, he could barely let any of himself peep out of his clothes for fear of giving offence. He began to wash obsessively.... To the end of his life, he would never be

> seen without socks and shoes and would prefer shadow to light, faded days to sunny, for he was suspicious that sunlight might revealed him, in his hideousness, all too clearly. (40)

Once the pride of his family and village, Jemubhai lives an isolated life in his large run-down house finding joy only in his dog, Mutt. When he is in search of Mutt, his pet dog, he thinks of his father whose strength, hope and love he had fed on, only to turn around to spit in his face. Then he thought of how he had sent his wife, Nimi, home. He recalled how his "anger, once released, like a genie from a bottle, could never again be curtailed" (305) and how he hit his wife because of his self-hatred.

The judge feels that the journey he had started so long ago had continued in his descendants. Perhaps he has made a mistake in condemning his daughter before he knew her. However, he feels that Sai, his granddaughter whom he doesn't hate is perhaps the only miracle fate has thrown his way. As Desai points out,

> But now he acquiesced to something in the past that had survived, returned, that might, without his paying too much attention, redeem him.... Despite himself, he felt, in the backwaters of his unconscious, an imbalance in his deeds balancing itself out. (210)

Sai, The Lovelorn

A lonely soul looking for love is Sai, the 16-year old granddaughter of Jemubhai. Her life mirrors the remnant influence of colonialism through her convent education. A girl pinched off life by the ultimate death of her parents, Sai is unable to care for her enough even when alive. When the orphaned Sai arrives with her battered trunk with the letters "Miss S. Mistry, St. Augustine's Convent" at her maternal grandfather's house in Kalimpong, little does she realize what life has in store for her. The judge is hiding from his own life and at a loss to provide the love and warmth the girl yearns for. He pours all his love on Mutt, his pet dog and leaves Sai's care to his chatty cook who speaks Hindi and their friendship composes of shallow things conducted in a broken language because Sai is a speaker of English. But she finds a ready friend and a confidant in the cook who tries his best in his own erratic ways to bring up Sai.

Sai does not dwell in the past and is happy with her present. She is glad to be out of the convent where she had lived when her parents were abroad. When Sai is four years old, her parents send her to St. Augustine's convent where they exchange newsy letters devoid of emotional content. Two years later she is still at the convent school when her parents immigrate to Russia where her father is striving to become an astronaut in the Soviet space programme. His mission however is never fulfilled as he and his wife are killed in a bus accident while crossing a street in Moscow. Orphaned at the age of six without seeing her parents for the last two years, Sai arrives at the door steps of Jemubhai Patel, a retired judge cum her grandfather she has never met in her life. The judge's cook takes a fatherly interest in Sai, perhaps a compensation for his absent son, Biju who is living in New York with his other illegal immigrant friends.

There is a sense of hidden excitement in Sai's life when Gyan, the young Nepali tutor comes into the picture to help her out with her maths. She falls in love with this misguided, if quixotic Nepali guy who is torn apart between his own love of Sai and his hatred of everything that Sai represents in Indian society. As Sai struggles with the fundamentals of mathematics, she develops a strange liking for Gyan who is also aware of her desire. As their romance flourishes, the political turmoil created by GNLF (Gorkha National Liberation Front) continues to remain in the background for them. Gyan's friends are actively participating in the revolt and also incite him to join the movement. As the trouble gets aggravated, there arises a note of unease in their relationship. Matters reach a head when Gyan finds himself inferior in status to her and finds Sai's actions as undesirable though they had charmed him earlier. Confused and disgusted, he joins the insurgents and marches across the streets demanding liberation of his homeland and wanting to oust all foreigners. Even as the dismayed Sai tries in vain to bridge the gap between her and Gyan she only ends up in humiliating herself. Their lives descend into chaos.

Sai is young enough to live in the moment, which helps her overlook some of the issues with her boyfriend Gyan—issues that lurk just under the surface of their affair. As an Indian of a formerly powerful, educated and Western-thinking family, Sai has an identity and her relationship to India is very different from that of Gyan. Gyan's Nepalese family lives in poverty, struggling to meet ends meet while providing him with good education. When his friends start to fight against, first peacefully and then with violence, the inequalities and xenophobia present in India itself, he is caught up in the furore and clashes with Sai. Though her romance provides her with an emotional escape from Kalimpong, it soon becomes complicated by Gyan's involvement with GNLF revolt. Shifting sands of political conflicts leave everyone struggling for footing, amplifying mistrust and prejudice. Loss is the currency common to all. Sai contemplates: "Could fulfilment ever be felt as deeply as loss? ...love must surely reside in the gap between desire and fulfilment, in the lack, not the contentment" (2-3).

As far as the judge is concerned, Sai's presence in the house serves to break down the barriers the sour old man has built up against the weight of deeply shaming memories. However, Sai is broken when Gyan abandons her. "What will happen to me? Gyan would find adulthood and purity in a quest for a homeland and she would be left forever adolescent, trapped in shameful dramatics. This was the history that sustained her: the family that never cared, the lover who forgot.... Sai cried for a while..." (265).

Gyan, The Radical

A Gorkha, sympathetic to the GNLF that is violently demanding an independent homeland in the Northern region, Gyan is the math tutor for Sai. Though he is born in a poor family, his parents have given him good education and he speaks fluent English. In the 1800s his ancestors had left their village in Nepal and arrived in Darjeeling. His great grandfather was inducted in the British Army and served in several countries. When Gyan was quite small, his family lived with his uncle in Kalimpong and his father was teaching in a tea plantation school beyond Darjeeling. They live in a small shattered house and Gyan is hesitant to talk about his family to Sai, though he shares his great grandfather's tenure in British army. Gyan comes across humiliation, mockery, upsurge, loss, excitement, etc., in his life.

During one of his visits to Sai's place, he had to stay back because of an unabated storm. It was then that he is humiliated by Sai's grandfather, the judge who says, "What made you come out in such weather, Charlie? You might be adept at mathematics, but commonsense appears to have eluded you" (109). Because of his lack of familiarity with the cutlery and the food that was offered by the judge, Gyan is further mocked at by him. He hates the dingy season that angered him as it had made a mockery of him and his ideals.

Initially Sai and Gyan did not pay much attention to the events on the hillside, the new posters in the market referring to old discontents, the slogans scratched and painted on the side of government offices and shops. But with the active role of youth wing, GNLF gains momentum in the hillside. Gyan is pulled in by old hatreds which are endlessly retrievable. "It suddenly became clear why he had no money and no real job had come his way, why he couldn't fly to college in America, why he was ashamed to let anyone see his house. Most of all he realized why his father's meekness infuriated him, and why he found himself unable to speak of him.... For a moment all the different pretences he had indulged in, the shames he had suffered, the future that wouldn't accept him—all these things joined together to form a single truth" (160). He voiced an adamant opinion that the Gorkha movement take the harshest route possible.

He shouts at Sai for her ridiculous middle-class upbringing and her ignorance. She in turn is shocked and feels betrayed on a singularly personal and intimate level...she has done nothing personal to elicit his vitriol. She merely belongs to a different group and is its representative in Gyan's limited life. Gyan ends up judging Sai for her connivance and her loyalty to the social class she's accidentally been born to. In other words, Gyan decides to despise her and her bourgeois ways. After failing to find out a sense of purpose in history and politics, Gyan feels, "Happiness has a smaller location".

Gyan breaks his affair with Sai because he feels the status difference that prevails between them.

> She who could speak no language but English and pidgin Hindi, she who could not converse with anyone outside her tiny social stratum.
>
> She who could not eat with her hands; could not squat on the ground on her haunches to wait for a bus; who had never been to a temple but for architectural interest; never chewed a paan and had not tried most sweets in the *mithaishop*, for they made her retch; she who left a Bollywood film so exhausted from emotional wear and tear that she walked home like a sick person and lay in pieces on the sofa; she who thought it vulgar to put oil in your hair and used paper to clean her bottom; felt happier with so-called English vegetables, snap peas, French beans, spring onions, and feared—feared—*loki, tinda, kathal, kaddu, patrel,* and the local *saag* in the market. (176)

Gyan thinks that "Sai had betrayed him, led him to betray others, his own people, his family. She had enticed him, sneaked up on him, spied on him, ruined him, caused him to behave badly" (262). However, he revisits what has gone through and feels guilty for what he has done and feels dizzy and nauseous.

Biju, The Pathetic Immigrant

Biju's life, like Sai's is a prisoner of his own conscience. Like Sai who lives in Cho Oyu as a virtual prisoner and pines for the love of elusive Gyan, Biju though lives in New York, hasn't had the time to see it, lives in poverty where he has to sleep in shifts, or on the floor of the hotel where he works, and has to serve beef which he detests. Like his friend Saeed, Biju is willing to undergo any torment to make ends meet. While Gyan and the insurgents are struggling for their rights and freedom in India, Biju is fighting for his own identity as he adapts to his life in New York. As he hops from one menial job to the other in the City, he finds that life in America is not as lavish as he had expected and he has left the servant's life in one country just to take a similar one in another country. He also realizes that though poverty in America is considerably less severe than it is in India, it is more difficult to live with because it is so obvious and noticeable, something that the members of the middle class actively work to separate themselves from. Biju's experiences reflect many of the problems with colonialism and globalization and when he decides to return to India, the message becomes very stronger when the American friend tells him:

> You know America is in the process of buying up the world. Go back, you'll find they own the businesses. One day you will be working for an American company there or here. Think of your children. If you stay here, your son will earn a hundred thousand dollars for the same company he could be working for in India but making one thousand dollars.... You are making a big mistake. Still a world, my friend, where one side travels to be a servant, and the other side travels to be treated like a king. (269)

He keeps his father live in his fantasy world writing letter after letter that he was doing fine though there was no improvement in his status in USA. This repeated letters of Biju and the repeated boasting of his father, provide a comfort for them. Biju works in run-down kitchens, sleeping in basements overcrowded with other illegal immigrants. During his second year in New York, he becomes a victim in the hands of Pinocchio's Italian restaurant owner whose wife hated his Indian smell. But he writes to his father, "Respected Pitaji, no need to worry. Everything is fine. The manager has offered me a full time waiter position. Uniform and food will be given by them. Angrezi khana only, no Indian food, and the owner is not from India. He is from America itself" (14).

Young Biju ekes out an existence as an undocumented worker in New York. Stumbling from one low-paid restaurant job to another, living in seedy squalor with groups of other immigrants Biju imagines what life would be like with "a sofa, a TV and a bank account". Spurred on by his father Biju came to USA thinking that he could achieve American dream, but the reality is quite different. He realizes that "this light was too brief for real succour and it seemed more the visitation of a beautiful memory than the real thing" (189).

We see the pathetic condition in which Biju lives in USA from many passages as the ones that follow: "Biju joined a shifting population of men camping out near the fuse box, behind the boiler, in the cubby holes, and in old-shaped corners that once were pantries, maid's rooms, laundry rooms, and storage rooms at the bottom of what had been a single-family home.... The men shared a yellow toilet; the sink was a tin laundry enough.... Biju had been nervous there from his very first day" (51-52).

> Looking at a dead insect in the sack of basmati that had come all the way from Dehra Dun, he almost wept in sorrow and marvel at its journey, which was tenderness for his own journey. (191)

Though he feels a flash of anger at his father for sending him alone to America, he knew he wouldn't have forgiven his father had he not sent him either. However, he finds no reconciliation with his father's expectations of life in America. His father's misguided belief in the American dream is obvious in his letters to Biju in which he implores his son to help the sons and daughters of neighbours as they arrive in New York illegally day by day. However Biju avoids them as he has no work, no food or no place for them to sleep. Life in New York is not a cake walk for Biju as he struggles immensely. Ultimately he feels fed up and left alone in a system that he knows nothing about and decides to return to his homeland with his meagre savings. When he reaches India, he thinks he is safe, breathes a sigh of relief and feels at home. "Biju stepped out of the airport into the Calcutta at night, warm, mammalian. His feet sank into dust winnowed to softness at his feet, and he felt an unbearable feeling, sad and tender, old and sweet like the memory of falling asleep, a baby on his mother's lap.... He looked out and for the first time in God knows how long, his vision unblurred and he found that he could see clearly" (300).

It is pathetic to see Biju being robbed of his meagre savings as well as his American clothes when he returns after his stress-borne life in America. In fact, Biju has failed to absorb anything positive from his life in America. Biju who goes to America with high hopes of returning with abundant wealth and new life is now "without his baggage, without his savings, worst of all, without his pride. Back from America with far less than he'd ever had" (317).

Cook, The Ardent Dreamer

Running parallel to Sai's life at Cho Oyu, is that of the old cook's whose thoughts always spin around his only son Biju who at present is in New York (www.hindu.com). The cook goes on recollecting the past and building dreams for his son. He keeps showering praises on Biju. He takes pleasure in boasting of him. He lives in a fantasy world typical of parents of immigrants. Even as the cook extols the virtues of America as a land of opportunities, little does he know the harsh truth of his son's banal, fugitive-like existence where each day brings in more despair than hope and life seems to be an endless hiding in smelly kitchens and rolled in newspapers for warmth.

The cook has no identity of his own except by his profession. He treasures his son, the pride of his life. A migrant worker from Uttar Pradesh, he has been living for survival at the judge's house and does household chores. Though he shows affection and love to Sai and takes full care of the judge, his dog, and Sai the *raison d'être* for his life at this old age is his son Biju. "Terrible", he says, "My bones ache so badly, my joints hurt, I may as well be dead. If not for Biju..." (3). When the police come to verify the robbery at the judge's house, we get to know a glimpse of the cook's untold life—the condition in which he lives. A few clothes hung over a string, a single razor blade and a silver of cheap brown soap, a Kulu blanket, a cardboard case with metal clasps that contained the cook's papers, the recommendations that had helped him procure his job, Biju's letters, papers from a court case fought in his village, a broken watch and two photographs—these are the only possessions of thc cook. His wife had died when Biju was seven years old and hence the entire responsibility of bringing him up has fallen on the cook.

At fourteen, he was hired by the judge at twelve rupees a month. The cook first starts a liquor business for Biju's sake because his salary has hardly been changed in years. In fact he has done this business for himself as well since he loves modernity: toaster ovens, electric shavers, watches, cameras, cartoon colours. He even dreams in modern codes, the digits of a telephone flying away before he could dial them, a garbled television.

When a recruiting agent appeared in Kalimpong four years ago, the cook had first made the effort to send his son abroad. He somehow ensured that his effort turned out to be a success by producing fake recommendations, a fake bank statement, etc., and finally sent Biju to USA fulfilling his long cherished dream.

The cook is thrilled and considers his son as the luckiest boy in this world. He lives in the hope that eventually his son would make enough and the cook would retire. He would receive a daughter-in-law to serve him food, crick-crack his toes, grandchildren to swift like flies (17). The story of the cook and his son runs through letters exchanged among them between the two worlds. As Biju agonizes in America, the cook in India establishes his status as the father of a son in USA and keeps sending recommendations to Biju asking him to take care of others as well. "Biju beta, you have been fortunate enough to get there, please do something for others... (94-95). Kiran Desai's masterly delineation of the cook's life reflects the real picture of how the Indian parents (like the cook) of US immigrants keep on building castles in air and live in a world of fantasy. They are unable to realize the miserable conditions in which their children live in USA but think that once their children reach America they live in luxury.

When Kalimpong is soaked in blood and bruises because of the insurgency by GNLF for an independent homeland, the cook feels insecure and fears that he may not be able to see his son Biju again. He feels guilty and thinks that he has ignored his duty when Mutt, the judge's pet dog disappears. He asks the judge to beat him: "Sahib, beat me. I'm a wicked man, a weak man, I'd better dead than alive. I'm a bad man, forgive me, forgive me..." (320).

Conclusions

The preceding discussion clearly illustrates how Kiran Desai's novel *The Inheritance of Loss* delineates the myriad shades of life through its major characters, namely, the Judge, Sai, Gyan, Biju and the Cook. A gamut of expressions such as brutality, humour, whimsy, harshness, delicate emotions, passionate commitment, humiliation, racial prejudice, pathos, outrage, etc., echo through their lives. Desai launches into a full-blown account of these distraught lives, buffeted by the winds of change—lives that hope to regain some of their lost assurances. But when everything descends into a chaos, each one needs to delve into their past to see what role they have played and how their actions have led to this final hour. Despite the unwritten hierarchy, their histories are intimately interwoven. Desai's depiction of their lives, longings and insecurities makes each one come alive just as they are—human, confused, loving, hating and longing—all at once. The spontaneous exchange of love between the cook and his son despite their poverty is contrasted with the lack of love that was visible in the judge-Sai relationship. Long for home, long for love and long for acceptance yet rarely they are skilled in locating any of these. Gyan's commitment to the insurgency offers an ironic contrast with the commitment of his family to the colonial British army in the earlier times just as the judge's hatreds learnt in England are ironically contrasted with his British affectations in his later life (www.amazon.co.uk). The threat of violence looms large throughout the novel, in the very words of its characters that seem to have nothing lacking in them, just the feeling that their lives are not fulfilled. But almost all of them realize that emotional fulfilment gives hope despite material losses and that the only thing that can sustain is human relationships (www.flipkart.com).

Works Cited

Desai Kiran, 2006, *The Inheritance of Loss*. New Delhi: Penguin Books.

http://www.amazon.co.uk/review/R1K7GFLXUTQZ3T

http://www.damaris.org/content/content.php?type=1&id=384

http://www.flipkart.com/inheritance-loss-kiran-desai/0143102788-xow3fses4b

http://www.hindu.com/lr/2006/10/01/stories/2006100100280100.htm

http://www.nytimes.com/2006/02/12/books/review/12mishra.html

Cyclical Temporality in Salman Rushdie's *The Satanic Verses*

Erin Warde

Salman Rushdie, through his novel *The Satanic Verses*, introduces his readers to a narrative that functions on multiple levels of theoretical understanding. Reminiscent of concepts from postcolonial theorists such as Edward Said and Homi Bhabha, Rushdie appropriately expresses the power play between the colonizer and the colonized in the construction of his characters and their respective symbolic natures as well as their identities. Rushdie problematizes the arbitrarily conceived duality of the East and West. The novel follows characters in a fashion that disorients the reader through shifts in psychic distance between the reader and character points of view. Through events that break the laws of the nature, *The Satanic Verses* stylistically attempts to subvert reality by using the trope of magical realism, bringing readers into a surreal world that reflects the reality of the history of colonization. Within the text, Rushdie makes strong theological and philosophical commentaries, often taking these concepts from both Western orthodox religion and the Eastern theological beliefs. In publishing this novel, Rushdie was catapulted into the realm of literary acclaim, yet had to die a metaphorical/symbolic death because of the strong implications articulated in the text, resulting in his own involuntary anonymity. Much the same way his novel caused his own figurative birth and death, the text also ushers his readers into the trope of birth and death. In

Salman Rushdie's *The Satanic Verses*, the concept of rebirth breaks the power structure of linear time by functioning cyclically, helping to shift focus from West to East, negating the normative linear temporality and thereby refusing to give the colonized a definitive end.

"To be born again...first you have to die;" the outset of the novel prepares readers for the influence of "rebirth" that is revisited continually throughout the narrative (Rushdie 1). This offers a divine link between death and life and sets the stage for a narrative in which linear time is broken; rebirth as a concept, claims Akhil Gupta, speaks to an "oriental" conception of time as being circular (191). Gupta explains this concept of Western and Eastern temporality when he writes, "time in industrial capitalism becomes abstract, homogenous, empty, linear, and progressive, shorn of 'nature's rhythms,' and unconnected to the task at hand" (196). Gupta continues by pointing out that throughout history, ancient cultures have embraced a very cyclical time—a time based in nature's flow (196). Rushdie believes that "unreality is the only weapon with which reality can be smashed, so that it may subsequently be reconstituted" —he calls for the death of the current definition of reality to give way to the birth of what he believes is the truth behind reality (Finney 5). The truth that asserts "uncertainty is the only unchanging certainty that Rushdie perversely posits in the novel" (Finney 5). By supplementing this idea of temporality, readers of Rushdie's text can see the concept of rebirth taking an upper hand in the power play between East and West, giving the East a mystical strength. By functioning cyclically, Eastern temporality does not fall victim to the "empty" linear time of the West.

By embracing nature's rhythms, cyclical time identifies with the eternal quality of nature—characters in Rushdie's text exist in their humanity, while similarly existing within eternity through a rebirth continuum. In death being the way to rebirth, there is a clear abandonment of linear time, allowing the East to triumph over Western temporality and never be given a definitive end. A good example of this would be indicated through novels from Southeast Asia winning major literary prizes such as the Booker that challenges the façade of Western authority—in this, the East "writes back" to the West and then, with this rebirth into discourse, refuses to see an end. The Eastern identity gets reborn to the West through Rushdie's fiction as he employs the concept of rebirth and its primary theme of non-normative temporality.

Rushdie employing this idea of *re*birth carries his readers through the theoretical realm of Edward Said's *Orientalism*. Said creates a theory about colonial power play between the colonizer and the colonized that is born out of Foucault's power/knowledge model (Childs and Williams 98). Rushdie's novel is reborn into discourse only because the Eastern identity has died at the hands of Western hegemony—the hegemony that attempts to control knowledge through discourse. Rushdie rises, a phoenix from the ashes of Western colonization, to insert a discourse of knowledge, and thus power, held by the colonized. Rushdie gives the East its rebirth. Childs and Williams quote Said in saying, "Orientals were rarely seen or looked at: they were seen through, analyzed not as citizens, or even people, but as problems to be solved or confined, or—as the colonial powers openly coveted their territory—taken over" (100). The East has been constructed by the West as a space that is a "repository of all those characteristics deemed non-Western (and therefore negative)" (Childs and Williams 100). Rushdie constructs characters that cannot be looked through and a discourse that cannot be reduced to problems to solve. The text is consistently carrying readers through their relationships and this constant shift in point of view acts as a disorienting agent that mimics the dislocation of the Eastern identity. The East experiences the *re*writing of their history—they are erased from their own space and redefined under Western authority. It is because of this violation that Rushdie must "reclaim the metaphor" from the Empire with a text that takes the West through dislocation and disorientation, which ultimately places the West in the cyclical and distinctly non-linear space of the East—a space the West attempted to negate, but instead, must inhabit (Rushdie 192).

Architectonically, Rushdie constructs a narrative that works cyclically, first through shifting characters in such a way that no one character defines the narrative, or how time progresses in that narrative. In doing this, Rushdie writes a narrative with no one centre, but instead, a circle of characters around the centre, which is undefined. Rushdie also distinctly does not place the British Empire as that centre. Again, this trope of cyclical temporality further promotes the novel's theme of rebirth that results in a breaking away from Western hegemony. In addition, as the point of view shifts from character to character, the reader is reborn into each character; in this way, the reader is reincarnated into the plethora of characters introduced by the text. The reader participates in the power play between the characters, especially those that serve as symbolic conflicts between the East and West.

For Rushdie, the chutnification of words shows the birth of new words that comes out of the death of old words. In Rushdie's very construction of words, he breaks away from the language of linear temporality; the Westernized English is abandoned and an Easternized English is embraced, an Indian "English" (Dayal 433). Samir Dayal's article "Talking Dirty: Salman Rushdie's *Midnight Children*" makes a strong commentary on *The Satanic Verses*, including quoting Rushdie and his ideas about how language and postcoloniality fuse together: "those peoples who were once colonized by the language are now rapidly remaking it, domesticating it...they are carving out large territories for themselves within its frontiers" (433). By Rushdie giving the English language Eastern accents, it becomes hybridized. This hybrid language "starts absorbing characteristics from the surrounding cultures, growing to such extent that no single culture can contain the cultural cross-references that inhabit this new being" (Rios 55). The new language cannot be called Western—it has progressed out of an amalgam, and gets reborn. By hybridizing language, the words Rushdie uses become part of a "copious language / A language trying to strangers" (Rushdie 438). This language is not easy to grasp because it is encoded with a language of voice for the East: the language of cyclical temporality. The novel asks, "How does newness come into the world? How is it born? Of what fusions, translations, conjoinings, is it made?" (Rushdie 8). Rushdie's answer is the entire novel—the entire novel's language, characters, plot structure, and development are the newness in the world, the fusions, the translations, and the conjoining. The language of the text creates newness and acts cyclically, thus creating a language like earth's movement. This hybrid tongue turns on the axis of the characters' lives, deaths, and rebirths; the language revolves around the trope of rebirth. Rushdie knows how newness enters the world—it is written into the world. Newness is a remake of the old; "Language is the courage: the ability to conceive a thought, to speak it, and by doing so to make it true" (Rushdie 290). He constructs a novel that brings that hybrid-newness into the world, and through such an action, re-defines temporality in the same cyclical fashion.

Aside from the motif of language to dislocate temporality, *The Satanic Verses* creates a binary between mysticism and history, which in turn creates the dyad of East versus West. The narrative puts history seemingly on the side of the West and mysticism on the side of the East, which sets up two competing concepts. In this, the reader gets to participate in this power play as s/he deciphers through the confusion of magical realism. The reader wonders: Is this real? Do I believe this is happening in the story? Is this a dream within the story? By creating a questionable text, Rushdie encourages his readers to either embrace the mysticism of magical realism, or constantly question the events of the story in order to make sense out of the nonsensical. Gibreel is also torn between the miraculous world and a world of dreams—this leaves Gibreel in a state of schizophrenia (Finney 4). This schizophrenia is similar to the dislocation of identity that the reader feels due to the rebirthing of psyches. Rushdie feeds on this psychological conflict, saying, "the imagination can falsify, demean, ridicule, caricature and wound as effectively as it can clarify, intensify and unveil" (Finney 5). Rushdie knows how the imagination works and uses magical realism to dilute the reader's understanding of reality just enough to let his own views spill in, but by hiding them deep within a sea of fiction and imagination.

Within the text, the characters question their own reality and the role of mysticism and history; they, like the readers, are dislocated in time and space. At times, characters, such as Mirza, as well as the readers participating in the action of Mirza, come to the conclusion that "it was better to put one's trust in reason than in miracles" (Rushdie 509). Hanif further encourages readers to "not fall into the trap of some damn mysticism", noting that they are "talking about history: an event in the history of Britain" (Rushdie 484). These characters, as the readers are reborn into their psyches, seemingly lead readers through the reasoning process of the events of the novel. On the other hand, Mishal guides readers into the Arabian Sea based on her faith in mystical forces. Readers entertain two mystical transformations of men into archangels and demons. Each reader is reincarnated into both the reasoned and romanticized view of the forces at work in the text. In short, s/he has the option to choose between history and mysticism with little to no help from the text, or specifically the characters, whom each embody a different opinion on these two conflicting topes in the novel.

Rushdie continually reinforces the trope of not just rebirth, but of reincarnation or being remade, through his characters. In continually shifting in their being, they are not being defined in linear time and are instead finding cyclical existence. Rushdie writes of the character Saladin Chamcha, "a new, dark world had opened up for him (or: within him) when he fell from the sky; no matter how assiduously he attempted to re-create his old existence, this was, he now saw, a fact that could not be remade" (Rushdie 433). Saladin cannot re-create his old existence, just as the colonized people cannot recreate their own existence; the colonized is stripped not only in identity, but also in history "in the moment when colonial power inscribes itself onto the body and space of its Others" (Childs and Williams 4). To further explain this concept, Rushdie introduces the character of Salahuddin—his being "remade" into someone who calls himself "Saladin" changes his identity and removes him from his own family history that he strives to escape from. Saladin's transformation/reincarnation into the satanic beast signifies that his desire to escape his own history succeeds; still, he escapes not only his history, but also his humanity. It is when Saladin finally returns home that he claims for himself again the identity that was taken from him. He is transformed back to his history, and in doing so he overcomes this erasing of identity and thus, overcomes the colonizer.

Throughout the narrative, multiple characters deal with disease, specifically cantankerous cancer. Mishal is stricken with cancer, and she believes she will be cured through passing through the parted Arabian Sea, with the parting of the sea being a common trope in religious texts—reminiscent specifically the Old Testament parting of the Red Sea. In Mishal's spiritual endeavour, her husband disagrees, causing a conflict between mysticism and history/reason. She functions as a representation of cyclical time, because she does enter into the sea, and thus enter into her death, but (as she believes) she also receives her life, regardless of her disease. Eyewitnesses to the event believe to see the people pass through the sea, though they are certainly passing through to a physical death. In this instance, while they die physically, readers are assured they do not truly die—but live. With a text full of rebirths, readers are certain that this death can only be telling of a new life.

In addition, Saladin is described as being evil that is "from some sort of recess of his own true nature, that it has been spreading through his selfhood like a cancer, erasing what was good in him, wiping out his spirit" (Rushdie 478). Saladin's evil is like a cancer because it takes him over, it overcomes his spirit—it erases his spirit, just as history being written into the colonized states does to the colonized. Saladin's father dies of disease, which brings him back to his home, and creates in him the appreciation for his home he never treasured. In his father's death, Saladin finds life within his home and new life in himself that respects his heritage. Generally speaking, the trope of cancer can function in such a way that reinforces the idea that linear time eats away at the characters by trying to force on them a definitive end—death. They escape this death—both their literal death and the death of their relationships—by being reborn, in whichever wide variety of ways Rushdie handles the death and rebirth concept.

To expound upon the trope of passing through the sea, in that section of the novel there are many mentions to "floods" and the characters undergo intense rain that can be seen as symbolic of a flood, which is naturally symbolic of death. While the flood may symbolize death, in narratives floods often lead to new creation and thus, new life. In orthodox Christian tradition, the concept of baptism explains that in the waters of baptism, a person dies, and rises out of the baptismal font as a new life, reborn into a life of community with God. In this narrative, the blending of religious traditions accounts for different interpretations of what this passing through the sea means.

Regardless of the flood-like rain, the characters pass through the Arabian Sea. The crowd moving towards the sea on their pilgrimage is described as "parting like the sea" (Rushdie 521). In this, readers see the group—united with one purpose—divide. In the same way, history has served to divide the identities of the colonized by imparting upon them a linear Westernized history. While this may leave the colonized disoriented, because they have no centre, this is not a death sentence—this is instead an opportunity for continual rebirth. Their lack of a centre births a cyclical being and liberates the colonized people; they are an unchained, mystical people. The crowd journeying to walk through the sea are persistent in their spiritual journey; in the issue of mysticism versus history, this parting of the sea shows mysticism overcoming history.

Rushdie uses the idea of falling to show characters and how they transition from one way of being to another. At the outset of the novel, both characters Gibreel and Saladin fall, which introduces readers to the two characters. These men are, instead of falling to their deaths, falling to new lives. The character of Gibreel has a sort of "fall from grace". He has a very physical event in which his body bleeds profusely that puts him close to death, yet he survives. Still, he renounces his faith. In this situation, we see him "reborn" not only physically, but also spiritually—though reborn into agnosticism. He is now a synthetic character, changed by the events and their reshaping of his psyche and ability to believe in a supernatural force.

The two characters, after their reincarnations at the beginning of the novel, "fall" in the eyes of the public, for whom they've served through entertainment. In addition, they've taken on different roles (been "reborn") in their families, as well as in their relationships. For example, in Saladin's life, he no longer is a husband to Pamela, but does finally become a true son to his father. This cyclical existence has disoriented the characters in their own lives, but also in how they are viewed by family, in their relationships, and by the readers. The two reborn characters, Saladin and Gibreel, are not only disoriented by their cyclical existence, but by the fact that they interact with other cyclical beings. Their breaking of linear time has created a vortex of identities that draws characters into the processes of death and birth. In the way the book is written, it's no surprise that as the shifts in point of view occur, readers "fall" into different narratives and perspectives, consequently also being taken into the narrative's vortex.

Works Cited

Childs, Peter and R.J. Patrick Williams. *An Introduction to Post-Colonial Theory*. Upper Saddle River: Prentice Hall, 1997.

Dayal, Samir. "Talking Dirty: Salman Rushdie's *Midnight's Children*." *College English* 54 (1992): 431-45. JSTOR. Troy University, Troy. 20 Apr. 2009 <http://www.jstor.org/stable/377839>.

Finney, Brian. "Salman Rushdie's *The Satanic Verses*." California State University, Long Beach. 1998. 05 May 2009 <http://www.csulb.edu/~bhfinney/SalmanRushdie.html>.

Gupta, Akhil and J. Patrick. "The Reincarnation of Souls and the Rebirth of Commodities: Representations of Time in East and West." *Cultural Critique* 22 (1992): 187-211. JSTOR. Troy University, Troy. 2009 <http://www.jstor.org/stable/1354088>.

Rios, Hugo J. Patrick. "Hybrid Moments in Salman Rushdie's *The Satanic Verses*." Atenea 24 (2004): 51-58. Literature Resources from Gale. Troy University, Troy. 24 Apr. 2009 <http://go.galegroup.com/ps/start.do?p=LitRG&u=troy25957>.

Rushdie, Salman. *The Satanic Verses: A Novel.* New York: Random House Trade, Paperbacks, 2008.

5

National Allegory, Reshaping Memory and Rewriting History: Salman Rushdie's *Midnight's Children* and *Shame*

John Nkemngong Nkengasong and
Magdelene Atanga Mafor

The relations between South-East Asia and Britain for several decades have been subject to various conflicting and controversial interpretations. The fact that colonialism merged nations with different ethnic, racial and religious identities made relations between India and Pakistan particularly tense. Indians have always asserted their Hindu majority status while the Pakistani, though minority, also set out to assert their Islamic ancestral origin. Each of the above groups desired to bring out a distinct national identity as a different religious entity. The issue of a national identity was inflamed by the independence of India in 1947 and the partition of Pakistan from India immediately after. The separation of India and Pakistan caused mass migration, political, social and economic upheavals between the two nations and the other ethnic groups in the sub-continent.

Salman Rushdie in *Midnight's Children* and *Shame* creates situations which can be considered as allegories of political events between India and Pakistan especially in his highlighting of the move from independence to the establishment of the new

Pakistani state on 14 August 1947 and the conflicts and controversies that arose thereafter. The question is: what prompted Rushdie to create characters and situations in his novels which allegorically evoke the historical, religious and socio-political crises that have characterized the two nations? The opinion held in this essay is that by reviewing the political course which both countries had taken, Rushdie was in a way reshaping memory to provide alternative visions for reconciliation and progress for India and the new Pakistani state in particular. He sets out in his novels to re-write an Indian and Pakistani nation through the events of the life of his narrators, Saleem and Omar in *Midnight's Children* and *Shame* respectively. The novels represent the reconstruction of the national identities following 1947 independence and partition. These identities however are revealed or exposed by different imaginations of India and Pakistan which are each contained within a broad sense of two separate nations, but which continually overlap each other.

The narrator of *Midnight's Children* Saleem Sinai in writing his own life is also writing the history of the nation. Saleem is born at the stroke of midnight of India's independence 1947 and as Teresa Hefferman remarks he "draws on the revolutionary legacy of apocalyptic nationalism as an obvious frame for his account of India's struggle of liberation" (472). The consequence of his double birth links the nation inextricably to his destiny "...I had been mysteriously handcuffed to my destinies indissolubly chained to those of my country (*Midnight* 1) Saleem, like the nation, begins to remake his life. By linking his life to that of the nation Saleem suggests that what his father Aadam Aziz passes onto him is also passed onto the nation and cannot be wiped out. Saleem represents a legacy to the future generation of midnight children as he becomes the leader of the Midnight's Children Conference. The Midnight's Children Conference is a symbol of India's diversity, a country with so many voices, languages, multiple races, religions and cultures. Like the children with different ambitions so is India "...a many headed monster, speaking in the myriad of tongues of Babel..." (220).

To rebuild Pakistan Rushdie in his works has to move back to the past ancestral roots. The breaking up of pre-colonial social orders and patterns of thought such as in the subcontinent, frequently evoke a widespread sense of social incoherence, chaos, fragmentation and disorder. After independence postcolonial writers in their works set out to chart out ways forward for the reconstruction of their societies. Postcolonial theory as explained by Lois Tyson makes clear the impact the inherited power relations, and their continuing effects on modern global cultures and politics and as Deepika Bahri explains, most of his [Rushdie's] novels allude to "postcolonial cultures and its eventual capitulation to modernity's temporal colonization" (491). Political and socio-economic questions in the postcolonial world are usually approached from the standpoint of national identity relations such as ethnicity, gender and representation which are made clearer when considered in the context of their relations with the past. Rushdie realized that it is through reshaping memory that the past can really be brought to understanding. Personal identity is built out of references to social, objects, people, events and institutions. No memory can be disconnected from society, from the language and the symbolic system patterned by the society over many generations (Funkenstein 1989). Rushdie in his novels reveals that the contents of the above system are selected and interpreted in socio-economic determined ways. We can retrieve the past by the use of the categories of our own collective culture (*Shame* 86). The narrator in the novel reveals how Pakistan has a historical origin which they can look to for reconstruction "We have floated upwards from history, from memory, from time" (85).

Collective memory has also to do with the beliefs about the past events that individuals recollect when defining themselves as members of a given group, and those memories are recalled by the individual not bound by the social communities. Not everyone belonging to a particular social group recalls exactly the same images when defining himself as a member of a given community. The revival of many collective memories results in contradictory narratives. This is exposed in Rushdie's

Midnight's Children and *Shame* where the narrative is not coherent. Rushdie uses different stories through different characters to bring out the understanding of socio-political and economic upheaval in Pakistan and India.

In *Shame*, Rushdie uses the family history of old Mr. Shakil and the three daughters—Chhunni, Munnee and Bunny. These three sisters are kept sealed up by their father to keep them from the outside world (1). The girls are brought up in a strict Muslim morality inside their labyrinthine. After the death of their father they become exposed to the outside world, one of them gets pregnant and bear a baby boy Omar Khayyam who becomes the protagonist of the novel and through him the political tyrant Raza Hyder in Pakistan is killed. The novel goes further to recount the history of Pakistan from independence involving three generations of people and focusing on the lives and families of Raza Hyder a military general and Iskander Harappa, a millionaire play-boy-turned-politician. Rushdie bases his characters on the real life story of the Pakistani former minister Zulfikar Ali Bhutto who was deposed by Zia ul Haq, his commander, in a military coup in 1977 and was later executed like Raza in the novel (Samir 39).

Rushdie breaks off in the novel to expose how Russia entered the subcontinent and merged India and Pakistan (*Shame* 185-89). This exposes the real history of India in the 15th century when Alexander the Great influenced a young Indian named Chandragupta Maurya to become king of India. Maurya later conquered the whole of northern India which included Pakistan and became the ruler of the above dynasty. The above exposes how Pakistan became part of India even before colonization (Wallbank and Schrier 216). Although history cannot really be constructed the way it was, Rushdie picks from such aspects which involve myths and artifacts, to imagine a past: "A name means continuity with the past and people without a past are people without a name" (86). This indicates that the modern nation can be reconstructed from the writer's imagination of the past.

Midnight's Children opens with the birth of Saleem Sinai which coincides with the birth of the New India in 1947.

Saleem's father begins by talking about an Indian true reconstruction which can only come from ancestral Mongul roots not British (123). He longs for a new state which will renew its old ancestral myths (124). Rushdie distinguishes the differences between India and Pakistan by indicating their different ancestral origins such as the Mohajir and the Mongul dynasties.

Rushdie examines the Muslims' desire which is to consolidate their position and exclude non-Muslims from a new Pakistani state. He discusses the role of Islam in the political paradigms of Pakistan "The Hummingbird was the founder, chairman, unifier and moving spirit of the free Islam convocation" (39). This convocation helped in the creation of an atmosphere of patriotism and cultural nationalism based on Islamism. Nationalism and religion are closely identified as such that to speak of the nation is to speak automatically in religious terms. Therefore, the Pakistani national discourse emphasizes religious affiliation and by extending a sense of religious nationality and language which supersedes any specific racial identity. Rushdie in *Shame* examines the role of Islam in an imaginary town named Indrasprastha. He says this place "Pakistan" had often been ruled by men who believed in "Allah, The God" (56). He further indicates how "Muslim artifacts are littered about in the city even from ancient times." Muslims reinforced the myth of racial democracy by writing various ethnic groups such as the Punjabis, Urdus and Sikhs which were either Hindus or Christians under Islam. This resulted to a larger Muslim population which eventually assimilated and consolidated a Muslim government.

The role of establishing a nation through language becomes very significant. Saleem describes the conflicts that were tearing the nation after independence by indicating how groups imagined their national identity based on the language they speak. "The nation's boundaries are no longer determined by physical features but the boundaries of these states were not formed by rivers...they were instead, walls of words" (216). The imagining of India in terms of language supports Ngugi's portrayal of language as an important tool in national identity:

> Culture embodies those moral ethnic and aesthetic values, the set of spiritual eyeglasses.... Values are the basis of a people's identity, their sense of particularity as members of the human race. All this is carried by language. Language as culture is the collective memory bank of a people's experience in history. (Ashcroft *et al.* 290)

The many heterogeneous languages bring out the conflicting struggles in India and how people sought to form a national identity united under their language barriers. Language thus becomes a political instrument of cultural identity as it evokes certain emotions through songs and words which disseminate information and marks out individual identity. Oral tales demonstrate ancestral origins and traditions in postcolonial communities, and portray how legends and histories are passed down from one generation to the other (*Shame* 74). Through memory characters reveal and maintain their cultural and historical ties with their nation. Thus, this enables generations to share a connection with their ancestral roots and thus define their national identity. Although nations embrace multiculturalism and ethnic diversities, there must be common claims about nationhood as Kymlicka says "...citizens are still expected to speak a common national language, share a common national identity, feel loyalty to national institutions, and share a commitment to maintain the nation as a single, self-governing community into the indefinite future" (236). Colonialism brought together communities with different histories, socio-economic, cultural and religious traditions submerged under the notion of the Indian nation against their wish. Gandhi wanted an independence which will unite the whole of India as one nation irrespective of ancestral religious origin in different states. This ideology was not supported by the Muslims who wanted a separate Muslim state of Pakistan. They formed a free Islamic convocation which tabled their grievances in the government of India arguing their representation and demanding an independent Muslim state. Jinnah advocated for an autonomous state of Pakistan under Muslim rule which will emphasize communal politics based on religion. He thought of a Pakistan completely separated from India in everything (86). In Pakistan, the Muslims reinforced the myth of racial democracy by uniting various ethnic groups such as the Punjabis, Urdus and Sikhs which were either Hindus or Christians under Islam. Islam is considered as the main political organ of the state which is seen as the only source of unity, success and development. Islamism to the Pakistani plays a very crucial role in the construction of the new nation as the people look back to their origin in the fifteen century during the reign of the Maurya dynasty. Therefore, the Pakistani national discourse emphasizes religious affiliation and by extending a sense of religious nationality which supersedes any racial identity.

Writers after independence stood out as the people's consciousness to make them know where they belong, who they are, who they want to become. This made the literature written in South East Asia and other postcolonial nations to cease to be colonial but independent and seeking to develop a distinct national identity. This results from the national consciousness as literary myths and folklores which deal with historical continuities have to resurface to help in rewriting the nation. Writers like Rushdie move backwards into history to remind us of the ancestral past which becomes the basis of national literature as Rushdie says "the past has dripped into me...so we cannot ignore it..." (*Midnight* 370). Nations therefore, are imaginary constructs which depend for their existence on an apparatus of cultural fiction in which imaginative literature plays a vital role. This is in support of Anderson's concept of the nation as an imagined community. An eminently constructed work of literature points to a practice from which society can take a stand. This mediation becomes a compromise between commitment and autonomy, which is a mixture of advanced formal elements with an intellectual content inspired by supposedly progressive politics. The content of a work of art should produce a historical reality as Rushdie reveals Pakistani origin from the Mohajir ancestors and makes us to understand that India and Pakistan are separate nations (*Shame* 86).

A work of art, according to Saleem Sinai, assesses what is barred to politics and makes politics to migrate into arts (*Midnight* 270). Rushdie's narratives do not only give a history of Pakistan and India, they provide a series of premises for interpreting events and set out rules for political and social behaviour. In *Shame*, Rushdie recounts a veiled satirical history of Pakistan and recalls historical events through the history of two families, the families of Iskander Harappa and Raza Hyder, former political rulers of Pakistan. This shows that events, feelings and experiences that build up our life and thought, can be described and even experienced through narratives. The rules of these narratives are to expose the past histories that indicate the sorts of culture that are legitimate for a particular society. Anthony Smith reveals that the ethnic community is a complex of myths, values, memories and symbols which constitute the ethos of identities and nations originate from these ethnic communities (22-31). We can say that nations seem to be modern phenomenon but from Smith's idea we see nations as myths of descent and historical memories.

The allegory of the twin birth in the novel indicates how individuals' histories together make up the history of nations. The birth of Saleem is the birth of a new nation which also involves the birth of 1001 midnight children. His birth and incidences surrounding his growth symbolize the trend of events which move in the nation. Saleem's birth introduces us to Aadam Aziz's grandfather who reveals to us about pre-colonial India during the Mughal Empire (4). Aadam Aziz is the founder of the family dynasty. His importance is prophesied early by Tai the boatman as one who holds the legacies to future generations (*Midnight* 8). Saleem inherits from Aadam Aziz a gigantic nose which is a dynasty mark and a fragmented identity. Aadam, schooled in a European university, cannot embrace the religious mythologies of his nation and this confusion is inherited by Saleem. The conflicts and inequalities in the construction of an Indian national identity are seen through events in the life of Saleem. Saleem describes the British presence inside his own personal history, intermingled with cultural and religious aspects which leak to the subcontinent. The influence of living abroad on Saleem's family is inherited from the family founder Aadam Aziz, his grandfather. Aadam returning from abroad after his education is unable to reconcile his European education with the customs of his childhood. He finds himself stuck between two cultures where he has to negotiate his identity. This double identity is passed onto Saleem Sinai and all aspects of Saleem's birth and ancestry are inherited by the nation. Many in the nation after empire like Saleem have been tainted with 'Abroad' and returning to the memory of an Indian heritage has become impossible. The issue of in-betweenness in the novel is what has to bring about the redefinition of the concept of homogeneous new cultures to negotiate selfhood and the collective experience of new nations. Bhabha sees the new postcolonial nations as the move away from fixed organizational categories of identification and the redefinition of subjectivity which encompasses human communities and the identifications produced in them (Bhabha 1). The postcolonial nation has to return to the essential past to assert a true national identity and accept the in-between geopolitical locale, institutional locations, theoretical innovative produced in the articulation of cultural differences. "These in-between spaces provide the terrain for elaborating strategies for selfhood-singular or communal that initiate new signs of identity, and innovative sites of collaboration, and contestation, in the act of defining the idea of society itself" (2). Saleem, raised a Muslim, is exchanged for the child Shiva from an improvised Hindu family into which Saleem was born. Saleem's identity is a synthesis of three identities, Moslem, Hindu and British as that of India.

From Bhabha analysis we see that the in-between identity forms the link between Saleem and the nation. In the novel Saleem and India have to negotiate identity from the broken pieces of colonialism and the pre-colonial ancestral past from Tai the boatman and Aadam Aziz Saleem's grandfather. Rushdie indicates that the birth of Saleem has to become a source of reshaping ancestral origin (45). A depiction of national identity reflects specific historical moments, which are not accidental but are part of a dynamic matrix that reflects and creates history, politics, development and myth. Stuart Hall looks at identity as linked to history and culture constructed through memory, fantasy, narrative myths. The past continues to speak to us (211). He says the tales, songs and proverbs do not reveal basic truths. They are used as a guide to show the people their society from the past and reflect their lost cultural aspects in the process of colonization.

In *Midnight's Children* Rushdie, memorizes the national life of India, its birth, growth and various pitfalls. He brings together various histories of origins and cultural differences in the subcontinent. These many histories are as a result of different ancestral origins and the influence of the colonialists. Colonization and the return to ancestral past form the national identity of the new nation. Saleem highlights the inherent heterogeneity and tendency for fragmentation. He has "eyes as blue as Kashmiri sky—which were also eyes as blue as methwold's—and a nose as dramatic as a Kashimiri father's which was also the nose of a grandmother from France" (130). The mixture found in Saleem portrays the many ethnic identities in the subcontinent. This multiple identities cause fragmentation in the individual and the nation. Rushdie compares this fragmented state to a broken mirror but he also sees that this broken mirror can still be used (*Imaginary Homelands* 11). The fragments when picked can still reveal aspects of the nation in the past just like that of the individual Saleem.

In *Imagined Communities* Benedict Anderson analyses the nation as a complex set of processes. He defines the nation as a social construct and as a product of a collective imagination not only in terms of history, geography and common language. It is "an imagined political community and imagined as both inherently limited and sovereign" (7). Writing India Saleem has to enter into an accumulated tradition. He himself becomes an emblem of the nation; his baby picture is produced and distributed to all Indian citizens putting him at the centre of the nation. The conflicting imagination of communal solidarities and the midnight children become the nation in narration.

As stated earlier, Rushdie in his novels sets out to write an Indian and Pakistani nation through the events of the lives of his narrators, Saleem and Omar who represent the construction of the national identities following 1947 independence and partition. These identities thus exposed by different imaginations of India and Pakistan are each contained within a broad sense of two separate nations which continually overlap each other. The overlap between India and Pakistan is seen in the life of Rushdie's protagonist as he poses as a child of three worlds: "I, too, know something of this immigrant business. I am an immigrant from one country India and a newcomer into two England where I live and Pakistan to which my family move against my will.... We have floated upwards from history, from memory, from time (*Shame* 84-85). Saleem like Rushdie also experiences this overlap as he is switched at birth from the Hindu-English parentage to Muslim parents. This triple identity which makes up their lives is what Bhabha indicates as "...the complex interweaving of history, and the culturally contingent borderlines of modern nationhood" (5). The national identities of Pakistan and India are the functions of the worlds of the narrator and author of the novels. The self, like the nation, receives images and a narrative from the world shaped by ancestral roots and colonialism. This indicates that the postcolonial self cannot be abstracted from its experiences and so cannot object the images it finds itself surrounded with.

Rushdie's narratives do not only give us a history of Pakistan and India, it provides a premise for interpreting events and a set of rules for political and social behaviour in the nations. Through the histories of families and individuals Rushdie rewrites the history of two nations both the triumphs and the downfalls. The narratives draw together histories past and present to expose the cultures that are legitimate for a particular society. The nation is remade through individual history and societal relationships. Identity is linked to culture as it reflects historical spaces, which are not accidental but are part of a dynamic matrix that reflects and creates history, politics, development and myth. These spaces make up national identities and differentiate them from each other. Stuart Hull links identity to history and culture as he says that identity is not a fixed essence at all, lying unchanged outside history and culture.... "The past continues to speak to us...always constructed through memory, fantasy, narrative myths" (211).

Like Hull, Rushdie in *Midnight's Children* and *Shame* use the traditional technique of the oral tale structure in narrating the nation. This technique moves back from present to past, building tale within tale. The narration does not follow a linear pattern as it follows the trend of activities going on inside the characters and the nation. To Rushdie the narration is like the nation:

> It goes in great swoops, it goes in spiral or in loops, it every so often reiterates something that happened earlier to remind you, and takes you off again, sometimes summaries itself, it frequently digresses off into something that the storyteller appears just to have thought of, then it comes back to the main thrust of the narrative. (Walder 399)

To Rushdie the narrative like the nation should move forward and backwards to indicate the influence of the past in the present. The writer narrates historical realities through memory by which means he brings in his thoughts the past and present intermingled with fiction to imagine the nation by which means he tries to negotiate the discourse of the seemingly illusory border between Islam and the West (Dayal 40). By so doing Rushdie redefines the concept of homogenous new cultures and collective experience in India and particularly Pakistan whose present he thinks should be based on the vestiges of ancestral past to create the new nations with legitimate cultures. As Rushdie himself explains, the title of *Midnight's Children* has become too many Indians "a familiar catch-phrase for defining the generation which was too young to remember the empire or the liberation struggle" (Qtd. Wenzel 27).

Works Cited

Anderson, Benedict. *Imagined Communities: Reflections on the Origin and Spread of Nationalism*. New York: Verso, 1991.

Ashcroft, Bill, et al. (eds). *The Postcolonial Studies Reader*. London: Routledge, 1995.

Bahri, Deepika. "Predicting the Past." *Modern Language Quarterly* 65.3 (September 2004): 481-503.

Bhabha, Homi. *The Location of Culture*. London: Routledge, 1994.

Dayal, Samir. "The Limitations of Nation and Gender: Salman Rushdie's *Shame*." *The Journal of the Mid West Modern Language Association* 31.2 (1998): 39-62.

Funkenstein, A. "Collective Memory and Historical Consciousness". *History and Memory* 1.2 (1989): 5-26.

Hefferman, Teresa. "Apocalyptic Narratives: The Nation in Salman Rushdie's *Midnight's Children*". *Twentieth Century Literature* 46.4 (2000): 470-91.

Hull, Stuart. "Cultural Identity and Diaspora." *Identity and Difference*. Ed. Kathryn Woodward. Thousand Oaks: Sage, 1995: 51-59.

Kymlicka, Will. "Nationalism, Transnationalism and Postcolonialism". *Liberal Values to Democratic Transition*. Ed. Ronald Dworkin. New York: Central European Press, 2004: 227-63.

Max, Weber. "The Origin of Ethnic Groups". *Ethnicity*. Ed. John Hutchinson and Anthony Smith. New York: O.U.P., 1996, 35-36.

Ngugi wa Thiong'o. *Writers in Politics: A Re-engagement with Issues of Literature and Society*. Oxford: James Curry, 1997.

Rushdie, Salman. "Imaginary Homelands". *Essays and Criticism 1981-1991*. London: Penguin, 1991.

Rushdie, Salman. *Shame*. New York: Knopf, 1983.

——. *Midnight's Children*. London: Penguin Books, 1991.

Smith, Anthony D. *Myths and Memories of Nation*. Oxford: O.U.P., 1999.

——. *The Ethnic Origins of Nations*. Oxford: Basil Blackwell, 1986.

Walder, Dennis, ed. *Literature in the Modern World: Critical Essays and Documents*. New York: O.U.P., 2004.

Wallbank and Schrier. *Living World History*. Chicago: Curtis Publishing Co. (nd).

Wenzel, Jennifer. "Remembering the Past's Future: Anti Imperialist Nostalgia and Some Versions of the Third World." *Cultural Critique* 62 (Winter, 2006): 2-32.

6

Subaltern Voices and Postcolonial Anxiety in Arundhati Roy's *The God of Small Things*

Diviani Chaudhuri

To argue, as some critics have, that Arundhati Roy's novel, *The God of Small Things*, is a re-articulation of Ranajit Guha's specific conjuncture of a statist historiography imbued with the oppositional binaries of 'big' and 'small' and 'elite' and 'subaltern' wherein "the motors of social, disciplinary, and epistemological transformation" are located "in the inherently or potentially resistant properties of the oppressed subaltern subject" is to assume that there are indeed two histories in actual existence—one 'official', deemed statist and hegemonic, and the other 'interpretative', resulting from a representational model that self-consciously seeks to subvert hegemonic impositions of power from below, and that both are viable forms of cultural production (Needham 370). In this theoretical configuration, then, for a given politics or culture or narrative, there must exist yet another corresponding counter-politics, counter-culture(s) or counter-narrative. The assumption here, of course, is that there is a history present in Roy's text and there is yet another history someplace else, *and these are mutually exclusive.*

Common sense tells us that 'history is always written by the winners', as do theoretical models proposed by postcolonial and subaltern theorists. Postcolonial Indian writing in English suffers from the malady of seeking to project itself into the person of this 'winner'. Ever since Thomas Babington Macaulay's infamous "Minute on Education" (1835) effectively robbed Indians of any science, history, language and culture, there have been innumerable attempts to represent that which will not be heard by the all-powerful at the centre—the Other, the voice of the periphery. Appropriating the coloniser's literary and linguistic resources, then, the colonised becomes engaged in the task of 'writing back'. Thus, in response to Macaulay's imposition of the English language (instead of vernacular languages) in all government schools in British India, Michael Madhusudan Dutt writes a *Meghnaadbadhkaabya* (1861), an epic in Bengali that self-consciously seeks comparison with Milton, and Bankimchandra Chattopadhyay publishes essays such as "Sakuntala, Desdemona and Miranda" attempting comparative studies of Shakespearian heroines and their classical Sanskrit counterparts while appropriating the Victorian novel form with commensurate skill, spawning writers like Salman Rushdie, who are still engaged in the endeavour of exorcising the ghost of Macaulay's minute by creating alternate, 'chutnified' histories.

Macaulay's indictment of the colonised culture was phrased thus:

> The question now before us is simply whether, when it is in our power to teach this language, we shall teach languages in which, by universal confession, there are no books on any subject which deserve to be compared to our own, whether, when we can teach European science, we shall teach systems which, by universal confession, wherever they differ from those of Europe differ for the worse, and whether, when we can patronize sound philosophy and true history, we shall countenance, at the public expense, medical doctrines which would disgrace an English farrier, astronomy which would move laughter in girls at an English boarding school, history abounding with kings thirty feet high and reigns thirty

thousand years long, and geography made of seas of treacle and seas of butter. (165)

The task before the colonised, then, was to somehow prove that they were indeed in possession of 'sound philosophy' and 'true history' to an audience that could not "deny that a single shelf of a good European library was worth the whole native literature of India and Arabia" (Macaulay 163).

In pre-independent India, thus, Raja Ram Mohan Roy wrote "Tuhfat ul-Muwahiddin" (1804), a treatise on a Hindu Unitarianism he would later call Brahmoism (which would become a major social reform movement) written in Persian that attempts to use Islamic principles of logic to reconcile seemingly polytheistic Vedic philosophy with monotheistic Upanisadic philosophy in order to construct a sense of continuity within the syncretic system of the various Hinduisms that have flourished throughout the ages in the Indian subcontinent. Decades later, Rabindranath Tagore would write "A Vision of India's History" (1923), wherein he would propose a version of the history of the Indian subcontinent from before the invasion of the Aryans to his contemporary historical conjuncture.

It is instructive to note that while formulating a probable account of Indian history or *histories*, to be more faithful to the multiplicity of historical narratives characteristic of the subcontinent, Tagore simultaneously embarks on an analysis of a literary historiography vociferously delegitimized by the coloniser. He uses the material in the pre-colonial culture of what Ngugi wa Thiong'o calls orality to embark on a system of historiography that would resist the structures of the coloniser. By identifying Indian oral epics such as the *Mahabharata* and the *Ramayana* with the national epics of the European canon such as the *Iliad* and the *Odyssey*, he succeeds in formulating an incipient Indian Nationalism and Indian historiography which would later turn out to be as exclusionary as the coloniser's systems. Yet it is to this inherently post-imperial impulse of re-imagining and re-envisioning a confiscated history that authors such as Rushdie, Roy and Ghosh owe their literary lineage.

The points to be noted here, are that (i) in the absence of History, there can only be Story and that (ii) as far as the Indian subcontinent is concerned, one cannot conceive of a History or even a system of mutually exclusive dual Histories. One must then conceive of polyphonic narratives and multiple histories. This is also what Roy asserts with her strategic deployment of a quote from John Berger in the very beginning of her novel: "No longer can a single story be told as if it is the only one." But this statement can be counterposed with another quote from Martin Heidegger: "Language speaks, man listens, but he can't hear everything" (71). Heidegger underlines the necessity of translating oneself into the thought of the other language, which in the postcolonial context is also the Other's language, in this case, English.

Are postcolonial publishing phenomena like Roy, Rushdie, Ghosh and Seth then peddling Macaulay's dream of a class that would act as an intermediary between the colonizer and the vast mass of the colonized, or, the mainstream and the marginalised, as the case may be? Are they the literary counterparts of Indian *babu*dom, "never challenging [systems of oppression], never appearing not to" (Roy 66)? Do activist-writers like Roy provide any means of positive intervention when they choose the private sphere as the medium of political résistance?

Like the canon of Indian writers in English, Roy too focuses on a temporal space (1947-75) within which the English-educated Enlightenment ideal emulating bourgeoisie was engaged in a process of constructing a cohesive identity of its "mongrel self" (Rushdie 404). Concomitant with this labour of producing a cultural identity was also the project of the imaginary of nationhood, and of a hybrid Indian modernity. Teeming as the novel is, with the Small Things and everyday features of Indian modernity—the figure of the maimed roadside beggar, (in the armless, legless Muralidharan) the coolie [through whose speech Roy deploys the famous blurb: "Big Man the Laltain sahib, Small Man the Mombatti," (89)] the street-hawker—the story it tells is that of the very same privileged bourgeoisie which has access to land and education, and crucially, the ability to traverse geopolitical boundaries of nation and state while the subaltern remains fixed in the backwaters of a rurality obscured by the shiny lure of the postcolonial city. It is this same class that Macaulay willed to spawn, well-nigh two centuries ago, through his trenchant espousal of a particular imperial educational policy.

Roy's novel is set in a sensually represented "immodest[ly] green" (3) rurality where the rhetoric of Nationalism as well as Communism is incapable of erasing the lines between ethno religious and socio-economic classes drawn by traditional dogma and where feudal structures are replicated despite the policies of "the first democratically elected communist government in the world" (67) such as the Land Reforms Ordinance (with the catchy slogan of "land for tillers") and the Education Bill which sought to empower the disadvantaged classes.

Roy's skill lies in exposing the exploitative practices inherent *within* the landlord class due to the patriarchal framework it espouses instead of roundly fixing the 'privileged' class with the responsibility of all the oppression it radiates outwards into the proletariat—in this case, the class of landless labourers. Furthermore, unlike earlier subcontinental writers in English, Roy explicitly acknowledges the existence of organised class struggles, with a specific conjuncture in the communist movement in Kerala forming the background to the novel. The question that begs to be asked, then, is how does one negotiate between these multiple subalternities and multiple configurations of state and capitalist power in Roy's novelistic universe? And how successful is an attempt, such as Roy's, at positioning representation as intervention in such a fraught socio-cultural milieu?

One way to approach the issues at hand can be through a reading of Velutha, the immediately identifiable subaltern paravan who is beaten to death because of transgressing the established 'Love Laws' which forbid a man of a 'lower birth' to enter into a sexual liaison with a 'high-born' woman. However, Ammu and Velutha are both outcastes after a fashion: she is a divorced Syrian Christian who has ruined her prospects by marrying a Hindu and bearing his children, and he is an emancipated paravan caste in a sensitive mould that ironically evokes western liberal modernity in stark contrast to the other colonised male figureheads such as the wife-beating Pappachi and the philandering and unconcerned Chacko.

Roy's narrative strategy is such that the sense of being unable to escape one's arbitrarily determined caste, class and gender identity permeates the entire text. Ammu's desperation to leave the insulated backwaters of Ayemenem only lands her back in Ayemenem House, humiliated and with no hope for recourse. Her transgressions with Velutha result in his death despite his "refusal to be interpellated as a Paravan" (Needham 374). Pappachi compensates for the nightly battery of Mammachi after being shamed by Chacko by flaunting his Plymouth by day, wearing a three piece woollen suit despite the tropical climate, because that is the stereotype foisted upon him by the appropriated structures of colonisation.

The wrath of the socio-political system that Ammu and Velutha operate in the margins of befalls them both with tragic consequences despite their state of excommunication from it because theirs is an act of resistance to the indoctrinated systems of behaviour that breed oppression. Regardless of their hithertofore status of 'outcaste,' once their transgression comes to light, their respective social identities engulf them with great swiftness as is evidenced by the treatment meted out to Velutha by the Police. Albeit an act that takes place in their private sphere, once committed and discovered, it spills into the larger public sphere as well.

In locating this act of transgression in the private sphere, Roy emulates the narrative strategies of many early Indian novelists writing in pre-independent India. In the temporally distant space and the private sphere alike, a sort of subconscious and surrogate resistance and call for revolt against the spatio-temporal reality of the present could be voiced against the humiliation of subjugation and the contempt of the power structures of the colonizer which stifled any assertion of indigenous cultural heritage in the public sphere. The European domination of public life and civil society left the home as the only conceptual space in which Indian men could act with some sense of autonomy and sovereignty over women and other social groups subordinate to them (Chakrabarty 215). The idea of the home therefore takes on a compensatory significance in the idea of modernity as experienced in the context of British colonization, for it is the home that is identified as the smallest unit of society wherein the possibility of independent change remains open.

What, then, has changed since the glorious throwing off of the oppressive yoke of colonisation? Have other, 'indigenous' systems of oppression replaced the old colonial spectre? How have systems of representation, then, changed to meet this new conjuncture? Can a character like Velutha meet with any fate other than death at the hands of the state machinery in a representational version of postcolonial India? Can such a representational text really speak for the Veluthas of postcolonial India?

Roy does not practice the elitist exercise in condescension by attempting to speak 'for' the subaltern. And this is why, even though Velutha has been argued to be the hero of the novel, the eponymous God of small things, it is still not *his* story. It is the story of Rahel, Estha, Ammu, or even their entire family. Velutha's motives and feelings are known only to himself (Chanda 131). He remains an unknowable other, mediated only through his relationship with the privileged class that while sympathetic to him is also exploitative. Ammu realises "I've killed him," but neither Ammu, nor her children are actors invested with the agency of resistance in the public sphere, and thus, cannot 'save' Velutha.

Another approach to the Janus faced questions that plague the postcolonial novel that attempts a "single-story-multiply-told" (Chanda 131) structure could be to revert to its assumption of representational historiography and examine whether it is indeed mutually exclusive to 'elite' official statist historiography. However, as Spivak notes, it is difficult to pinpoint any given account of facts as the hegemonic version, since each and every exercise in historiography is informed by the choice of the writer (24-28).

This is indeed the problem of 'the permission to narrate' discussed by Said (1984).... Within the effaced itinerary of the subaltern subject, the track of sexual difference is doubly affected. The question is not of female participation in insurgency, or the ground rules of the sexual division of labour, for both of which there is 'evidence'. It is, rather, that, both as object of colonialist historiography and as subject of insurgency, the ideological construction of gender keeps the male dominant. If, in the context of colonial production, the subaltern has no history and cannot speak, the subaltern as female is even more deeply in shadow (Spivak 26).

Spivak suggests that subalternists must sometimes, for the sake of sheer pragmatism, accept "strategic essentialism" in their academic discourses, insisting that past subaltern voices have been silenced even if the subalternist her/himself is unable to entirely speak for those subaltern subjects (2196). On the other hand, perhaps sometimes the best thing Subaltern Studies can do is insist that the past itself exists only in silence ["At the time, there would only be incoherence. As though meaning had slunk out of things and left them fragmented," (Roy 215)] buried beneath competing discourses of the present. Priyamvada Gopal writes, "The grandest, though surprisingly definitive, act of them all is that of 'refusal'—not just to write foundationalist histories, it would seem, but to write history at all; for at the end of the day, any act of knowledge production or historiography becomes, by definition, damningly 'foundational'" (160).

Moreover, Partha Chatterjee's conception of a 'perceptual distance' between the state and peasant communities acting autonomously against it (34) draws one to the inevitable conclusion that the Indian crowds before and at independence were indeed the unknowable Other excluded from the principal format of the elite *babu*-dominated Indian nationalist movement and subsequently from the process of nation-building. This distance was both real in terms of everyday politics as well as perceived in the sense of being deprived, even marginalised, from the momentous process of decision-making that eventually shaped the future of Indian polity. It is true that without a sense of identity a popular movement cannot even begin properly, let alone sustain itself over time. Such an identity is a reference point that can decide the level of efficacy of any particular movement. However, whenever subaltern movements tried to identify themselves with any issue or institution, they were generally manipulated by their elite leaders and diversified into channels of unknowable othernesses by foisting factionist and/or communal identities to these movements so that their aims may be obfuscated by polemics and internecine feuds.

Thus, there are hierarchies of oppression to be considered instead of a monolithic conceptualisation of the other as conceived by the coloniser, an oppositional binary which now appears to be replaced by that of the subaltern as conceived by the elite. Caste, class, and gender oppressions are not fungible forms of violence, and therefore care must be taken to avoid allotting interchangeable representational spaces to each of these.

Roy accomplishes in her novel by choosing to situate her critique of patriarchy within that of gender and caste. Roy's nuanced portrayal of the dynamics between Ammu and the twins on the one hand, and Velutha on the other do not allow gender based oppression to subsume caste based exclusion, or *vice versa*, and neither are responses to oppression uniform in Roy's characters. This is evident in the difference in the modes of response—rebellion as well as collusion—that Ammu and Mammachi deploy in the face of the marital violence and exploitation that they both face. While Ammu repudiates her husband's attempt to prostitute her to his English manager thereby denying the offering of her flesh to the dominant patriarchy, Mammachi endorses it by adhering to the rigid and hegemonic system of caste based hierarchy when she condemns Ammu's relationship with Velutha.

Furthermore, Roy offsets Velutha's resistance to interpellation as a Paravan with his father's ready acceptance of the established order of things and a servile reluctance to overturn it. Vellya Paapen goes to Mammachi and offers her the glass eye that she had arranged to have made for him, out of a sense of shame for Velutha's indiscretions with her daughter because, as far as he is concerned, the sin of the Untouchable Velutha's sexual liaison with her divorced daughter could only be expiated if he told her the truth and returned the eye she had given him. But Velutha's attitude is that of a quiet defiance characteristic of his ability to sense the injustice meted out to him as well as the forms of redress supposedly available to him as a citizen of an independent India generally and as a card carrying member of a Marxist organisation specifically. Thus Roy draws upon the resources of the realist novel to problematise the uniform and stable conception of the subaltern as a monolithic entity devoid of internal plurality and difference of positionality.

To her credit, Roy fixes the culpability of Velutha's death on *all* the characters and systems the reader encounters in her novel instead of merely placing the blame squarely on the official state sponsored punitive system as espoused by Foucauldian analyses of subalternity: "Esthappen and Rahel both knew that there were several perpetrators (besides themselves) that day. But only one victim" (182). Velutha variously serves as a sacrificial lamb for both the landlord class—the orthodoxy of which he challenges—as well as "Indian Communism," which crept into Kerala insidiously. As a reformist movement that never overtly questioned the traditional values of a caste-ridden extremely traditional community. The Marxists worked from within the communal divides never challenging them, never appearing not to. They offered a cocktail revolution. A heady mix of eastern Marxism and orthodox Hinduism, spiked with a shot of democracy (Roy 66).

Velutha's mysterious involvement in the violent Naxalite rebellion reflects his proactive fervour in rebelling against a certain type of oppressive social structure, but his identity as Untouchable Paravan still foreshadows his demise. He has no control over the kidnapping and murder charges levelled against him, and in the aftermath of his death, the same members of the Communist party who betrayed him attempt to use his death to further the party's political cause (286-87).

Velutha does not disappear from the text in a flurry of activity at the final moment of his fatal beating in the History House; he is constantly disappearing into the text's literal and metaphorical darknesses.

> This tendency of all visible traces of Velutha's presence to disappear can be understood to be a result of his Untouchable Paravan status, a kind of social discrimination that demands the ritualized removal of a person's traces in order to avoid the defilement of his social superiors; or, alternatively, a deliberate ignoring and overlooking of his footprints and presence by those in a more elevated social position than his. (D'Souza 118)

Velutha appears multiple times in Ammu's dreams as the eponymous God of small things, a mysterious and silent entity which "left no ripples in the water" and "no footprints in the sand" (274). As foreshadowed, it is his father Vellya Paapen who informs Baby Kochamma of Velutha and Ammu's love affair, in effect sweeping away his own genetic lineage. Following the double betrayal by the Communist party and by his father, it is the betrayal by the confused and traumatized Estha in speaking with Inspector Matthews that seals Velutha's fate:

> The Inspector asked his question. Estha's mouth said yes.
>
> Childhood tiptoed out.
>
> Silence slid in like a bolt.
>
> Someone switched off the light and Velutha disappeared. (303)

In this erasure, then, lies the redemptive transmogrification of the subaltern into an "irreducible, internalised idea," a recurring problematic that Victor Li suggests afflicts postcolonial Indian texts which seek to depict subalterns such as Roy's Velutha and Amitav Ghosh's Fokir (*The Hungry Tide*):

> The sacrificial logic discernible in their deaths transforms them from struggling, uncertain actors into symbols of

> counter-hegemonic resistance and alterity. Defeat turns into redemption as death immortalizes the subaltern's defiance. (Li 2007)

Such texts, then, are bound to grapple with multiple competing subalternities, those of *dalits, adivasis,* Scheduled Castes (SCs), Scheduled Tribes (STs), Other Backward Classes (OBCs), of the women belonging to all of these castes as well as those who belong to the privileged classes and yet, like Ammu, are excluded from the fruits of their 'privileged status' because of their gender identity within a dominant patriarchy.

However, in self-consciously touting themselves as the 'authentic' version of events, or as the 'voice' of the subaltern, such texts can only re-enact the repression and silencing faced by such subalternities in the public sphere of the larger nation within the potentially freeing novelistic universe. In such a case, representation as an interventionist technique fails utterly and exposes the incipient neo-orientalist tendencies inherent in the postcolonial imaginary. It participates, then, in what Timothy Brennan in *At Home in the World: Cosmopolitanism Now* calls literary cosmopolitanism, which is nothing less than the "interlocutor" for "what enters metropolitan literature as a 'third world literature'" (37). He goes on to provide a formulaic definition of this intermediary genre which comprises, amongst other things, an irreverence towards national politics and literatures of national liberation, forms of transculturation and dialogic abundance, and an often magical-realist combination of epic scope and personal, impressionistic memory (Tickell 75).

When the disconnect between the novelistic universe and the larger world gains such proportions that, the answer to the simple question, "who is the subaltern in the novelistic universe?" can give rise to conflicting answers, one must begin to appreciate the subtle delineation between the two categories of historiography and fiction. In Roy's novel, Velutha, Ammu and her children and even Sophie Mol may be argued to be the ones addressed as the subalterns. However, these characters in themselves are elites amongst their own ethno religious groups due to the access they enjoy to education, a privilege denied to

36 per cent of the Indian population. If Roy's novel speaks for such subalterns, why then, does it speak to the very discriminatory machinery of hegemonic power to the exclusion *of* the party or parties it claims to represent? Is not the postcolonial novelist, by denying a non-idealised space to the representational figure of the subaltern in the novelistic universe, then reproducing the colonial imaginary of the Other and reinforcing the imbalance of power in favour of the elite?

Negotiating such a double bind of a palimpsest of potential misrepresentations of the emancipated subaltern aware of his or her rights but incapable of defending them and the impulse of mimetic fidelity to the original of these representations can become not only problematic, but quite simply an impossible task to accomplish. The areas in which *The God of Small Things* succeeds in this representational acrobatics are those of its portrayal of a gendered patriarchy and caste-oppression. Furthermore, Roy insulates herself from narrative failure by investing a female child with the narratorial voice, thus underwriting her own limitations as an author within Rahel's childhood vision of a particular conjuncture. Perhaps then, we might venture to hope, that the subaltern does speak, but not to or through a cosmopolitan writer-activist.

Works Cited

Chakrabarty, Dispesh. *Provincialising Europe: Postcolonial thought and Historical Difference*. New Jersey: Princeton University Press, 2000, 215.

Brennan, Timothy. *At Home in the World: Cosmopolitanism Now*, Cambridge MA: Harvard University Press, 1997, 37.

Chanda, Ipshita. "The Tortoise and the Leopard, or the Postcolonial Muse." *Comparative Studies of South Asia, Africa and the Middle East* 23.1-2 (2003): 128-40.

Chatterjee, Partha. "Agrarian Relations and Communalism in Bengal, 1926-1935." Ranajit Guha (ed.), *Subaltern Studies: Writings on South Asian History and Society*. Vol. 1. Delhi: Oxford University Press, 1982, 9-38.

D'Souza, Florence. "Silences and Ellipses in *The God of Small Things*." Eds. Carole and Jean-Pierre Durix. Reading Arundhati

Roy's *The God of Small Things*. Dijon, France: Editions Universitaires de Dijon, 2002.

Gopal, Priyamvada. "Reading Subaltern History." Ed. Neil Lazarus. *The Cambridge Companion to Postcolonial Literary Studies*. Cambridge: Cambridge University Press, 2004, 139-61.

Heidegger, Martin. *On the Way to Language* (New York: Harper & Row, 1971), 71.

Li, Victor. "Death and the Subaltern." *Literature For Our Times*. The University of British Columbia (UBC), Vancouver, British Columbia, Canada, August, 2007. Available at http://ocs.sfu.ca/aclals/viewabstract.php?id=135

Macaulay, Thomas Babington. "Minutes on Indian Education". *A South Asian Nationalism Reader*, ed. Sayantan Dasgupta. Delhi: Worldview Publications, 2007, 163-65.

Needham, Anuradha Dingwaney. "'The Small Voice of History' in Arundhati Roy's *The God of Small Things*." *Interventions: International Journal of Postcolonial Studies*. 7.3 (2005): 369-91.

Roy, Arundhati. *The God of Small Things*. New Delhi: Penguin, 1997.

Rushdie, Salman. "In Good Faith." Imaginary Homelands. London: Granta, 1994.

Spivak, Gayatri Chakravorty. "A Critique of Postcolonial Reason." *The Norton Anthology of Theory and Criticism*. Ed. Vincent B. Leitch, et al. New York: W.W. Norton & Co., 2001, 2197-2208.

——. "Can the Subaltern Speak?" Bill Ashcroft, Gareth Griffiths and Helen Tiffin (eds.), *The Post-Colonial Studies Reader*. London/ New York: Routledge, 1995.

Tickell, Alex. "The *God of Small Things*: Arundhati Roy's Postcolonial Cosmopolitanism". *The Journal of Commonwealth Literature*, 2003, 38-73.

7

From Backward to Forward: Self-upgrading in Contemporary India

Alessandro Monti

Domestic migration from the countryside to the big city is a subject not easily taken by Indian fiction. A first and rather sketchy overview highlights a seminal work such as *A Fine Balance* by the expatriate writer Rohinton Mistry (1995), perhaps an ultimate assessment concerning the past campaigns of urban and social beautification. India has known a tremendous change after its rather authoritarian Seventies—in particular it tried, and it is still trying, to cope with its huge areas of economical and I would say human backwardness. The juxtaposition I refer to concerns what is left of the welfare state featured by Nehru after the Independence, in opposition to the contemporary rush towards social success and wealth.

The White Tiger by Aravind Adiga (2008) tries to illustrate critically this double-edged tension between a spread condition of extant backwardness, whose unchangeable location seems to be the so-called Darkness, and the upward individualities which want to get finally rid of the stifling heritage constituted by casteism, feudal tyranny and obsolete social and economic machinery. Albeit grounded on mutinous acts of individual social ascent, the novel by Adiga should be understood and analysed within the pale of the constitutional frame defining castal identities in relationship with their possibilities of progress. As a matter of fact I would focus on the Other Backwards section defined by Ambedkar and further institutionalised by the Mandal Commission with its splitting between Backwards and Forwards.

We should be able to translate such terms into a Western lexicon speaking of rural destitute and urbanised migrants, even if this process still implies subaltern positions that are the sheer impossibility of reaching a somewhat middle class status. The main character in the novel presents himself as a regressive *halwai*, one whose family has sadly lost the comfortable station of vendors of sweets. Being consequently reduced to the unsavoury role of drudge for a seedy roadside *dhaba*, the protagonist needs some purview to improve himself. Of course his first move mimics the bureaucratic procedures operated by the Mandal programme, insomuch he must privately use the agency of reservation—in other words he has to manage, by means of money, his own access to the closed group of drivers. He has to acquire a new-fangled professional identity—one, however, still within castal (or castal-like) hierarchies.

To start with, his own self-made forwarding procedure does not make him evade the feudal backlash that controls the economy and the lives of the single persons as well, within the Darkness. He enters in fact the service of one of the three leading families in the area, in a way that allows him to exchange the soiled rags of a famished *chai-wallah* with the more socially dignified clothes of a servant. As a matter of fact he just wears a different kind of livery, according to a pattern of instructed forwardness that earmarks people no more, or not only, through their caste names, but primarily by means of their institutionalised uniform-like clothes: from backwood rural to bus or car driver to, finally for a few, professional politicians. This updated reflex of traditional casteism stands high as the ruling motive within the apparently modern picaresque of *The White Tiger*—we should view it as the percolating agency between the Darkness and Delhi, between the archaic economic background of the *mofussil* areas and the rampant corruption in the capital city.

Both locations deploy a structural lack of flexibility which rather indicates authoritarian conformity within the national framework. Given this substantial fixity the character cannot but move across disconnected layers of professional competence. His first step does not evade however the feudal imposition, since to pledge his fidelity he has to pawn the lives of his family circle. This act of jeopardy makes havoc of the current notions concerning the self-effacing duty, or service, that according to Hinduism one should show towards the elder or the other members of the family. However, in the novel the rural family is just seen as a domineering and pitiless institute, more subservient to the dry rules of domestic exploitation, rather than promoting or protecting individual improvement—indeed a real extended burden and an impending clog in the wheel of emancipation. Caste heritage and family constitute in the novel a sort of counter-Hindutva pastoral, one in which selfish hegemony rules both in the private and public spheres, these concerning either human or social relationships.

To avoid such crude impositions of raw power the *halwai* turned to budding driver through self-promotion, and without any external purview, updates his role within the hierarchical archive of the modernised nationhood, switching his position from rural subaltern to domestic servant in a modernising setting, as I have told before. As a matter of fact, his first forwarding move seems to lead him to a further dead end. By leaving the *mofussil* for Delhi the driver is still dangerously perched along the precarious edges of social improvement. To escape hell he has to proceed on his subterranean behaviour of self-taught survival.

To achieve his aim he becomes the silent and mimicking stranger who enters as a migrant the walls of the ruling city, a place he will finally be able to conquer. An uncanny metaphor reflects as it were the competitive rush towards affluence and corruption which marks contemporary Indian society.

I mean the voracious cockroaches that every night crunch off the eatable concrete walls of his cellar-like room, in the basement of the posh mansion in Delhi. This image reminds me strikingly of the concealed worm that in a well-known poem by William Blake gnaws at the very heart of the budding rose. An analogous invisible cancer eats cruelly away at the roots of Indian society. The frenzied devouring activity of the nocturnal vermine highlights to me a composite backdrop of unsatiated greed and darkened destruction.

We should compare this bleak imagery of impending ruin (perhaps someday the whole building will crumble down) to the everlasting fire that is said to be burning in the deep entrails of the coal district. The former stands high as a suggestion of precarious and threatened beautification, whereas the latter rather suggests a myth against change and impermanence. Indeed, this invisible or fabulous flame, one which burns perennially without destruction or consumption, could represent aptly the social stillness of the "Dark" land. On the contrary, the apparently tasty walls in the basement of the mansion enforce intimations of social entropy. They give us a glimpse of what might happen in the future. The metaphor acts disturbingly like a kind of grim time machine which anticipates the events to come—of self-destroying corruption and cannibalising greed.

At the very heart of the disease stands again the conflictual relationship between master and servant. We should understand it in sheer terms of colonial procedure that is a poisoned mix of distanced friendship and invidious mimicking on the part of the inferior. This pattern of insincere behaviour defines the social gap in terms of semi-clandestine conflict, one grounded on individualised mutinous attitudes, of which the murder in the story is the logical and extreme consequence. *Havālā*, that is the black money of corruption, is the turning agency that opens the door of the forward world to the driver—once in Bangalore, the so-called Silicon Valley of the new India, he takes advantage of the infrastructural inadequacy concerning transportation to start his own network of cabs for the computer-literate white collars.

Thus the driver seems to have finally reached the inner core of competitive India. The apologue in the novel should perhaps be understood as a nasty reaction against the features of select inequality which have been inherited by casteism and above all against the alliance between statal bureaucracy and both the feudal lords and the political *goondas*. This shared background of power constitutes the argumentative side of the novel, beyond its merely satirical bias. By focusing on specific slices of Indian reality (that is, the forgotten countryside, the circle of urban drivers, the cosmopolitan feudal lords) the writer gives lurid life to a circumscribed contemporary comedy of manners. Its analysis goes well beyond the sociological representation of changing modes such as takes place in previous Indian fiction—let's say *The Sari Shop* by Rupa Bajwa (2004), perhaps a pioneering instance of social self-promotion, or the more recent *No God in View* by Altaf Tyewala (2005).

To understand properly *The White Tiger* we should turn to the *Reluctant Terrorist* by Moshin Hamid (2007)—a novel which tackles in a rather bitter way with the issues of revengeful violence inside a split world. Perhaps individual terrorism is the possible key to *The White Tiger*, whose main character should be included in the endless list of social bandits, these leading a private war of their own against society. His act of belligerent murder shifts to individual reaction the insurgent nature of such groups as the naxalites—by being an urban dacoit he re-introduces these uncouth reactions of re-compensative resistance against dispossession which the new Indian state had erased out of its imagined tableau.

So, the rural and domestic epic of the film *Mother India* (1957), one celebrating shared nationhood through a self-sacrifying mother, refuses disrupting intimations of violent revolt, endorsing however the murder of the rebellious son, a pre-naxalite character, on the part of his fond mother. As a matter of fact *Mother India* should be viewed by us according to hierarchical measures of conformity to unprogressive type—the same which are shamelessly broken down in *The White Tiger*. Recent films in the age of globalised competition move their focus from a stylised countryside to the urban rat race. Once again a driver is the plotting hero of the dark filmic comedy *Maharathi* (2008), in which the pseudo-murder of a man who has committed suicide is the too astute trick to inherit his money.

Notwithstanding Bollywoodian easiness, the film raises issues of self-promotion in contemporary society quite akin to the killing strategies adopted by the driver in *The White Tiger*. Both narrations deal with triumphant actions of private purview, these replacing public agencies of social improvement such as reservation and the likes. Not casually the summarising jacket of *Maharathi* epitomises the situation like this, "Subhash recognizes this [the suicide committed by his master] as on opportunity to rid himself of a lifetime of middle class mediocrity and poverty."

An even more recent filmic comedy, *Oh, My God!!* by Saurath Srivastava (2008) tries to come to terms with one's big dreams. The juxtaposition here is between the wish "to make it big in life but through ethical ways" and the refusal of *artha* in favour of financial renouncing. In other words, the film makes a strong plea for an updated and urbanite figure of Hindu spirituality. A sheer stroke of luck is not considered ethical enough, although operating through the help of God. On the other hand, frenzied strategies of self-financial improvement are bluntly equated in the film to procedures leading to alienation and loss of spiritual balance.

The message looks clear enough—competitive India has to come back to her spiritual heritage, if she wants to survive. However, *The White Tiger* makes definitive havoc of the timeless grounding values which emphasise the ruling importance of the family circle and of the community in general. Social climbers, like the two drivers both in the novel and in the film *Maharathi*, are thus obliged to move surreptiously in-between the constituted hierarchies that shape the cline of identities in India. This interstitial position foregrounds the schizophrenia which is latent in the failed compromise which should have harmonised conformity to traditional values with dreams of personal improvement. The triumphant progress from the Darkness to Bangalore which takes place in *The White Tiger* does not efface hell from the map of India—it simply adds a new grain of sand to the contemporary wasteland. At the very background of the voyage of conquest the reader should acknowledge a dreary sequence of thematic parks—these including the half-starved village and the neglected *mofussil*, the lousy colony in Delhi and booming Bangalore. The "Backward's Progress" intimates a few considerations concerning the role of the national archive and the related issue of social descent and shared values of nationhood. You cannot simply wash out your past, the character says. It is again the "Mark of the Beast" of Kipling and the Anglo-Indian discourse, a revealing indication of marginal belonging and unbalanced social status. A Backward is tokened, i.e. is "marked" for life, in a way that betrays disturbingly his humble origins—this badge of social impurity (one which evokes the original Biblical taboo against any mixed complexion) in the diseased skin of the drivers, either blanched by vitiligo or blotched in pink patches by scalding tea. This unhappy lineage deregulates even the seminal issue of fatherhood—the protagonist cannot identify himself with a hen-pecked and failed *pati*, one who is worked to death by a cannibalising family circle. Also a possible father-son relationship with his partly benevolent master turns sour at its very beginning—given how the driver assumes surface hybridisation of manners as his constant behaviour. We should take the fateful term hybridisation by focusing on the in-between stance to which a colonial servant is obliged in his daily public (or working) life.

He apparently discards his own culture and his own customs and manners, being constrained as he is to wear a double livery, outside and inside, in dress and behaviour. This ambiguous duality makes a cannibal serving at table of him, or, as far our resistant driver is concerned, a murderer. From a metaphorical point of view by killing his master (a *crorepati* by all means) he erases step-fatherhood out of his biographical archive and at the same time renounces globalisation. A reader should keep in mind how fastidiously the driver reacts to exotic Western food, and how he comments sourly on the disgusting smell of a pizza. Whereas imported liquor stands as a shared value, one that intimates social prestige and accomunates in tastes both rich and poor. Foreign liquor and controversial pizza indicate respectively standards of accepted colonial heritage and a bitter refusal of contemporary globalisation.

The implied archive of food (greasy deshi food against disgusting *phorein* fare) goes well beyond the plain issue of diet—it rather deploys a divide in class through difference in the cultural habits concerning nutrition. One should perhaps draw a sharp distinction opposing backward food (chunks of brown meat and vegetables dripping reddish oil) and the *phorein* masala dish represented by pizza. I would like to observe that the notion of pizza as food reaches back to ancient Rome, one in its line of ancestry answering to the definition of *atellana*, a term foregrounding a mixed filling or topping and a sort of comical play as well. The old term might stand for *masala*, insomuch today the pizza acts as a social leveller, being eaten as it is both by Western upper and lower classes.

By rejecting mundane sophistication in food the protagonist of *The White Tiger* personifies the crucial figure of the *am admi*, the common man still beyond the range of globalised modernisation. Albeit a financially successful entrepreneur the protagonist still belongs to the Darkness, that is an unchangeable hell of feudal exploitation and marginal lives. It is a location prior to social mobility and flexible identity. However, a reader should not understand the novel in terms of caste. Since the Indian Constitution, the order of the Government of India in 1990 and the Mandal Judgement in 1992 it is held that caste is class in the sociological sense. Consequently, *The White Tiger* is not a novel about casteism but rather concerns the backdrop of failed shared belonging in post-Independence India and of his politics of equality. As such, the novel moves on the mimicking edge of parody, since it transposes the rush of economical globalisation into less sedate terms of unchecked leaps of social upgrading. As a matter of fact, the character does not move across himself—he just pushes forward his identity as driver, but not yet a SAPS (Socially Advanced Person and Section) and always a creamy-layered SEBC (Socially and Educational Backward Class).

8

The Subaltern as Hero in Aravind Adiga's *The White Tiger*

Anita Myles

The Man Booker Prize of 2008 was conferred upon Aravind Adiga for his debut novel *The White Tiger*[1] inviting several reviews, views and opinions as a customary practice though no solid literary criticism attracted the work. However, my approach in this paper towards the novel is going to be a critical exercise, a deviation entirely distinct because I have scrutinized the work impartially without being prejudiced by either the individual or nationalistic narrow centricism. Like most of the reviewers, majority of the Indian readers may find Adiga's blatant and bold analysis of the contemporary Indian scenario and system repulsive but I will be concentrating on what exactly the writer has portrayed attempting to offer a balanced evaluation. To be precise, the central character of the novel is a subaltern who gradually rises to the level of a white collar entrepreneur by deploying a wide variety of *anti-deregle* ruses and actions.

The novel adopts the epistolatory tradition, the letters being written on seven nights to the Chinese Prime Minister, Mr. Wen Jiabao who plans to visit India for a week with the specific purpose of wanting to know the truth about Bangalore and a keen desire for interacting with some Indian entrepreneurs and hearing their story of success in an attempt to create some successful Chinese entrepreneurs. Balram Halwai, the author of these letters informs the premier that he may not get an accurate representation of India in the company of the Prime Minister and the Foreign Minister of India whereas a common man, who by his grit and skill has risen to be an accomplished businessman may be the right person to narrate the success story to the Chinese Prime Minister. Balram assumes it to be farcical that the Chinese who are more progressive than the Indians in diverse fields should turn to India for practical lessons. To quote the novelist,

> And our nation, though it has no drinking water, electricity, sewage system, public transportation, sense of hygiene, discipline, courtesy, or punctuality, *does* have entrepreneurs. Thousands and thousands of them. Especially in the field of technology. And these entrepreneurs—*we* entrepreneurs—have set up all these outsourcing companies that virtually run America now. (4)

Balram Halwai then emphatically discloses his observations about an accomplished businessman in India bursting out unhesitatingly,

> My country is the kind where it pays to play it both ways: the Indian entrepreneur has to be straight and crooked, mocking and believing, sly and sincere, at the same time. (8-9)

The bold veracity about the Indian economy emerges from Balram's personal experiences; hence he narrates in the seven letters his personal adventures branding these, "The Autobiography of a Half-Baked Indian". He designates himself half-baked because circumstances prevented him from completing his formal education. However, he is proud to admit that he learnt much and many more practical things about life from the India roads and pavements.

Balram Halwai alias Munna, son of Vikram Halwai, a rickshaw puller was born and raised in the darkness as he sees two Indias, one of darkness and one of light. Both his parents succumb to fatal diseases. Being left to fend for himself, Balram discontinued going to school and started working in a teashop near the coal mines of Dhanbad. Vikram Halwai, though a rickshaw puller, had higher plans for his son while his mother could also visualize that her son had adroitness and aptitude to make a mark for himself. Balram was certainly a distinguished student much above the others, something that was instantaneously perceived by the Inspector of Schools who asked Balram several questions ultimately concluding,

> You, young man, are an intelligent, honest, vivacious fellow in this crowd of thugs and idiots. In any jungle, what is the rarest of animals that comes along only once in a generation?

I thought about it and said:

> The white tiger.
>
> That's what you are, in *this* jungle. (35)

The inspector was so delighted by Balram's intelligence and determination that he bestowed a scholarship upon Balram for pursuing his education. However, the death of his parents and the instable financial condition of the family compelled him to find work.

Balram has aptly been referred to as 'The White Tiger'—a freak that occurs occasionally and is a rarity,

> The creature that gets born only once every generation in the jungle. (276)

White tigers are stronger than the golden variety, are intelligent and rare to find, hence treasured and protected with utmost care. The protagonist in the story is the white tiger of his generation, an uncommon rarity because he has the capacity, the strong will power and the aspiration to rise above his class and transcend his poverty. Thus the novel delineates his life as a progression from the subaltern to a hero. The novel is structured in the picaresque tradition showing Balram itinerating from place to place, adding on to his experiences and learning how to survive on his own, surmount adversities and overcome vicissitudes. The story of his life also follows a convention of a bildungsroman for his varied encounters help to build his character as a successful entrepreneur in the silicon valley of India that is Bangalore.

Balram resolves to become a car driver after listening to the conversation of other drivers at the teashop and acquiring the information that a driver is paid a salary of at least Rs. 1500 per month, manages to get the training and begins working as a driver in the house of a landlord from Laxmangarh, popularly known as 'the stork'. Later, he moves to Delhi along with the landlord's son, Mr. Ashok and the daughter-in-law, Pinky where he gets ample opportunity to intermix with other drivers of the affluent class thereby learning myriad lessons and survival techniques. He wins the confidence of the young couple as he cooks, cleans and drives for them. While driving Mr. Ashok around he discovers that his master keeps the family business going on by monetarily gratifying various officers and dignitaries of influence. He was entrusted to carry suitcases full of currency, later witnesses the separation of Ashok and his wife, the latter ultimately migrating to America to live with her parents. One day while driving Mr. Ashok with a red bag containing seven lakh rupees to be given as bribe, Balram considers it an opportune moment to kill his master and disappear with the money which he does discreetly on the rainy night by slitting Ashok's throat with a broken bottle of whisky which he had hid in the glove case of the car. Then he escapes to Bangalore changing his identity to Ashok Sharma. He says:

> There—I'm revealing the secret of a successful escape. The police searched for me in the darkness: but I hid myself in light. (118)

A turning point emerges in his life as he has walked out of the cage, earned his freedom, is no more a servant but becomes the master of his destiny. Balram has rich experience to back up his adventurous dreams which he proceeds to convert into reality gradually but carefully. He has successfully moved from darkness to light. His parents belonged to the darkness for they were poor; moreover they lacked the courage to fight for their betterment and were deprived of their paternal land by the upcoming feudals. Even as a driver Balram observed the suppression of the poor—often a driver was framed for charges that were untrue, put in jail for accidents caused by the master. Ironically Balram reminds himself that in spite of all deceptions, injustices and gratifications, India, his motherland is the "world's greatest democracy".

Balram portrays realistically the plight of suppressed working class in India as 'The Great Indian Rooster Coop' explaining the nuance in detail through a comparison with the chicken market behind the Jama Masjid in Old Delhi where hundreds of birds are stuffed tightly into wire cages with hardly any breathing space spreading unbearable stench. Nearby sits the butcher displaying proudly the flesh and the organs of recently slaughtered birds. Other birds smelling the blood realize that it could be their turn next. Being resigned to their fate they make no attempt to get out of the cage. Similar is the predicament of thousands in India as not many have the courage to revolt and escape the cage in order to gain their freedom. It would take a white tiger to do so and Balram is one such person. Initially trapped in the Rooster Coop of a suppressed 'subalternism', he craved for liberty and hence by using his subtle mind, courage and determination eventually discovers a way out even though it is not the right way which he realizes and bursts out in self-indignation,

> The rest of the narrative will deal mainly with the sorrowful tale of how I was corrupted from a sweet, innocent village fool into a citified fellow full of debauchery, depravity and wickedness. (197)

He recalls how his innocent master too had been corrupted in the same way.

Balram's encounters in Delhi assist him to discern the rich from the poor, the 'Big Bellies' from the 'Small Bellies'. While the poor dream of getting just enough to eat and looking like the rich, the rich dream of losing weight and looking like the poor, indicating a process of constant marginality in a nation pressed between tradition and modernity and crushed by the ideas compromising between the western and the native. At one time Ashok had confided in Balram,

> I'm sick of the food I eat, Balram. I'm sick of the life I lead. We rich people, we've lost our way, Balram. I want to be a simple man like you. (238)

The history of the world is actually a chronicle of an eternal conflict between the rich and the poor, a global process in which each side attempts to hoodwink the other. Consequently a few battles favour the poor though victory mostly sides with the rich. Balram was unlike the others for he looked upon himself as a 'working-class hero'. In Bangalore he carves a niche for himself skilfully, begins to run a taxi service owning a fleet of vehicles as he claims proudly:

> Once I was a driver to a master, but now I am a master of drivers. I don't treat them like servants—I don't slap, or bully, or mock anyone. I don't insult any of them by calling them my 'family' either. They are my employees, I'm their boss, that's all. (302)

All along Balram is cognizant of his achievements and attainments being vigilant and prudent enough to maintain his status. He says "a White Tiger keeps no friends. It's too dangerous".

He had traversed a long and difficult path from social ostracization to the level of an accomplished entrepreneur. He had also hauled himself from the darkness to the light by learning a secret that dishonesty is a preservative and a tonic for a man's life in India. He too had grown a 'Big Belly' for which only a little manipulative skill was required and felt enlightened for he had woken up from his sleep of slavery and suffering while the rest were still slumbering. This is how he was different from the others—a white tiger. He claims,

> All I wanted was the chance to be a man—and for that, one murder was enough. (318)

The murder had darkened his soul no doubt, but it also earned him a significant status in society. Balram is overwhelmed by his success intending to move into real estate business and later to start an English medium school for the poor in Bangalore:

> A school where you won't be allowed to corrupt any one's head with prayers and stories about God or Gandhi—nothing but the facts of life for these

> kids. A school full of White Tigers, unleashed on Bangalore! (319)

These were his dreams but the stark reality was that he had actually 'broken out of the coop'. He doesn't regret the murder as it was worthwhile and he is no more a servant. He had "...changed from a hunted criminal into a solid pillar of Bangalorean society".

Later, he was able to pay the police enough to stop pursuing the murder case realizing that money could get you everything making the world move as per your own wishes. Indeed the main thing was of ignoring one's conscience though the efforts had to be coupled with courage and determination which he had right from the beginning. He was indeed the white tiger of his generation, a subaltern who transforms himself into a hero.

Aravind Adiga, in his maiden attempt at fiction writing seems favourably inclined and sympathetic towards the neglected classes of India. The narrative throws ample light on the plight of the poor in India whom Adiga considers as 'subalterns'. Economically exploited, socially condemned, medically neglected and educationally ignored these vanquished sons of the soil struggle to keep body and soul together while people in power make merry at their expense. Most villagers are like bonded labourers of the landlords who take undue advantage of their poverty and ignorance. They are subalterns in the true sense of the word.

Mention should be made of at least three novelists other than Adiga who have written significantly about the subaltern. Mulk Raj Anand leads the list as in his novel *Untouchable* Bakha, the protagonist belongs to the suppressed class yet he is like the 'white tiger' because his desires and tastes are different from the other youngsters of his group. He has the inclination to learn, to improve and to rise above his established low status. However, he lacks the cunning of Balram and hence remains static in his position with his dreams unfulfilled. In Bhabani Bhattacharya's *He Who Rides a Tiger,* Kalo, the protagonist is a subaltern who decides to show the world that he is the master of his own destiny. Like Balram he has the grit and the courage to hide his past. In the process, he hoodwinks the masses emerging as a *sadhu* having miraculous powers. He is different from his fellow beings who remain satisfied in riding the sheep, but Kalo proves the fact that if one has the courage to ride the tiger he can change his life. Velutha in Arundhati Roy's *The God of Small Things* stands midway between Bakha and Kalo. He has the desire to rise, falls in love with a woman who is socially above him but then loses the courage to face the world. He is condemned for what he has done. While we sympathize with Velutha, we have words of admiration for Bakha, Kalo and Balram. Aravind Adiga's protagonist is similar to the others and yet he stands apart owing to the progression traced in his character. He is not afraid to take the risks involved and soon rises by hook or by crook because that is the sole mission of his life.

The subalterns in these novels have been treated like being physically handicapped as life's chances are limited for them. They cannot singly overthrow their suppressors due to the inherent social system. The portrayal of these characters raises awareness in the readers towards an age-old problem as the dates of publication of these novels will justify: *Untouchable* published in 1935, *He Who Rides a Tiger* published in 1954, *The God of Small Things* published in 1997 while *The White Tiger* some ten years later in 2008. These novels cover a long span of time though the status of the subaltern remains unchanged. All these four novelists have based the titles of their novels on the character of the protagonist; Bakha is the untouchable, Kalo is the man who rides the tiger, Velutha is the god of small things, while Balram is the white tiger. The protagonists are gifted, different from the rest of their caste and are in many ways indispensable for their masters. However, a noteworthy fact is that Bakha and Velutha suffer remaining where they are for they lack deception and cunning. Kalo and Balram break open the cage because they have the courage to kill the conscience and use deception and cunning to find their way to the top. Kalo is the miraculous *sadhu* has powerful politicians at his feet while Balram becomes an entrepreneur par excellence and considers himself as an apt person to enlighten the Chinese premier about India entrepreneurs. Both Kalo and Balram hover between feelings of fear and ecstasy for quite some time. Both have to suppress the voice of their conscience. Both desire to rescue their fellowmen from the exploitation of the rich. Both the novels are significant documents of socio-cultural realism in disclosing the bitter truth about the vice of neo-colonialism in contemporary India.

Postcolonial theories and literature occupied the centre-piece up to the last decade of the earlier century. Writers felt free to demonstrate the evolution of protagonists taken from the suppressed and neglected masses under the erstwhile imperialist masters and began to ventilate their views fearlessly inhaling the sweet smell of liberation expecting new horizons and fresh opportunities to open out for everyone. However, the anticipation proved chimerical as a new class of feudalists started emerging in India. This new colonialism tends to be more banal, detrimental and destructive as now the natives suppress natives just for personal gains and selfish ends. An in-depth study of the subaltern, therefore proves to be significant in the light of the contemporary Indian social structure which is beset with class struggle, caste wars, religious intolerance and ethnic alienation. Aravind Adiga's *The White Tiger* portrays an excellent picture of such a coetaneous reality.

Reference

1. New Delhi: Harper Collins, 2008. (Page numbers of textual references pertain to this edition only.)

9

Dislocation and Identity in *The Inheritance of Loss*

Nishi Pulugurtha

Kiran Desai's *The Inheritance of Loss* won the Man Booker Prize in 2006 and the National Book Critics Circle Fiction Award in 2007. Written over a period of seven years, Desai's second novel, explores issues that are of importance in postcolonial literature. Homi Bhabha's definition of postcolonial criticism is of importance from the perspective of this paper:

> Postcolonial criticism bears witness to the unequal and uneven forces of cultural representation involved in the contest for political and social authority within the modern world order. Postcolonial perspectives emerge from the colonial testimony of Third World countries and the discourses of "minorities" within the geopolitical divisions of east and west, north and south. They intervene in those ideological discourses of modernity that attempt to give a hegemonic "normality" to the uneven development and the differential, often disadvantaged, histories of nations, races communities, peoples. They formulate their critical revisions around issues of cultural difference, social authority, and political discrimination in order to reveal the antagonistic and ambivalent moments within the "rationalizations" of modernity.[1]

This definition highlights the central themes of *The Inheritance of Loss*. The novel brings into focus the differences between the East and the West through two parallel stories, one set in Kalimpong and the other in New York.

The rise of the Gorkha movement is an important aspect in the novel and reveals that the negotiation of national identity and belonging, are not features of the diaspora abroad, but also in Kalimpong where ethnic identity becomes all important. The Gorkha movement affects the lives of all the characters in the novel. This is what the novel says about the movement:

> In Kalimpong, high in the northern Himalayas where they lived—the retired judge and his cook, Sai and Mutt—there was a report of new dissatisfaction in the hills, gathering insurgency, men and guns. It was the Indian-Nepalese this time, fed up with being treated like a minority in a place where they were the majority. They wanted their own country, or at least their own state, in which to manage their own affairs.[2]

One of the themes of the novel is the displacement that the characters undergo in the course of their lives. Almost every character in the novel is unhappy in the environ he/she inhabits. Their displacement creates problems of assimilation, a sense of alienation and a crisis of identity. This paper is an examination of the dislocation and cultural alienation that each of the characters undergo. The story of each is different given the fact that situations and circumstances each character is in are different. The environs in which they all live are hostile to them and their identity is hence troubled. Ashish Nandy in an essay says that,

> ...nationalism does not come free in a society like ours. Firstly it comes bundled with official concepts of state, ethnicity, territoriality, security and citizenship. Once such a package captures public imagination, it is bound to trigger in the long run, in a society as diverse as ours, various forms of 'subnationalism' [...] the idea of the nation in the 'official' theory of nationhood can be made available in a purer form to culturally more homogeneous communities such as the Sikhs, the

> Kashmiri Muslims, the Gorkhas and the Tamils. As a result, once the ideology of nationalism is internalized, no psychological barrier is left standing against the concepts of new nation-states that would be theoretically even purer, homogeneous national units—in terms of religion, language and culture.[3]

The various ethnic and religious upheavals that India has witnessed in the past few years could be seen as part of an attempt by Indians to reconstruct their political and cultural identity. It is this idea that finds concurrence in the depiction of the Gorkha movement that rears its head in the quiet Himalayan town and brings about great changes in the lives of its inhabitants.

The idea of nationhood is often grounded on pride in native culture. Indian identity is multiple and is complicated further by the colonial influence. Sai, in the novel notes this:

> In contrast to the National Geographic's order, this part of the country that the characters find themselves in is a part of a messy map, particularly with the insurgency gathering momentum, "What was a country but the idea of it? She thought of India as a concept, a hope, or a desire. How often could you attack it before it crumbled?"[4]

Many of the characters in the novel have been stunted by their encounters with the West. The judge had been to England as a student and it is there that he becomes completely isolated. His race begins to matter a lot and there are times when he feels "barely human at all" and leaps "when touched on the arm as if from an unbearable intimacy".[5]

> ...For entire days nobody spoke to him at all, his throat jammed with words unuttered, his heart and mind turned into blunt aching things.[6]

He is unable to find a house for several days in England as no one is willing to rent a house to someone who is racially inferior.

On his return to India, he begins to despise his wife. He creates a huge uproar when his power puff goes missing. In

England he learns the way of the British and begins to believe in the supremacy of British society. Homi Bhabha points out that the influence of a different culture often causes tension between the desire of holding on to one's identity and the demand for a change in identity and that mimicry is a compromise to this tension.[7] In his endeavour to be like them he begins to study hard. He has tea every afternoon, speaks English with a British accent, and uses the powder puff in an attempt to hide his real skin colour. In spite of all his attempts to fit into British society, he remains an outsider. The judge hence suffers from a double isolation and it is this that causes an identity crisis. However, he still believes in the superiority of the West.

In the United States Biju becomes aware of the ugly, disorderly state of the West. His life is miserable, moving from one restaurant job to another and living with many others in appalling conditions. His father, the cook at Cho Oyu imagines him to be leading a wonderful life in the United States with every modern amenity that one can dream of. Biju finds that Indian men in New York restaurants order beef, something that he does not like: "One should not give up one's religion, the principles of one's parents and their parents before them. No, no matter what. You had to live according to something."[8] His reaction toward the West becomes a little more forceful when later he understands that he, along with many other illegal immigrants like him in the restaurant, is actually being exploited. When he applies for his visa at the U.S. embassy, he is with a group of Indians struggling to reach the counter window. The biggest pusher among them tries hard to impress the U.S. officials that he is civilized:

> He dusted himself off, presenting himself with the exquisite manners of a cat. I'm civilized, sir ready for the U.S., I'm civilized, man. Biju noticed that his eyes, so alive to the foreigners, looked back at his own countrymen and women, immediately glazed over, and went dead.[9]

This is possibly one of the most agonizing scenes in the novel. The eagerness for a U.S. visa results from a preconceived notion of the West.

Lola and Noni are two Anglophile sisters who grow broccoli with seeds got from England, listen to the BBC and read nineteenth century British novels. Lola is proud that her daughter is an anchor at BBC and she asks her not to come back to India. In this she is very much like the cook who makes every possible attempt to send his son Biju to the United States and dreams of the wonderful life that his son is leading there. The judge asks Noni to teach Sai instead of sending her to a public school in Kalimpong because he believes that Sai will learn the Indian-accented English in school, which he does not approve.

The death of her parents brings Sai to Kalimpong and her grandfather, thrusting her from her convent school environ to a lonely life in her grandfather's mansion, Cho Oyu. Her meeting with Gyan, the Nepali tutor, brings a change in her life. Culturally they are very different and it is this that causes differences of opinion which creates a rift in their relationship. Gyan is aware of their differences when he first eats with Sai—he eats with his hands while she uses a fork. Later when he dines at the judge's house, his awkwardness with the fork and knife makes him very conscious and uncomfortable. He begins to feel ashamed about it and this leads to a sense of inferiority.

> "I am not interested in Christmas!" he shouted "Why do you celebrate Christmas? You're Hindus and you don't celebrate Id or Guru Nanak's birthday or even Durga Puja or Dussehra or Tibetan New Year."[10]

Gyan finds Sai and the judge's ways superficial and prefers to retreat to his own culture and way of life so much that he shuts himself off from any other culture. As he stands in the market watching a procession of the Gorkha movement pass by, "Gyan had a feeling of history being wrought."[11] He joins in the procession, shouting slogans as they move ahead, and begins to feel a sense of oneness with the cause, "he was pulled back into the making of history".[12] Among his own kind of people he seems to find a sense of identification by mocking on the judge's western lifestyle. However, this attempt to isolate oneself from other cultures is not always possible. Bill Ashcroft, Gareth Griffiths and Helen Tiffin, in *The Empire Writes Back*, say that "within the syncretic reality of a post-colonial society it is impossible to return to an idealized pure pre-colonial cultural condition".[13]

Having been to a convent school, Sai, like her grandfather, speaks English fluently and leads a western lifestyle. However, she is not an anglophile like her grandfather or Noni and Lola. She gets angry on reading about the advice given by an English writer, asking Indian gentlemen not to enter into the compartment reserved for Europeans—"A rush of anger surprised her. It was unwise to read old books; the fury they ignited wasn't old; it was new."[14] Unlike the judge, we find in her an amalgamation of the west and the east. There is no sense of isolation as she is able to accept the differences of both the cultures and is happy at that. The judge had been a bit wary about taking Sai into his household, afraid that he might treat her as he had treated his wife and daughter. Sai, however, was a lot like him as the judge soon found out.

> There was something familiar about her, she had the same accent and manners. She was a westernized Indian brought up by English nuns, an estranged Indian living in India. The journey he had started so long ago had continued in his descendants.[15]

The conversation between Noni and Lola reveals that many of the upper-class residents of Kalimpong see the region's disintegration as a result of illegal immigration—placing the blame on the Nepali speaking population who had been brought to work on the tea plantations and in the British army. There is, hence, a differentiation between 'us' and 'them' which actually fuels the separatist movement. A parallel can hence be drawn between the stories of Nepali immigrants in India and Indian immigrants in the States, all struggling with questions of identity. In 'Nation and Narration', Bhabha demonstrates the lack of national consciousness in the postmodern era of ethnic communities.[16] He says that the nation will lack unity and homogeneity and that it is doomed to be unstable. Lola says in the novel,

> This state-making, [...] biggest mistake that fool Nehru made. Under his rules any group of idiots can stand up demanding a new state and get it, too. How many new ones keep appearing? From fifteen we went to sixteen, sixteen to seventeen, seventeen to twenty-two...?[17]

All of the novel's characters eventually come to share Sai's belief that life is often defined by loss. "Could fulfilment ever be felt as deeply as loss?"[18]

> The country, Sai noted, was coming apart at the seams: police unearthing militants in Assam, Nagaland, and Mizoram; Punjab on fire with Indira Gandhi dead and gone in October of last year;....[19]

The characters in the novel long for home and love, but rarely achieve it. There are moments of tenderness and pleasure in their lives though. When Gyan fails to find a sense of purpose in history and politics he says something that is important and applicable to all the characters in the novel, that "happiness has a smaller location".[20] In the end, it is the landscape that remains, of course, there are changes to it as well. Darjeeling is literally "going downhill,"[21] there are landslides everywhere. The rebels say that it is not their tents but the big houses that endanger the hillside.

Almost all the characters in *The Inheritance of Loss* contribute towards the issues of identity that are of importance in a postcolonial and multicultural society. The Gorkha movement that soon overtakes the place brings about rapid changes in life in the once calm hills. Tourism is hit and hence business is bad. There is no water supply, no electricity and no cooking gas. People are afraid to leave their homes and often innocent people are arrested and tortured on flimsy grounds. Everyone is terrified and it becomes even more difficult for the poor people. Lola and Noni are discriminated against, humiliated and ridiculed, they lose most of their property to the movement, who see their estate as "free land".[22] When Lola visits the head of the organization for the Kalimpong area to discuss her situation, she is discriminated against because of her ethnicity and class. It is for the first time in her life that she is able to recognize the poor and understand their difficult situation: "the sisters had never paid much attention for the simple reason that they didn't have to. It was natural they would incite envy, they supposed, and the laws of probability favoured their slipping through life without anything more than muttered comments".[23]

> It did matter, buying tinned ham roll in a rice and dal country; it did matter to live in a big house and sit beside a heater in the evening, even one that sparked and shocked; it did matter to fly to London and return with chocolate filled with kirsch; it did matter that others could not. They had pretended it didn't, or had nothing to do with them, and suddenly it had everything to do with them.[24]

Uncle Potty and Father Booty also represent the privileged class. Uncle Potty belongs to the English upper class and studied at Oxford. His parents settled in India post retirement. He bought his land from the judge years ago, and now spends his days drinking. Father Booty is from Switzerland and keeps a dairy. Like the other characters, the Gorkha movement affects his life too. Having lived in India for forty-five years, it is suddenly discovered that he does not have a valid residence permit, and hence is an illegal immigrant—"He knew he was a foreigner but had lost the notion that he was anything but an Indian foreigner...."[25] The parallel with Biju's life in the United States is obvious, though, of course, their individual experiences as immigrants are very different. Father Booty had been able to assimilate in Kalimpong, having lived there for forty-five years, unlike Biju who had to spend his days hiding from the authorities lest he is found out and deported. When Biju gets his ticket to return to India, he is told by Mr. Kakkar that he is making a mistake in taking this decision, that in spite of all the problems and difficulties, it is "Still a world, my friend where one side travels to be a servant, and the other side travels to be treated like a king."[26]

Notes

1. Bhabha, Homi K. "The Survival of Culture". *Redrawing the Boundaries: The Transformation of English and American Literary Studies*. Ed. Stephen Greenblatt and Giles Gunn. New York: The Modern Language Association of America, 1992, 437-65.
2. Desai, *The Inheritance of Loss*, Penguin Books, New Delhi, 2006, 9. All quotations are from this edition of the novel.
3. "Unity in Nationalism: Pitfalls of Imported Concepts," *Times of India*, Bombay, October 4, 1995.
4. Desai, 2006, 236.
5. *Ibid.*, 40.
6. *Ibid.*, 39.
7. *Location of Culture*, Routledge, London and New York, 1994, 86.
8. Desai, 2006, 136.
9. *Ibid.*, 183.
10. *Ibid.*, 163.
11. *Ibid.*, 157.
12. *Ibid.*
13. Routledge, London and New York, 1989, 108.
14. Desai, 2006, 199.
15. *Ibid.*, 210.
16. Routledge, New York, 1990, 7.
17. Desai, 2006, 128.
18. *Ibid.*, 2.
19. *Ibid.*, 108.
20. *Ibid.*, 272.
21. *Ibid.*, 197.
22. *Ibid.*, 240.
23. *Ibid.*, 241.
24. *Ibid.*, 242.
25. *Ibid.*, 221.
26. *Ibid.*, 269.

10

Worlds within Words: A Study of Rushdie's Use of Allusions in the *Midnight's Children*

Garima Gupta

The Indian Writing in English has travelled a long way from its genesis as an anti-colonial and fervently nationalistic genre to a cosmopolitan and multicultural voice. In this span the one novel that is taken as watershed event is Salman Rushdie's *Midnight's Children* which won the writer not only a Booker but also a Booker's Booker and changed the entire direction of the future generation of Indian writers. Thus this novel has been one of the most researched one. One of the most discussed aspects of Rushdie is his innovative use of the English language to provide an Indian sensibility. His use of language in this novel particularly, is so dense and multilayered that only one of its aspects can be discussed in detail in the space of a research paper and this paper will explore his use of allusions in the novel.

Allusion as a figure of speech and its usage in creative writing has been explicitly discussed by Prof. Syal in her doctoral dissertation. Allusion has been defined as a 'tacit reference' to another literary work, history, contemporary figures, events, etc. It differs from source borrowing because allusion requires the reader's familiarity with the original for full understanding and appreciation. Allusion also differs from ordinary reference because it is sometimes tacit, and fused with the new context (of the text/speech situation) in which it appears. Various critics have opined differently about whether an allusion is always tacit. Bloom does not uphold the view of allusion as direct overt reference. However, Perri and Wheeler accept the view that allusion is marked in a text in an overt manner, and that "allusion is a generic term for quotations and references, and for the act of quoting and referring" (3). Matthews provides a scale of allusion where quotation is at one end of the scale, followed by misquotation, echo and trace. However, we are concerned here with allusion that is explicitly marked in linguistic form, as opposed to echo which is not so clearly marked.

The second aspect of allusion is its most distinctive feature, and it is the fusion within a new context, as the allusion is used for a specific purpose in the new text. Thus allusion is a form of reference to persons, places, events or literary works by naming them in a new utterance or text. It can be considered as allusion, even though it is overtly specified. Even, if the significance of a name may not be clear to a reader who is not familiar with the thing named, the fact that it is a grammatical marker for something is clearly recognizable.

If we make a categorization of allusion according to levels of simplicity and varying complexity, then we can differentiate between simple and complex types. Thus the non-tacit and directly indicative nature of direct reference makes it the simplest form of allusion. For instance, proper nouns by which 'Christ', 'Krishna', 'the Apocalypse', 'the themes' are named directly in a text, point to specific frames of reference that exist independently and externally to the text, in a real or imaginary world, which the reader must be familiar with in order to understand their significance when used in the text.

Indirect reference of various kinds is what has normally been understood as an allusion, where the indication of poems, texts, etc., is made not by naming, but by indirect means, such as description of attributes or comparison to something else. For instance, if Christ were referred to as 'the saviour' or Satan as 'fallen angel', the reference is made by mentioning the attributes of something not named.

Tacit suggestion of such links is the most characteristic quality of allusion. Higher in their degree of complexity are those allusions that signal towards not only one but two or several sources. Such allusions may be called dual or multiple reference or ambivalent reference. One of the referents may be referred to directly and others may be recoverable from the context in which they occur. Two or more connotations belonging to that object in more than one previous context can be applied thus, such as two interpretations of a myth, or two versions of a story or character. Many instances of these can be found in the works of writers who have made adaptations of myths or characters of myths based on both their Homerion and Virgilian versions.

Apart from being confined to a small part of a text as in quotation, allusion in literature can also be more extensive through imitation of the entire structure of a previous work. The use of poetic conventions and literary genres and sub-genres, is in itself on extended use of allusion, whether it is for serious or comic purposes. A mock epic, for instance, systematically exploits all the devices used in an epic. Again, as in the case of other types of allusion, understanding is enhanced by more knowledge.

In case of Salman Rushdie one notices an absence of ambivalent allusions. This is probably so because writing for an international audience he wants to avoid references which the readers might find too difficult to comprehend. In this paper I have divided the allusions used by Rushdie into naming or direct and indirect. In addition I have divided them according to the source of their borrowing which brings up categories like mythological, literary popular historical, political, etc. The objective of this analysis is to bring out the eclectic dynamism of Rushdie's texts wherein he brings different contexts together—sometimes as diverse as mythological and popular and imbues his characters, places or situations with multi-dimensional and multi-layered meanings. To illustrate, what I mean, I'll take the example of the character of Ormus Cama in *The Ground Beneath Her Feet.* He is in the novel, through allusions, related on one hand to the mythological figure of Orpheus and on the other to the popular figure of Elvis. This is the magic and the realism of Rushdie which expands the character and enriches it. Another characteristics feature of Rushdie's use of allusions that can be seen is that one kinds of allusion predominate in his novels. To illustrate, the allusions in *Midnight's Children* and *Shame* can be said to be predominantly historico-political while in *The Ground Beneath Her Feet* and *Fury*, use of popular allusions exceeds all other categories.

TABLE I

Use of Allusions in *Midnight's Children*

Mythological	Popular	Historico-Political	Literary
Naming Christ, is a Ravana, Vishnu, Mumbadevi, Valmiki, Ramayana, Musa, Moses, Mount Hira, Indra, Pandavas, Shiva, Kurukshetra, Radha and Krishna, Rama and Sita, Purana, Shaitan, Ganesh Chaturthi.	Dev Anand, Lata Mangeshkar, Bano Devi, Dara Singh, Korma, Dahi, Cumin, Chowpatty Beach, Batman, Superman, Clark Kent, Tenzing, Pashmina Shawl, Filmfare, Times of India, Illustrated Weekly of India.	Emperor Jehangir, Shah Jahan, Mumtaz, Mahmud Ghazni, Tughlaq, Iltutmish, Mughals, Brigadier Dyer, Jallianwalla Bagh, Muslim League, Five-Year Plans, General Zulfikar, Prime Minister, Shastri, Sheikh Mujib, Emergency.	Scheherazade, A Watery Caliban, Lenins, What is to be done, Pinocchie, C.G. Jung, Romeo and Juliet, Hero and Leander, Saint Joan in Shaw's play, Ali Baba Forty Thieves, Alladdin, Hatim Tai, Sindbad.
Indirect Lingam fashion, goddess of wealth, dung lotus, age of Darkness, Thirty different species of birds.	Dilli-dekho' machine, a little black blister, on a khaki hill, fisherman's pointing finger, Snotnose, Brass Monkey, Hairoil, Sharabi	The Great War, Green and Saffron Widow, Labia-Lips, Commander of Pepperpots.	Genie of the lamp, Open sesame, 'There are no strings on me', Schecherazade.

Midnight's Children, the *magnum opus* of the author contains a wide variety of different types of allusions, each having a role and purpose in the text. We may group these allusions into different types according to the classification given in Table I. The table, which is only illustrative and by no means exhaustive, shows how the different types can be grouped according to their distribution in the text. It must, however, be borne in mind that though this classification is useful for purposes of understanding how allusions are linguistically realized in the text, they are embedded in the text and to understand their functions we have to look at their position and immediate environment within the text.

Direct References

Rushdie's use of language in constructing a composite structure of narration in *Midnight's Children* involves a comprehensive use of lexical structures—chiefly the device of naming which is an important aspect of any culture. Rushdie has exploited its suggestive and semiotic powers to the maximum by using it in varied ways. Allegorical names like Sharabi, Singer, etc. and symbolic names like 'Lifafa Das' are included in indirect reference. In addition name-calling is also categorized under indirect reference as it in a way exploits an undesirable attribute of a person to indirectly refer to him.

In the present category are included only direct references in the form of nouns. These are subcategorized as mythological, popular, historico-political and literary. These categories bring out the eclectic sources wherefrom he borrows the references and also how he mixes categories to expand the referentiality of the text.

A glance at Table I reveals that Rushdie has used the device of naming as direct reference extensively. A look at the mythological names brings out the fact that the writer has extensively used Hindu mythology and he has used it in two ways—one he has named his characters after the mythological figures and secondly he has directly referred to mythological figures, places, important days, etc. Thus there are characters like Shiva, Parvati, Padma, Musa, etc. on one hand and references to Christ, Isa, Indra, Kurukshetra, Ganesh Chaturthi, etc. on the other.

Mythological allusions indicate the cultural focus of the context and require on the part of the reader a certain amount of familiarity with the original source for its complete comprehension. However, Rushdie being well aware that his audience in the west might not be familiar with the myths he has used, has embedded within the text of his novel some explanation of the myths used by him so that the unfamiliar reader is not completely at loss. Thus he tells in the novel that Shiva is a God both of creation and destruction and his character Shiva plays a similar role—both of the destroyer (he emasculates the midnight's children) and of the creator (he himself procreates in immense numbers). However, the novelist is not simply borrowing the myths. He is also working on these myths and adding to them. Thus Shiva, apart from his mythological attributes, is also representative of something else i.e. the raw energy of injustice—that is not derived from the myth, but is part of the semiosis of the novel, which in turn is a semiosis created from the social dynamics of a newly independent nation. Rushdie also freely subverts various myths. Thus Parvati, the Goddess and consort of Lord Shiva is 'Parvati-the-witch' in the novel and although she consummates with Shiva, it is with Saleem that her heart lies. The mythological son of Shiva and Parvati is Ganesha and in the novel Aadam, the son of Shiva and Parvati has big flapping ears like an elephant, like Ganesha.

Rushdie, typically, names his characters after mythological figures but uses the attributes they suggest freely to expand, follow or subvert their meanings. Rushdie has not invited himself to Hindu mythology alone. Since he is speaking of Mumbai and wants to convey the cosmopolitan and secular flavour of the city, he has used Muslim, Parsi and Christian allusions as well. Thus, we have characters like Mary, Joseph, Ibrahim, Musa and of course the Sinais. Rushdie's own elaboration on the significance of names comes in the chapter entitled "Drainage and Desert", through Saleem. As he says:

> Our names contain our fates; living as we do in a place where names have not acquired the meaninglessness of the West and are still more than mere sounds, we are also the victims of our titles. (304)

In addition to using mythological allusions for naming his characters, Rushdie has also used direct mythological references to create the flavour of the culture which forms the context of his characters. Thus he refers to Kali Yuga, Ganesh Chaturthi, Hadith, Om symbol, Kurus, Pandavas, Ramayan, Ramjan, Eid-ul-Fitr, Christ, Isa and the like. He uses an allusion in a single context to convey more than one meaning. For example, he has named the racecourse, Mahalaxmi. Laxmi, in Hindu mythology is the Goddess of wealth, a connotation which is self-evident. But a hidden connotation can be discerned in the fact that Laxmi is a pious name given to racecourse, a place which Amina Sinai regards as sinful. Another example can be seen where the protagonist is describing the meeting of Lila Sabarmati and Homi Catrack. Here the allusions he uses are Radha and Krishna, Rama and Sita, Laila and Majnu, Romeo and Juliet, etc. All these are love stories of the highest form of love whereas Lila Sabarmati is having an illicit affair with Homi Catrack. Thus, the contrast is highlighted. Moreover, another characteristic of Rushdie's use of allusion that can be seen in this example is his mixing of various categories. Thus Radha and Krishna are mythology, Laila and Majnu folklore and Romeo and Juliet literary. The postmodern writer does not maintain a distinction between high and low allusions and mixes them up freely. This expands the referentiality of the text. In the present example, the diversity of the allusion seems to convey that love is a universal phenomenon and may be so is an illicit affair.

In the category of popular allusions, Rushdie has used direct references to everything from media, advertisements, clothes, food and above all the Bollywood. Food allusions are extensively used throughout the novel. Chutney and pickle are preserves and symbolise the preservation of history in the jars of narration—'the pickling of time'. It is the power of food into which Rushdie's characters mix their emotions that alienates Saleem's family from each other, but the chutney becomes the link through which Saleem is able to rediscover his family. Along with the traditional cuisine we also have references to popular food items like 7 Up, Coca-Cola, Kwality Ice Cream, etc. From the world of media and advertisements Rushdie mentions *Times of India*, *Pakistan Times*, *Jang*, *Illustrated Weekly of India*, *Filmfare*, *Screen*, etc. thus giving a window into the popular reading of the people in the subcontinent. He also refers to various ads and in fact he names one of his chapters after a very famous advertisement of the times—The Kolynos Kid.

This expansion of an allusion into an entire chapter can again be seen in the chapter entitled 'Snakes and Ladders' which refers to a game popular among the children. However, it can also be termed as a multi-referential allusion because snakes in the Indian context are culturally and mythologically prominently placed. The multiple semantic and semiotic implications of 'snakes' and the game of Snakes and Ladders is shown as an elaborate semiotic, as a representation of life, and of the characters who alternate between sliding down snakes and climbing up ladders. Snakes are also associated with the God Shiva, and the character Shiva in the novel is the 'snake' who threatens Saleem. Further, the snake is both feared and worshiped: thus in the novel, snake-poison is shown as both healing (Saleem) and killing (Joseph). Picture Singh is able to scare away the political speech-maker with his snake charming abilities. Saleem compares himself to a snake, when he follows his mother, and puts a deadly note, like snake-poison, into Commander Sabarmati's pocket. Thus, this is a perfect illustration of how Rushdie exploit an allusion in all its connotations.

The most pervasive source of popular culture in India is Bollywood or Hindi movies and Rushdie has fully utilized it in his writings. The renowned sociologist Ashish Nandy firmly believes that "Only a handful of writers have matched the insight with which Rushdie speaks in *Midnight's Children* of elements of the new popular culture in urban India such as Bombay films" (15). Thus Rushdie has used Bollywood allusions directly such as Dev Anand, Lata Mangeshkar, Vaijayantimala and he has also alludes to the Boollywood techniques as applied by him to his text. Thus we have alternate editing, which allows consecutive sequences passing from the night of prodigious births on August 15, 1947, from the streets of Delhi to Lahore, from Narlikar to Nehru; these consecutive episodes resemble TV soap operas. The announcing effects the Saleem calls movie trailers...trumpeting 'Coming Soon' are also previews. Certain chapter headings such as "Love in Bombay" ironically evoke popular movie titles and this chapter recounts Saleem's unrequited love with the American girl Evie Burns. The cinematic stylistics also allows for convenient narrative acceleration which Saleem explains, during one of his narrative digressions:

> while Padma is holding her breath. I will allow myself to introduce here a close-up as in Bombay films.... A

calendar blown by the wind (where the pages... disappear marking the passage of years). (346)

In the category of popular allusions I've also placed popular figures of the day like Tenzing, Dara Singh; clothes like Pashmina shawls, games like Shatranj; places like Chowpatty beach, Juhu, Trombay and comic figures like Batman and Superman. Rushdie uses popular allusions as mere documentary backdrop or to flesh out his characters and to evoke the challenges they face or to give a flavour of the milieu. He intertwines his use of popular culture to enrich his use of history, politics or mythology and he challenges the division of the high art and the low.

When *Midnight's Children* was published, it was heralded as a powerful voice of the subcontinent; in the story of Saleem Sinai, the writer had written the story of the subcontinent. Thus the main narrative framework of the novel is historico-political. Consequently, the narrative abounds in historico-political allusions. The narrative spans the period from 1915 (the Kashmiri years of Aadam Aziz, Saleem's grandfather) to roughly 1977 (the end of emergency). How the novel is divided structurally to cover this period and the important points of intersection between the protagonist's life and the historico-political happenings of the subcontinent is explicitly highlighted by Prof. Pushpinder Sayal as follows:

TABLE II

	Individual/Personal	Historical
Book one (seven chapters)	Background	1919-Jallianwalla Bagh
Book two (Thirteen chapters)	Birth and Growing up (In India) (In Pakistan)	1947-Independence 1956-Language riots 1958-Coup in Pakistan
Book three (Eight chapters)	Adulthood (Amnesia and after)	1965-Indo-Pak War 1971-Bangladesh 1975-Declaration of Emergency 1977-Lifting of Emergency
Total 30 Chapters/Pickle Jars	30 years in the life of the protagonist/narrator	30 years after independence completed.

In this broad outline of the framework we can see how historico-political allusions form an integral part of the text.

Nearly all major events have been alluded to. Since the historico-political strand is an integral part of the fabric of the novel, these allusions are not extrinsic but made to appear as integral parts of the narrator's consciousness, more so because they are linked with the protagonist's life. For example when the language riots are alluded to, the narrator is intrinsically connected to them and says: "In this way I became directly responsible for triggering off the violence which ended with the partition of the state of Bombay" (192).

Moreover, as against a partisan, nationalistic, religious or cultural point of view, he refers to the various historico-political incidents from a humane point of view. For example, his description of the Jallianwalla Bagh incident is not narrated with a nationalistic fervour but to bring out the inhumanity of the incident.

> They have fired a total of one thousand six hundred and fifty rounds into the unarmed crowd. Of these, one thousand five hundred and sixteen have found their mark, killing or wounding some person. 'Good shooting', Dyer tells his men, 'we have done a jolly good thing'. (36)

Further, Saleem's voice is neither that of an Indian, nor of a Pakistani nor of a Bangladeshi. He covers all the three countries and alludes to their politics and history and he is equally critical of all the three. Another characteristic of his use of these allusions is that he is not always factually correct. The most glaring example of this is that the time of Mahatma Gandhi's assassination is given incorrectly. But the narrator is aware of the mistake, which seems to be deliberate on his part since he refuses to rectify it thereby challenging the official version. Thus, the writer uses his allusions to expose the political version of the subcontinent.

Literary allusions are few and far in the text. The reason for this is obvious. Rushdie is trying to outline a subcontinent to his audience and mythology, popular culture and history/politics help further his task. However, literary allusions would only be an embellishment and not help in furthering or explicating the context. However, we do have allusions like 'A watery Caliban', 'Saint Joan in Shaw's plays', 'Romeo and Juliet', 'Hero and Leander' and the like. Rushdie, here as well, mixes them up frequently with allusions from the other categories. For example, 'Romeo and Juliet' and 'Hero and Leander' are mentioned in the same breath with 'Radha and Krishna' or 'Rama and Sita' (Literary and mythological) or 'Hatim Tai' and 'Batman' or 'Sindbad' and 'Superman' are clubbed together (literary and popular). By such means Rushdie manages to make his literary allusions more than mere embellishments and also add to their referentiality.

In this category I would also like to include allegorical and symbolic names. It is a common practice among many cultures in India to name people after their occupation. Thus amongst Parsees we have 'Batliwalas' though they might not necessarily deal in the business of bottles. Similarly, in the novel the writer exploits a quality to name a person. Thus, we have names like 'Sharabi', 'Singer', etc. Another kind of naming in the novel is symbolic and suggestive within the framework and context of the novel. To illustrate 'Lifafa Das' is one such name. Lifafa in Urdu means an envelope and Lifafa Das does carry around the world enveloped in his peepshow. Similarly, we have Ram Ram Seth when the rhythm in his name recurs in his prophecies.

Indirect References

Name calling

Name calling is an integral part of the culture of the subcontinent and can be described as a mischievous way of referring to someone, using any one of the attributes of his character or personality to coin a pejorative, sarcastic or funny distortions to call him instead of his actual name. Rushdie exploits this practice to the maximum and for different effects. For example, in the category of the political he uses such names mostly to deflate, ridicule and present the characters in a bad light. Thus 'Widow' is used for Indira Gandhi, Sanjay Gandhi is 'Labia-Lips' and Ayub Khan is 'Commander of Pepperpots'. In the category of popular, the narrator has used nick names for his childhood friends, his sister and he introduces even himself by a string of a nicknames. Thus his sister is 'Brass Monkey' and his friends are 'Eyeslice' and 'Hairoil'. His string of nicknames can be connected to the various events in his own life. He is, thus, 'Stainface' (because of his birthmarks), 'Snotnose' (his leaky nose), 'Sniffer' (his olfactory powers), 'Buddha' (Premature grey hair as also his numbness to the world around him) and 'Piece of the Moon' (endearment term used by Mary). Thus, all these names are indicative of different phases in the life of the protagonist. When he regains his memory, he remembers all these but is not able to recall his actual name. The different names are indicative of the multiple personalities of the character and amongst all these he seems to have forgotten his real self. His inability to name the dying soldiers amongst the heap of bodies as his childhood friends also points to his dehumanization as indeed the narrator describes himself, having changed from Saleem to 'man-dog'. The narrator uses even mythological borrowing mischievously for the purpose of name calling when he refers to Padma as dung lotus frequently in his narration.

Other Indirect References

In comparison to the direct references, the use of indirect references by the writer is sparse. Moreover, these references can be considered 'anaphoric' and that the text to a large extent plays a part in filling out the meaning of the references. Moreover, it is the meaning that the writer chooses to convey. This can be seen in almost all the categories. For example, 'goddess of wealth' as already explained is Laxmi or 'dunglotus' is Padma as in mythology. In the popular allusions 'Dilli-dekho machine' is the Lifafa Das's peep show as already mentioned before or 'fisherman's pointing finger' is the portrait of Raleigh pointing referred to before. In the category of literal if 'Genie of the lamp' is mentioned, then so is Aladdin and with the phrase 'there are no strings on me', Pinocchio is mentioned. Similarly in the category of historico-political, 'Green and Saffron' are alluded to in the context of the moment of independence thus making clear its implication.

The reason for Rushdie's limited use of indirect references is clear. His writing is aimed at a wide range of international audience. Thus he doesn't want any ambiguities or such information in his text that makes the reader lose out on its meaning due to his inability to comprehend it. Although a familiarity with the original context of the allusion does add to the knowledge of the text but an ignorance of the same does not render the text incomprehensible. It is for this reason again that most of the indirect references in the text are used anaphorically by the writer. This can also account for the absence of any ambivalent allusions in the text.

The midnight's children are presented by the writer as India—the polyglot, multilingual, multiple plurality which is both a country and a concept and it is in 'allusions' that the writer finds the most apt means to realize his theme and uses it with a coruscating virtuosity.

Works Cited

Arnold Matthews. "Explorations in the Stylistics of Dramatic Literature with special reference to Fletcher and Massinger's 'Prophetess' and the problem of allusion and echo verification", *Unpublished M.Phill Dissertation*, University of Hull, 1983.

Ashish Nandy. "Satyajit Ray's Secret Guide" *East-West Film Journal*, 4:2, 1990.

Harold Bloom. *The Anxiety of Influence—A Theory of Poetry*. London: Oxford University Press, 1973.

M. Wheeler. *The Art of Allusion in Victorian Fiction*, New York, Barnes and Noble, 1979.

Pushpinder Syal, Prof. "A Stylistic Analysis of Idanre by Wole Soyinka and Relationship by Jayanta Mahapatra, in the Context of Non-Native Literature in Literature in English", *Ph.D. Dissertation*, University of Lancaster, 1986.

——. *Structure and Style in Commonwealth Literature*. New Delhi: Vikas Publishing House, 1994.

Salman Rushdie. *Midnight's Children*. London: Jonathan Cape, 1981.

——. *The Ground Beneath Her Feet*, Jonathan Cape, 1999.

11

Democracy and Dictatorship in Salman Rushdie's *Midnight's Children*

Prakash Chandra Pradhan

I

Democratic ideals and values are congenial for a nation to move forward, and they also help in the enlightenment of its people. Contrarily, violations of these ideals are detrimental to the growth of democratic institutions thereby causing immense hardships and sufferings for them. Such a system prevailing for a long time, there will be curtailment of liberty and freedom of expression which are essential for nourishment of human values, and the much needed progressive ideas for overall development of a nation. Such things happen only when there is misrule by the rulers who misuse their authorities and power to inflict oppressive measures on their subjects to their own advantages and survival. Consequently, progressive, independent thinking, that helps in movement of human culture and civilization forward, is censored. In this perspective, it is perhaps pertinent to refer to the intellectual tradition of the seventeenth and eighteenth centuries when such enlightened thinkers as Francis Bacon, John Locke, William Godwin [England], Descartes, Voltaire, Diderot [France], Leibniz and Immanuel Kant [Germany] (Abrams 1993: 52-53) emphasized the importance of rational thinking for dissipating the darkness of superstition, prejudice and barbarity to liberate humanity from its complete dependence on an earlier unfounded and unexamined irrational tradition. The enlightened, progressive writers in the literary tradition produce such texts that are of immense significance to inculcate free spirit in the people. In the context of production of literary texts, some of the twentieth century philosophers/ thinkers/Marxist critics/New Historicists/Cultural materialist critics viz. Althusser, Pierre Machery, Frederic Jameson, Raymond Williams, Greenblatt, Spender and many others put forth the argument that a great literary text subverts the ideology from which it is produced (Jefferson and Robey 1986: 166-203; Abrams 1993: 241-46, 248-55). They further plead that a literary text also exposes the contradictions that are inherent in an ideology. A political and cultural reading of a text therefore reveals the ironic vision of the writer that elucidates the subversion of ideals, values and ideologies in relation to socio-political-economic-cultural conditions of the society in which it is produced. Contextualising Salman Rushdie's seminal novel *Midnight's Children* in this perspective, we understand that the author, while portraying the socio-economic growth of the Indian subcontinent, remains rather ironical to the implementation of democratic policies of governance. In the perspective of the theme of the Conference, this paper therefore seeks to explore how Rushdie delineates the fact that the democratic doctrines and procedures remain merely theoretical resulting in substantial sufferings of the marginalized sections because of the illusory, falsified value systems in which they were thrust upon to survive.

This paper is thus an effort to focus on the political aspects of pre-independence [1915-1947] and post-independence [1947-1977] periods of the Indian subcontinent as portrayed in Salman Rushdie's novel *Midnight's Children*. We will examine how these aspects have affected life and society of its people to a considerable degree because of violation of democratic norms by the colonial as well as postcolonial rulers. Rushdie has covered a wide range of political aspects in relation to freedom struggle such as Jallianwalla Bagh massacre, *Hartal* called by Mahatma

Gandhi, Rowlatt Act, Partition politics and Communal violence during the colonial period [1915-1947]. He has also highlighted how during the postcolonial period [1947-1977], the sufferings of the people due to poverty, ignorance and disease, still continued. That happened so because the political corruption, unscrupulousness in business and commerce, violence in public life, misrule and Emergency due to the self-interest of the politicians in India as well as Military coups operated in Pakistan, have shattered the high aspirations for the subcontinent groomed by the freedom fighters. In other words, mere political freedom is not effective in raising the living norms and economic standards of the majority of the people in the postcolonial period. What was essential for them was to gain economic freedom if they were to live with dignity as human beings.

It has always been a fact that free expression of an individual has been suppressed time and again by the despotic rulers. In politics the ends are more important than the means. As in his other novels such as *Grimus, Shame, The Moor's Last Sigh* and *The Satanic Verses*, Rushdie has emphasized how individual freedom has been smothered on a large scale in *Midnight's Children* too. The use of politics in his writings enables him to scrutinize the functioning of contemporary governance and thereby criticizing the misrule by which the democratic norms have been violated. Stylistically he portrays political events as inter-texts. Rushdie's treatment of history and politics in his novels is both contextual and inter-textual as it explores the long-term political and economic effects on its people. He, therefore, addresses the question of politics, social strife, oppression and liberty. That is, therefore, Rushdie writes: "Liberty is herself in chains" (*Grimus* 140). His strong affinity to an interest in the contemporary politics have motivated him to refer to the contemporary political events, and the long-term economic impact on the people of the Indian subcontinent. His political inclination in *Midnight's Children* lends this novel a postcolonial and postmodern orientation as he discusses the contemporary issues of politics of freedom struggle, partition, migration, communalism, colonialism and multiculturalism. The political realities have a strong and direct bearing on the social and moral ethos of the people of pre-independence as well as post-independence milieus.

II
PRE-INDEPENDENCE CONTEXT AND ISSUES

The Imperial administration in India by 1919 has been rather ruthless by adopting a number of oppressive measures such as lathi-charging, firing, jailing and so on to suppress all types of rebellious activities by the "colonized other". Mahatma Gandhi calls *Hartal* against the British Raj in 1919 so as to protest against injustices and exploitations inflicted upon the "natives". His call was to demonstrate the protest quite peacefully. However, the call was turned into violence resulting in the "ruthless firing order" by General Brigadier Dyer. In this context, Rushdie portrays oppressive measures of the "dominant Empire" on the "dominated natives" when they were mourning "in peace, the continuing presence of the British" (*MC* 33). Rushdie thus narrates the incident in a sarcastic tone:

> Brigadier Dyer's fifty men put down their machine-guns and go away. They have fired a total of one thousand and six hundred and fifty rounds into the unarmed crowd of these, one thousand five hundred and sixteen have found their mark, killing or wounding some person. 'Good shooting' Dyer tells his men, 'We have done jolly good thing'. (*MC* 36)

Rushdie's reference to Jallianwalla Bagh massacre is to expose the excesses of the 'State Apparatuses' of the British Raj on innocent natives who were protesting against the injustices done to them. The colonial administration controlled the "colonized other" by resorting to all types of oppressive measures. Such a stand is rather the reflection of the dominant, authoritarian governance of the Colonials. They suppressed all democratic rights of the natives, who were not even allowed to protest peacefully against the unjust actions of the British Empire. Such brutality and hegemonic domination were very often central to the colonial rule in India. According to Althusser hegemony and dominance over the people were achieved through "Repressive State Appartuses" such as the army and the police. The resistance of the natives to achieve decolonisation often resulted in such offensive consequences as threatening and terrorizing the native struggles to make them ineffectual. People must have to be more organized to challenge the colonial authorities not only in physical and intellectual levels, but also in the "emotional plane". In this context, Loomba's emphatic remarks against colonialism are worth mentioning:

> Anticolonial struggles therefore had to create new and powerful identities for colonized peoples and to challenge colonialism not only at a political or intellectual level, but also on an emotional plane. In widely, divergent contexts, the idea of the nation was a powerful vehicle for harnessing anticolonial energies at all these levels. (155)

To counter the oppressive measures of the British Raj as per the Rowlatt Act, the natives were to be united emotionally as if belonging to a single nation and fight for their rights. The Raj exploited the situation to their own advantages because the natives were far from being enlightened and organized as well. Their ignorance and irrationality helped the Empire to instigate and intensify the communal violence among the bigoted Muslims and Hindus. "During the time of World War II i.e. by 1942-43, there were serious group clashes between the two opposite Muslim groups e.g. Muslim League and the Free Islam Convocation group led by Mia Abdulla resulting in the murder of the latter, who opposed the Partition Politics of the former. Even the British attitude to him (Mia Abdulla) was always ambiguous" (*MC* 47). The Rani of Cooch Naheen, like Dr. Aziz loathed the Muslim League too:

> That bunch of toadies...landowners with vested interests to protect! What do they have to do with Muslims? They go like toads to the British and form governments for them, now that the Congress refuses to do it! 'It was the year of "Quit India" resolution.... And what's more,' the Rani said with finality, 'they are mad. Otherwise why would they want to partition India?' (*MC* 46)

Rushdie points out how the opposition to the Muslim League by some enlightened Muslim leaders was spontaneous because they did not want a "partitioned India" which was an instigated creation by the British Empire:

> Mian Abdullah, the Humming bird, had created the Free Islam Convocation almost single-handedly. He invited the leaders of the dozens of Muslim splinter groups to form a loosely federated alternative to the dogmatism and vested interests of the Leaguers. (*MC* 46)

In reference to the Hindu-Muslim conflict during the pre-independence period it is interesting to discuss here the role of "Ravana gang" in terrorizing the Muslim businessmen and "peepshow" of Lifafa Das. The "Ravana gang" is "posed as a fanatical anti-Muslim movement" (*MC* 72) who "sent men out at dead of night, to paint slogans on the walls of both old and new cities: PARTITION OR ELSE PERDITION! MUSLIMS ARE THE JEWS OF ASIA" (*MC* 72). They also burnt down the "Muslim-owned factories, shops, godowns" (*MC* 72). In this context, Rushdie gives us a graphic description with a teasing tone of satire:

> ...behind this façade of racial hatred, the Ravana gang was a brilliantly conceived enterprise. Anonymous phone calls, letters written with words cut of newspapers were issued to Muslim businessmen, who were offered the choice between paying a single once-only cash sum, and having their world burned down. Interestingly, the gang proved itself to be ethical. There were no second demands. And they meant business: in the absence of grey bags full of pay-off money, fire would lick at shop fronts factories warehouses. Most people paid, preferring that to the risky alternative of trusting to the police. The police, in 1947 were not to be relied upon by Muslims. (*MC* 72)

Through these remarks, Rushdie points out his fingers at the bad governance of the "Empire". Due to their misrule the natives suffered to an intolerable level, and led a life of traumatic insecurity. On the other hand, there was always threatening of the muscle-power and blackmailing for which these Muslim businessmen were to lead a life of anguish and restlessness. In the name of Anti-Muslim movement, the Hindus of the 'Ravana gang' inflicted torture on the common businessmen and the so-called "Empire" was not keen on protecting their interest by maintaining Law and Order. Rushdie is not only critical to the intention and functioning of the Ravana gang, he is also satirical towards the biased and bigoted Muslims who attacked the innocent common Hindus without any substantial reasons. Even the small school children of Muslim community were encouraged to develop hatred towards Lifafa, the Hindu "peepshow" man. The small Muslim girl shouted at him: "You have got a nerve, coming into thith Muhalla! I know you: my father knows: everyone knows you're a Hindu!" (*MC* 76). Instantly other school boys spontaneously shouted: "Hindu! Hindu! Hindu!" (*MC* 76). The girl's father furiously abused Lifafa by shouting "Mother raper! Violater of our daughters"! Zohra, the distantly related sister of Ahmad Sinai made a loud noise: "Rapist! Arre my God they found the badmash" (*MC* 76). Then the communally surcharged Muslim crowd attacked Lifafa who ran away to save his skin.

This is how the functioning of the colonial Government has been graphically portrayed in *MC*: the natives of both the communities were neither secure nor protected. They rather remained irrational without enlightenment. They were encouraged to be communal, violent and divisive. The tall claims of civilizing the "colonized other" by the "colonizer" were false and baseless slogans. The police remained indifferent and cool to such communal violence and riots. It is significant to note that Rushdie is deeply anguished in describing the woes of the people vividly. In book I, he highlights how the natives suffered considerably during the colonial rule. He elaborately portrays that colonial social structure was rampant in mob violence, insecurity, communal disharmony, unscrupulous business practices, blackmailing, crime and murder, irrationality and ignorance, and erosion of human values. Through such elaborate descriptions and the technique of magic realism, Rushdie perhaps makes a point that the colonial regime in India was not much concerned with the public welfare. It did not even bother much for eradication of ignorance, poverty, disease and irrationality. A good governance by a progressive government would have been interested in cultivating the high ideals of enlightenment as well as freedom of expression through proper political, social and educational measures by which the natives could have lived with safety, security and dignity. In other words, the colonial regime was based on self-interest and exploitation of the natives, rather than taking any genuine welfare measures to improve their socio-political, cultural and economic conditions. It was only a government which was oppressive and opportunistic without any genuine concerns to make the colony progressive by improving the mental and socio-economic standards of the people. The situation of the Indian subcontinent was rather more serious when the country was granted freedom on 15 August 1947. Communal violence was at its peak. That was the legacy of the British Empire. Rushdie's disillusion on Indian independence are conspicuous through Mary's utterances:

> This independence is for the rich only; the poor are being made to kill each other like flies. In Punjab, in Bengal. Riots, riots, poor against the poor. It's in the wind. (*MC* 104)

The British regime has brought the country to such disaster and catastrophe while granting the country its long-cherished freedom. While ruling the natives, the Empire was indulgent in their oppression and exploitation, and while leaving, they instigated the people to indulge in violent riots, communal hatred and divisive practices. They, therefore, indulged in the gimmick of bringing the nation into permanent disintegration. As rulers, they were not interested in dispelling the darkness from the natives and illuminating them with enlightenment.

III
NEO-COLONIAL ILLS OF THE INDIAN SUBCONTINENT DURING 1947-1977

Rushdie has further depicted a vivid picture of the Neo-colonial ills of the two young nations, India and Pakistan, from

1947 to 1977 in Book II and Book III. His anguish is obvious when he narrates the deplorable conditions of these two countries because of partition, migration and violence. In India, the early years are marked by communal violence, divisive politics, language violence, regionalism, communism, corruption in public offices, election malpractices, nepotism, defective five-year plans, self-interest of the politicians, unscrupulousness in business practices, illiteracy, disease, ignorance and starvation-deaths. In the name of democracy and political freedom, the rulers often indulged in exploring the methods and possibilities of amassing ample wealth and acquisition of absolute power at any cost. In Pakistan, the situation was even worse. The politicians became millionaires overnight by indulging in corruption. The military coups toppled the democratically elected governments. Martial Law was imposed, and people lost their liberty and freedom of speech as well. Even in India, Indira Gandhi encouraged corruption and unscrupulous practices among her colleagues to remain in power. Subsequently, she declared Emergency in 1975 so that she could remain at the helm of affairs. Rushdie has shown that the two young nations have adopted democratic methods in theory and followed despotism and tyranny in practice. In the process, they demolished all the ideals and values of democracy. The principles of democratic governance did little to dispel the darkness from the ignorant to make them enlightened.

We have already discussed communal violence prevailing during the pre-independence period. Such violence even continued after the achievement of independence. The secular credentials were under threat when both the communities took revenges on each other. Rushdie exposes the naked side of this communal politics, and questions the viability of Indian secularism after independence when selected affluent Muslims were targeted:

> These are bad times, Sinai bhai-freeze a Muslim's assets, they say, and you make him run to Pakistan, leaving all his wealth behind him. Catch the Lizard's tail and he'll

> snap it off! This so-called secular state gets some damn clever ideas. (*MC* 135)

The author's pungent satire on the political corruption is quite obvious. He is anguished to note the degradation in politics and morality in the society. In this context, the encounter between Shiva and Saleem further exposes the political corruption: how the money power and goondaism play prominent role to win elections through booth-capturing and threatening. By referring to the general elections of 1957, Rushdie notes with great concern for the steady rise of regionalism, communalism, goondaism, religion, and communism in political life and its impact on our society. In this context, the strategies of different parties of Anna DMK in Tamil Nadu, Communist Party of E.M.S. Namboodripad in Kerala (food for everybody), Jan Sangh (rest homes for aged sacred cows), Congress (Hindu Succession Act to give women equal rights of inheritance) point to the narrowness in the political agenda which is a deviation from the national interest. Politics in India after independence has therefore gone away from the high ideals and morals set by the great freedom fighters who had sacrificed their lives to get freedom for us. There is also language politics to divide the country on the basis of different languages. As a result, politics has degenerated by embracing the evil aspects of regionalism, religion, communism, communalism, division on linguistic basis, Partition politics, booth-capturing, corruption, violence, and so on. Politics is no more an ideal to sacrifice for the sake of people and the nation; on the other hand, it becomes a game to gain popularity by resorting to narrow populist measures and arousing narrowness in people on the basis of region, religion, communism and community. As a fall out of such tendency after the death of Nehru, there was struggle for power in the Congress. Though Indira was prevented from assuming power, she could however succeed to control the Congress Party after the death of Lal Bahadur Shastri. While such narrowness in politics was going on in India, there was more corruption and instability in Pakistan. The unscrupulous politicians there amassed ample wealth and the military resorted to coups to dethrone the elected governments.

The Military Coup conducted by Ayub Khan, the Commander-in-chief of Pakistan with the help of Major Zulfikar throws light on the deterioration in the socio-political system of Pakistan. Despite being a pure Islamic nation, corruption had become a way of life in Pakistan politics, thereby resulting in a continuous conflict between the civilian political parties and military dictatorship. General Ayub assuming supremacy over the civilian rulers declares: "To night therefore.... I am assuming control of the state" (*MC* 289). Consequent upon this declaration of Martial Law, General Zulfikar on a midnight threatens the democratically elected president at gun point to go on exile. The narrator therefore sarcastically writes:

> Midnight has many children; ...the offspring of Independence were not all human. Violence, corruption, poverty, generals, chaos, greed and pepperpots. (*MC* 291)

During the four years coup, there was greater tension in the Indian subcontinent. The Pakistan Govt. encouraged hatred towards the Indians. As a result the relationship between the two young nations grew worse. By 1965, General Ayub's fame was declining due to corruption charges such as his son becoming multi-millionaire through his Gandhara Industries. Greater tension precipitated between India and Pakistan on the issue of Kashmir and War was declared in 1965. However, the War came to an end because both sides went shortage of ammunitions. Before UNO's announcement of the war "India had occupied less than 500 square miles of Pakistan and Pakistan conquered just 340 square miles of its Kashmir dream" (*MC* 344). The Post-1965 period in Pakistan forced Ayub to make room for Yahya Khan to be the President. Yahya and Bhutto diverted the attention of the people to East-West Pakistan conflicts. Mujib's popularity forced these two West Pakistani leaders to resort to a Military Coup in Bangladesh resulting in overthrow of Mujib. Indira Gandhi by this time in India assumed power by winning the 1971 elections by a landslide victory.

Sanjay Gandhi, the son of "the Widow", though not an elected representative, misuses power. Saleem, the narrator therefore, enquires:

> I did not, at that time know what I now set down: that certain high-ups in that extra-ordinary government (and also certain unelected sons of Prime Ministers) had acquired the power of replicating themselves...a few years later, there would be gangs of Sanjay all over India! No wonder that incredible dynasty wanted to impose birth control on the rest of us.... (*MC* 345)

It has rightly been remarked that Rushdie's "vast sense of historical imagination is the key to his aesthetic purposes" (Rao 1992: 155). Rao justifiably furthers this discussion by considering that the "contemporary history acts as a sort of narrative backdrop and milieu", and the "historical sense retreats into the mythical past of the Indian subcontinent" (155). Through his aesthetic imagination, Rushdie builds his political and cultural value-systems into this history. In his own way of using irony and subversion of fantasy, Rushdie portrays the emerging political scenario of post-independence Indian reality with vivid, authentic descriptions, and deals with the larger political issues of India's growth as a young nation. In this context, the observations of Rao are significant to quote: "Rushdie develops the theme of democratic experiment and the social and economic planning with patience and hope, yet becomes the ironic critic of its falsified value system" (168). As the nation starts growing, it faces so many challenges from the socio-economic and political fronts. Its secular credentials are threatened; its strength as a military power is challenged by China and Pakistan, its immediate neighbours. In the post-Nehru era, there are certain glorious moments of national developments because of some long-term democratic and political measures. But then, the success of democratic experimentation is jeopardized due to dissensions, political corruptions, ideological clashes and self-interests of power-monger politicians. This attains the climax when Indira

Gandhi, "the Black Widow" proclaims Emergency Rule in 1975 to silence her critics. She imposes a long "midnight" of more than two years on the Indian Nation pushing its people to suffer in the continuous, hellish pitch Darkness. It was such "midnight darkness" that it did not allow any light to the people of Indian nation. Rushdie thus narrates the birth of Emergency in India with a sarcastic tone:

> ...the word Emergency was being heard for the first time, and suspension-of-civil rights, and censorship-of-the-press, and armoured-units-on-special alert, and arrest-of-subversive elements; something was ending, something was being born, and at the precise instant of the birth of the new India and the beginning of a continuous midnight which would not end for two long years.... (*MC* 419)

The author has also been sarcastic when he writes about Indira and her Emergency Rule:

> Bùt she had white hair on one side and black on the other; the Emergency too, had a white part—public, visible, documented, a matter for historians—and a black part which, being secret, macabre untold, must be a matter for us. (*MC* 420)

The sufferings of the people have been symbolized by imposition of continuous darkness:

> Endless night, days, weeks, months without the sun, or rather (because it's important to be precise) beneath a sun as cold as a stream-rinsed plate, a sun washing us in lunatic midnight light.... (*MC* 423)

Saleem, the narrator describes how the prime minister was empowered absolutely with alteration of the Constitution to impose a despotic rule and tyranny in the country:

> When the Constitution was altered to give the Prime Minister well-nigh—absolute powers, I smelled the ghosts of ancient empires in the air...in that city which was littered with the phantoms of Slave Kings and Mughals, of Aurangzeb the merciless and the last, pink

> conquerors, I inhaled once again the sharp aroma of despotism. (*MC* 424)

Through such alterations of the Constitution Indira assumed absolute power, and hence she became India: "Indira is India and India is Indira" (*MC* 424). After that the dissident politicians were imprisoned and the people of the country were deprived of their freedom:

> ...although there is considerable disagreement about the number of political prisoners taken during the Emergency, either thirty thousand or a quarter of a million persons certainly lost their freedom. The Widow said: "It is only a small percentage of the population of India." (*MC* 434)

In a teasing tone, Rushdie points out how Indira was quite happy in her oppressive measures and autocratic governance during the period of Emergency. Through her *Rule of darkness* the sufferings of the Indian people multiplied just like their sufferings during the British rule. People were completely deprived of liberty and freedom of speech. In this context, it is relevant to refer to the thinking of Alexis De Tocqueville in his book *Democracy in America* Vol. II:

> And I perceive how under the dominion of certain laws, democracy would extinguish that liberty of the mind to which a democratic social condition is favourable, so that after having broken all the bondage once imposed on it by ranks or by men, the human mind would be closely fettered to the general will of the greatest number. (13)

IV
CONCLUSION

The *Rule of Emergency* is therefore not meant for the welfare of the people by eradicating poverty, ignorance and disease. It is not even good governance which aims at promoting development of the nation. It is in contradiction to the principles of good governance by a ruler as elucidated in Kautilya's *Arthasastra*: "In the happiness of his subject, is his happiness, in their welfare, his welfare; whatever pleases himself he shall not consider as good, but whatever pleases his subjects, he shall consider as good." Even the Preamble of the Indian Constitution suggests that the basic principles of good governance are "to secure all its citizens justice, social, economic and political". The ultimate aim of good governance is to secure a social order for promotion of welfare of the people, adequate means of livelihood, prevention of accumulation of wealth and creation of congenial atmosphere for enlightenment of its people. True Democracy facilitates all these to the people for sharing power. It also prevents catastrophes falling on the nation. It, therefore, builds physical and economic infrastructure for development of education, health, employment, social welfare, empowerment of women and marginalized sections as well as shelter for all (Joshi 1979; Jalal 1995; Shapiro and Hacker-Cordon; Shrimali 1970; Narang 1986). Rushdie however shows us how the rule of Emergency in India and Military rule in Pakistan deprived the people of all these benefits which would have helped them to be Enlightened enough to substantially contribute to the growth and development of the two young nations. Even the Imperial rule by the British Raj was least interested in the enlightenment of the colonized natives to enable them to lead a life of freedom and dignity. Contrarily, the colonial administration indulged in sucking the blood of the Indian subcontinent and exploitation of her people for its own prosperity and welfare.

Works Cited

Abrams, M.H. *A Glossary of Literary Terms* 6th edn. Bangalore: Prism Books Ltd., 1993.

Althusser, Louis. "Ideology and Ideological State Apparatus", 1970.

——. *Contemporary Literary Theory.* Dan Latimer, ed. Harcourt Brace Jovanich, 1989, 60-102.

Adami, Esterino. *Rushdie, Kureishi, Shyal: Essays in Diaspora.* New Delhi: Prestige, 2006.

Brenan, Timothy. *Salman Rushdie and the Third World: Myths of the Nation.* Macmillan, 1989.

Chatterjee, Chandra. *Surviving Colonialism: A Study of R.K. Narayan, Anita Desai, V.S. Naipaul.* New Delhi: Radha Publications, 2000.

Colebrok, Claire. *New Literary Histories: New Historicism and Contemporary Criticism.* Manchester: Manchester UP, 1997.

Cuddon, J.A. *A Dictionary of Literary Terms and Literary Theory.* 1976, 4th edn. rept. by C.E. Preston, Blackwell Publishers Ltd., New Delhi: Maya Blackwell/Doaba House, 1998.

Cundy, Catherine. *Salman Rushdie.* Manchester: Manchester UP, 2001.

Eagleton, T. *Literary Theory: An Introduction.* Oxford: Blackwell, 1983.

Fletcher, M.D., ed. *Reading Rushdie: Perspectives on the Fiction of Salman Rushdie.* Amsterdam, Atlanta: Rodopi, 1994.

Grant, Damien, *Salman Rushdie.* Northcole House & British Council, 1999.

Harrison, James. *Salman Rushdie.* New York: Maxwell Macmillan International, 1992.

Harton, John. *Liberalism, Multiculturalism and Toleration.* New York: St. Marti's Press, 1993.

Jalal, Ayesha. *Democracy and Authoritarianism in South Asia: A Comparative and Historical Perspective* (CUP, 1995). New Delhi: Foundations Books, 1995.

Jefferson, Ann and David Robey, eds. *Modern Literary Theory: A Comparative Introduction* (1982, 1986), 2nd edn., London: B.T. Batsford Ltd., 1986.

Joshi, N.C., ed. *Democracy and Human Values.* New Delhi: Sterling Publishers, 1979.

Khan, Fawzia Afzal. *Cultural Imperialism and Indo English Novel: Gender and Ideology in R.K. Narayan, Anita Desai, Kamala Markandya and Salman Rushdie.* Pensylvania: Penn State UP, 1993.

Latimer, Dan, ed. *Contemporary Literary Theory.* Harcourt Brace Jovanich, 1989.

Loomba, Ania. *Colonialism/Postcolonialism.* 2nd ed. (India reprint, 2007) London and New York: Routledge, 2007.

MacDonald, Steve. *The Rushdie Letters: Freedom to Speak, Freedom to Writ.* Ireland: Brandon Book Publishers, 1993.

Mittapalli, Rajeshwar and Kuortti, Joel. *Salman Rushdie: New Critical Insight*, Vols. I & II, New Delhi: Atlantic, 2003.

Mongia, Padmini, ed. *Contemporary Postcolonial Theory: A Reader* (1996). Oxford: OUP, 1997.

Narang, A.S. *Democracy, Development and Distortion.* New Delhi: Gitanjali Publishing House, 1986.

Rao, M. Madhusuddan. *Salman Rushdie's Fiction: A Study.* New Delhi: Sterling, 1992.

Rice, Philip and Patricia Waugh, ed. *Modern Literary Theory: A Reader.* (1989) 4th ed. London: Arnold, 2001; Rept. 2002.

Rushdie, Salman. *Imaginary Homelands: Essays and Criticism.* 1981-1991. London: Granta Books, 1992.

——. *Grimus.* Vintage, 1996.

——. *Midnight's Children.* Vintage, 1995.

——. *Shame.* Vintage, 1995.

Ryan, Kiernan, ed. *New Historicism and Culture Materialism: A Reader.* London: Arnold, 1996.

Said, Edward W. *Orientalism: Western Concepts of the Orient with a New Afterward* (1978, 1995). New Delhi: Penguin Books, 2001.

Sandel, Michael J. *Democracy's Discontent: America in Search of a Public Philosophy.* Cambridge: Harvard University Press, 1996.

Shapiro, Ian and Casiano Hacker-Cordon, Eds. *Democracy's Value.* Cambridge: Cambridge University Press, 1999.

Shrimali, K.L. *The Prospects for Democracy in India.* Carbondale and Edwardsville: Southern Illinois University Press, 1970.

Tocqueville, Alexis De. *Democracy in America.* Volume II. (1945). New York: Vintage Books, 1954. 3rd Print, 1955. Trans. Henry Reeve (Revised by Francis Bowen, further corrected and edited by Phillip Bradley).

——. *Democracy in America,* Volume I. New York, London: The Colonial Press, 1900.

(Trans. Henry Reeve, Spl. Int. by Hon. John J. Morgan and Hon. John J. Ingalls. Revd. Edition).

Vesser, H. Arams, ed. *The New Historicism.* New York, 1989.

Viswanathan, Gauri, ed. *Power, Politics, and Culture: Interviews with Edward W. Said.* New York: Vintage Books, 2001.

Williams, Raymond. *Problems in Materialism and Culture: Selected Essays.* London: Verso, 1980.

Wolfreys, Julian, Ruth Robins and Kenneth Womack, eds. *Key Concepts in Literary Theory* (2002). New Delhi: Atlantic, 2005.

Young, Robert J.C. *Postcolonialism: A Very Short Introduction* (2003). Oxford: Oxford University Press, 2006 (Indian Edition).

12

The Unsafe Edge: Ammu's Agency in *The God of Small Things*

Christina Bertrand Firebaugh

In a 1998 interview, Arundhati Roy asserts, "since the dawn of time, human society has found ways in which to divide itself, to make war across these divisions, to make love across these divisions. There will always be those of us who make these divisions and those of us who argue against them" (Abraham 91). In Roy's novel *The God of Small Things*, the character Ammu actively "argue[s] against" the divisions ingrained in her society despite the many forces seeking to uphold social stratifications. These divisions, caused by a combination of colonial discourse and caste, class, and gender differences, cast Ammu into a position in which her ability to exercise personal agency is in danger of being stifled. Ultimately, however, she demonstrates that she resists and defies these forces to the best of her ability. *The God of Small Things* reveals that the discourses of the patriarchal caste-based culture that predates colonialism in India in many ways dovetails with the (similarly) patriarchal racially stratified colonial system. Focusing on only one of these aspects would oversimplify Ammu's plight; rather, it is the complex combination of factors that illuminates her position. Despite the existence of hegemonic narratives of power and patriarchy, Ammu's counter-narrative works against and seeks to dismantle (or at least offer an alternative to) dominant discourses. This novel can be read as one example of "counter-narratives of the nation that continually evoke and erase its totalizing boundaries—both actual and conceptual—[that] disturb those ideological manoeuvres through which 'imagined communities' are given essentialist identities" (Bhabha 213). By analyzing the extent to which Ammu is able to exercise her personal agency given the confines of her sex, her social upbringing, and the unique position of her family in greater Indian society, one can see that although immense imbalances of power do exist that work against her, Ammu is neither completely powerless nor voiceless.

The question of female agency in *The God of Small Things* is complex not only because of the myriad of social factors that its female characters must negotiate but also because each female character in the novel understands her own position differently. In their discussion of agency, Annie E. Coombes and Avtar Brah observe that "a number of commentators... insist on the need also to recognize agency as a *conscious choice* and as a means of rescuing the colonial subject from perpetual victimhood by acknowledging their ability to act as progenitors of resistance against the violence of colonialism in different ways" (11, my emphasis). Agency, therefore, is intrinsically tied to one's awareness of her position; she then uses this awareness as motivation for rebellion against both her own position and the socio-political structures that cause subalternity in the first place.

Other critics have mentioned the forces that work to dictate Ammu's role, but they have not focused exclusively on her resistance to these social and cultural demands. In her examination of classification in the novel, Florence Cabaret points out that Baby Kochamma exhibits a "gradual and cornering classification of Ammu...[that] ends up marginalizing [her]" (77). But in her analysis, Cabaret does not take into consideration the ways in which Ammu resists this marginalization. Cabaret focuses on how traditional systems of classification are undone and challenged in the novel, but Ammu's particular resistance is unrecognized. Similarly, Susan Stanford Friedman highlights the gendered opposition between Ammu and her brother Chacko, arguing that a "double standard" exists in Kerala that leaves little room for women to exercise personal freedom (255). Friedman's parallel comparisons—for example, that "the family's money sends Chacko to Oxford, while Ammu's only escape from Kerala is to marry" (255)—illuminate the stark contrast between the relative positions of women and men in Kerala. However, this parallelism does not explore the evidence of resistance or personal agency on Ammu's part. It seems that much of the scholarship on *The God of Small Things* sidesteps the question of agency, either addressing it momentarily or subordinating it to other issues. This leaves room for a much-needed discussion of female agency in the novel.

Roy's tightly controlled depiction of Ammu reveals that she contests the gender and social boundaries characteristic of the position into which she is born and, in doing so, exercises her own personal agency. Although Kerala has been called one of the more liberal states in India and one in which the position of women is comparatively positive, Ammu continually makes remarks throughout the novel that clearly elucidate her dissatisfaction with her lot in life.[1] These comments provide shape to a character who otherwise is only understood through momentary glimpses into her life. Much of the reader's understanding of Ammu is through the eyes of her seven-year-old children, so we see her primarily in the role of a mother. The narrator does provide details that give further dimension to Ammu (for example, the scene in the bathroom in which Ammu envisions her body as that of an old woman), but these details come later in the novel, after her role as the mother of Estha and Rahel has been foregrounded. This technique serves two purposes: first, it forces the reader to identify mainly with Rahel so that the focus remains on Rahel's coming of age. More importantly, by establishing Ammu's role as primarily that of a mother automatically subordinates Ammu's other roles, such as those of lover, wife, or independent woman. Here, Roy aligns Ammu with the primary role traditionally allotted to women in her position and in doing so calls attention to the assumption that this *should* be Ammu's priority. However, it is through the sharing of intermittent intimate moments in Ammu's life that Roy highlights the antagonism between Ammu's primary role as a mother and the other ways in which she sees herself.

This gendered conflict arises from the dual influences of caste and colonialism. In her introduction to *Allegories of Empire*, Jenny Sharpe discusses how concepts in colonial discourse such as the "myth of white womanhood" or the "threat of the dark rapist" emerged as ways of maintaining control over the colonized (3). Rape, especially, figures significantly in colonial discourse, particularly the "sexual threat Indian men posed to white women" as a "highly charged trope that is implicated in the management of rebellion" (2).[2] But it is not the *act* of rape itself that constitutes a major part of colonial discourse in India. It is the *idea* or *threat* of rape—real or perceived—that has far greater effects on colonial Indian society. This perceived threat positions white English women at the top of the "racial hierarchy of colonialism," while dark-skinned Indian men are placed at the bottom of it (12). Sharpe argues, "a crisis in British authority is managed through a circulation of the violated bodies of English women as a sign for the violation of colonialism" (4). As a result, English women in India become representatives for the entire English colonial project in India. They stand for that which should be protected and revered. This representational status is contingent upon the existence of its opposite: the dangerous, lust-filled, dark-skinned Indian man.

For the colonial project to survive, this dichotomy must exist in the minds of English and Indians alike. Power structures are not only forced onto the Indian population, but they must be internalized by the English as well. In other words, white English women must both believe in the importance of their position and act accordingly, and the native men must also internalize their inferiority and start to believe in their prescribed role. While constant struggle and insurrection throughout the history of imperialism shows that this ideal was never fully realized, the establishment of fixed roles for both colonizer and colonized was what buttressed

English colonialism in India. Nevertheless, the myth of white womanhood had lasting effects on Indian society, even after colonialism had officially ended.

However, the English colonists were not innovators in using social stratification to maintain control over the masses in India: the caste system had already existed for thousands of years, and has resisted change over time. As the English introduced their own form of social control to India, colonialism (and the accompanying fears regarding the protection of the white woman from the dark native) became enmeshed with the caste system, producing a hybridization that further imposed order on a social system that already was extensively ordered. Homi Bhabha's description of hybridity helps define the meeting of these two structures:

> ...elements that are *neither the one* (unitary working class) *nor the other* (the politics of gender) *but something else besides*, which contests the terms and territories of both. There is a negotiation between gender and class, where each formation encounters the displaced, differentiated boundaries of its group representation and enunciative sites in which the limits and limitations of social power are encountered in an agonistic relation. (Bhabha 41)

While this definition seems to emphasize the differentiation or "third space" created as a result of the meeting of cultural boundaries, it seems that other interpretations of this meeting ground are plausible. "*Something else*" suggests that this third thing is characterized by its *difference* from the original elements or social constructions, but another phenomenon results from the intersection of two discourses. Instead of becoming "something else" entirely, postcolonial India, as represented in Roy's novel, joins elements of patriarchy, caste, and colonialism that operate *together* and *simultaneously* (as opposed to "contest[ing] the terms and territories of both") to exert pressure on the lives of women. As a result, those that inhabit this hybridized space exist under the domain of not one but two social systems that have been synthesized to some extent. Bhabha explains this meeting ground as a "Third

Space" which is simultaneously marginalized by larger cultures and productive in its own way: it is the location where the larger culture begins to be changed (53). So although the characters' experiences may seem to be disjointed from the larger culture, this sense of disjointed-ness is productive.

What I would like to suggest is that, as a result of the combination of caste and colonialism, Ammu can be seen as signifying the role of the "white English woman," while Velutha can be seen as the "dark native". Though there are obvious differences between a white English woman and Ammu, the comparison offers a provocative perspective on Roy's novel. The Ipes, upper class Syrian Christians, are admittedly "Anglophiles"—people who, in Chacko's account, are "pointed in the wrong direction, trapped outside their own history and unable to retrace their steps because their footprints had been swept away...[by] a war that has made us adore our conquerors and despise ourselves" (51-52). This family has been conditioned to believe that the English are at the top of the moral and social spectrum, and the Ipes therefore emulate English behavior and raise their family accordingly. However, these beliefs combine with the influence of caste, which explains the precarious position Ammu, as a woman, inhabits in her family. In this family, and in Ammu, caste, gender, and the mix of English and Indian culture all blend to cast Ammu in a role in which she is treated as the mythologized white woman is in colonial discourse: she is the representative linchpin that holds together her family's position as both Syrian Christians and as upper caste. She is not white and therefore cannot be seen as an exact match, but when viewing her social position in terms of the caste system, Ammu is not exactly the "subaltern shadow" of the quintessential English woman; (12) rather, she occupies the role Sharpe describes as "the sexed subject of colonial discourse" (12). Sharpe's position that "English womanhood emerge[s] as an important cultural signifier for articulating a colonial hierarchy of race" (4) can be taken a step further to illustrate caste-based distinctions in the novel. Upper-caste women such as Ammu, although they are not white, serve a purpose similar to that of the white English woman in postcolonial India.

Viewing Ammu's subject position in this light changes the understanding of Ammu's agency. She is not just a victimized woman oppressed by both patriarchal and colonial discourses. Rather, Ammu's role gives her unique power in her culture. Since her elevated position holds together her family's (and, by extension, her caste's) status, her choices to step outside the boundaries carry more weight and are therefore more dangerous to the existing structures. Ammu's decision to marry outside of her caste already transgresses boundaries and sullies her family's image. But her affair with Velutha, an Untouchable, is an unforgivable offense. This would have been the case under a system only mandated by caste, but colonial discourse adds the element of race:

> Racial explanations occur when historical conditions make it difficult to presume the transparency of race—which is to say, "race" is all the more necessary for sanctioning relations of domination and subordination that are no longer regarded as "natural." When we deploy race as a transhistorical category of difference, we tend to read racial constructions according to their own truth effect—that is, to locate inequalities in the immutability of human nature. (5)

While race of course produces a set of issues different from caste, Sharpe's observations on the "use" of racial categorization provide a helpful model for discussing caste in postcolonial India. Ammu's actions even before her affair with Velutha reveal her disregard for conventional social divisions in her society—she marries (and then subsequently divorces) a Hindu man whom her parents have never met, much less approved of. Her rebellion shows that she does not believe that class or caste are factors that should dictate one's actions without question, because by using her marriage to subvert the expectations of her parents and her community, Ammu challenges the beliefs that underlie such social expectations. To Ammu, these expectations are not part of the "natural" social order, which is why her actions enrage her family. Ammu's rebellious decisions call into question the social foundations that keep her family securely in power, and two of these seemingly solid foundations—the assumed inequality between castes and between races—are shaken as a result.

By contrast, many of the other characters in the novel (such as Mammachi, Pappachi, Baby Kochamma, and Inspector Thomas Mathew) operate under the belief (or at least the unchallenged assumption) that caste and class are vital to Indian culture and must be maintained. To them, caste operates as a "transhistorical category of difference," something intrinsic to humanity (Sharpe 5). For example, Mammachi comments that Velutha "might have become an engineer" "if only he hadn't been a Paravan" (72), and Vellya Paapen believes whole-heartedly in his place as an obedient, grateful Paravan. This attitude of unquestioning belief on the part of both upper and lower caste Indians in the novel suggests that caste, like race in Sharpe's text, is taken to be simply a part of the "immutability of human nature" (Sharpe 5).

These characters' internalization of social expectations is compounded by their internalization of colonial discourse, resulting in a hybridized value system that interprets an affair between a Syrian Christian and a Paravan as multiply subversive. The Ipe family embodies this hybridized value system, evidenced by their description as "anglophiles". The Indian Ipe family is described as mimicking English traditions in many ways. Here, mimicry is not necessarily used as act of subversion (as in Bhabha's sense of the term) but almost as unconscious subservience to colonial order. Postcolonial India retained many characteristics from the British occupation, and the "British" and "Indian" elements can no longer be distinguished from one another. This can be seen in Pappachi's photograph, in which he wears "khaki jodhpurs though he had never ridden a horse in his life" and "an ivory-handled riding crop lay neatly across his lap" (50). The Ipe family does not simply ape English values; they fuse values derived from caste politics with the newer English model, and effectively support a hybridized category of "anglicized" Indians.

On another level, the Ipe family's status as anglophiles complements Sharpe's theory regarding the issue of protection of the white woman: Indian society seems to have adapted the myth of white womanhood so that it applies to upper-class *Indian* women. Ammu can be seen as occupying the role of the European white woman, in terms of the need to protect her from the native savage (Velutha). Therefore, Ammu is placed by her family in a role that she is expected to occupy but ultimately cannot conform to, for she is aware that her family members are not in fact white Europeans. Ammu mocks Chacko's attitude about his time spent at Oxford:

> Chacko said:
>
> (a) You don't *go* to Oxford. You *read* at Oxford.
>
> And
>
> (b) After *reading* at Oxford you *come down*.
>
> "Down to earth, d'you mean?" Ammu would ask. (55)

Ammu's unmasked sarcasm reveals not only her disgust at her brother's pomposity, but it also shows her opinion of the futility of his going away to England to gain an education: for all his "reading" at Oxford, Chacko still cannot run the pickle factory profitably (54). To Ammu, the desire to conform to English ideals seems out of step with the reality of life in India. If Ammu recognizes the falsity of her family's Englishness [she even goes so far as to call her father an "incurable English CCP" ("shit-wiper") (50)], then she is also inherently calling their Indian-ness into question since their identity has been so thoroughly infused with English customs.

Ammu is also aware that caste compounds the role that she is expected to fulfill. The myth of the white woman can be applied here because she is part of the upper class and must protect her family's upper caste status through her marriage. Her first violation (marrying a Hindu) infuriates her family, but the major tragedy of the novel (her affair with Velutha) results from her utter disregard for her expected role as guarantor of her family's social status. This helps to explain why Ammu and Velutha's relationship is so problematic: Ammu, an upper-class woman, needs to be protected from untouchables in order for the traditions of the caste system to stay intact.

How, then, can Ammu's (and, by extension, Velutha's) actions be explained? Both characters have personal traits that place them in the role of rebels: Velutha is described as having "a lack of hesitation. An unwarranted assurance.... The quiet way in which he offered suggestions without being asked. Or the quiet way in which he disregarded suggestions without appearing to rebel" (74). Ammu also resists being categorized according to her upbringing or her gender. The narrator informs us, "Ammu had not had the kind of education, nor read the sorts of books, nor met the sorts of people that might have influenced her to think the way she did. She was just that sort of animal" (171). She is further described as being "an unmixable mix. The infinite tenderness of motherhood and the reckless rage of a suicide bomber" (44). Described as such, it would be easy to conclude that Ammu's actions throughout the novel can be attributed to an essential element of rebelliousness in her character, instead of attributing them to her frustration with her social position. However, it is the combination of both her personal characteristics and her social position that produces a character that is able to *choose* to rebel. Education and literature were not necessary catalysts for Ammu's way of thinking because the source of her frustration is so prevalent in her life. Written this way, Roy reveals the extent of Ammu's dissatisfaction and provides a reason for her actions that extends beyond her character to include social structure.

Throughout the novel, Ammu makes sarcastic comments about her position as a woman in India. For example, Ammu knows that she has no legal standing, "thanks to [her] wonderful male chauvinist society" (56). Comments like these reveal Ammu's feminist tendency, due to which she continuously and sharply criticizes patriarchy. Ammu's criticism of both patriarchy and Indian society symbolically threatens her society, because she challenges the assumptions that her status as upper-caste Indian, and female necessarily correlates with certain expected behaviors. A woman in Ammu's position traditionally serves as one means of holding together the fabric of her society: through marriage to the "right" man (meaning, desirable caste, family, and career), a woman can secure the position of her family and hopefully even strengthen it. But Ammu disregards these kinds of concerns that monopolize the thoughts of other women in the novel, such as Baby Kochamma and Mammachi.

In contrast to the other women in the novel, Ammu embodies this keen social awareness and acts accordingly. Because of Ammu's heightened awareness of her own position, she cannot be examined as simply an objectified subaltern Indian woman. It seems that Ammu's knowledge of her own position is one of the causes of her demise. Her rebellion against caste and gender subordination that is encapsulated in her visit to the police station ends in defeat, and her attempt to defy social stratification causes the police officer to further objectify her and reinscribe her role [shown when he taps her breasts with his baton as if he is "choosing mangoes from a basket" (10)]. She cannot shake her upper-class family status or the ingrained caste system, because organizations such as the police have a more significant function than simply investigating crimes: they are there to protect the dominant culture. And in the case of Ammu's affair, her actions so greatly threatened that culture that it is necessary, in the eyes of the state, to quell her type of rebellion.

Ammu's rebellion can be compared to the Naxalite marchers at the beginning of the novel—and as threatening as the marchers appear to people such as Baby Kochamma, Ammu's subversive act can be seen as much more dangerous to the status quo. The Naxalites represent a faction of society that, while violent and threatening, is still a faction of the Communist party (which was the ruling party at the time). They also still abide by traditional forms of rebellion, utilizing fear tactics and ridiculing the bourgeoisie. The Naxalites could be seen as, in Comrade Pillai's words, "mechanics who serviced different parts of the same machine" (248). However, Ammu and Velutha's affair can be seen as a challenge to one of the core structures in Indian society: the caste system. Although the caste system had at this time been outlawed, it still directs much of the social interaction in Kerala, and therefore challenging this structure has far more serious implications.

The caste system is scrutinized throughout the novel, and not just by Ammu: the idea of the "Love Laws" encapsulate the unspoken laws ingrained in the lives of the characters. The narrator describes these laws as existing since the beginning of time:

> ...it actually began thousands of years ago. Long before the Marxists came. Before the British took Malabar...before Vasco da Gama arrived...long before Christianity arrived in a boat and seeped into Kerala like tea from a tea bag.
>
> That it really began in the days when the Love Laws were made. The laws that lay down who should be loved, and how.
>
> And how much. (33)

The Love Laws are not to be questioned. No matter who is in power in India, the governmental system works *around* the caste system. For this reason, Ammu's subversion poses more of a threat than a governmental protest—she and Velutha break the unspoken, ingrained social laws that have dominated India for centuries. No one counted on the possibility that Ammu would betray her class and caste and come to Velutha's defense. It is unclear what Ammu hoped would be the outcome of her decision to go to the police; however, it is her "Unsafe Edge" that provides the impetus for this decision (44). Before the Terror, Ammu already felt the scorn of her family for being divorced and having half-Hindu children: "a woman that they had already damned, now had little left to lose, and could therefore be dangerous" (44).

The question arises, then, of whether Ammu's actions reveal her agency, or if she ultimately lacks any agency. She and Velutha both die by the end of the novel, and the family is fractured as Estha and Rahel are separated for twenty-three years. First, Ammu's aims (or causes for her actions) should be considered. As was previously stated, Roy has created a character that is acutely aware of her own subordinate position within her family and her society. She openly expresses her dissatisfaction verbally and through her actions: she marries a Hindu without the consent or approval of her family and is not shamed by her divorce. She returns to her parents' home with two "half-Hindu Hybrid" children, disappointing both her brother and her Aunt (44). Even though she returns, it is evident that Ammu is still dissatisfied and unhappy, revealed in the moments when she listens to her tangerine radio and "walk[s] out of the world like a witch, to a better, happier place" (43). At these times, Ammu retreats further from the roles ascribed to her (even the established role of mother), and the descriptions of Ammu here become a combination of transcendence and sorcery. It seems that Ammu's frustration prompts her to seek mental escape when physical escape is impractical or impossible.

However, Roy's choice to end the novel on a hopeful note, in an intimate scene in which she and Velutha are happy, signals to the reader that her actions were not futile. While the chronological order of the novel indicates that Ammu is broken by the effects of her affair with Velutha, the novel closes on a scene that suggests intimacy and hope—further signifying that the transgression of social boundaries in order to exercise personal agency takes precedence over conforming to the multiple restrictions placed on Ammu's life. She is aware of the cost of her decision—she knows that Velutha's arms are "the most dangerous place she could be" (319)—however, she consciously chooses to risk the danger. Despite the multiple forms of repression operating in her life, Ammu reveals her own agency and therefore embraces her role as one who, in Roy's own words, chooses to battle the ways in which society "divides itself" (Abraham 91).

Notes

1. The official website of the Government of Kerala highlights the advanced position of women (see "Status of Women". Public Relations Department, Government of Kerala <www.kerala.gov.in/education/status.htm>). However, others such as Vanessa Baird report that "...on paper the women of Kerala are much better off than their sisters in the rest of India..." but in reality the position of women is far from ideal. (See Baird, Vanessa.

"Respect and Respectability" *New Internationalist* 241, March 1993 <http:// www.newint.org/issue241 /respect.htm>).

2. The rest of Sharpe's study provides examples of the manifestation of this concept throughout colonial (and postcolonial) literature and discourse over the past two centuries.

Works Cited

Abraham, Taisha. "An Interview with Arundhati Roy." *ARIEL* 29 (1998): 89-92.

Bhabha, Homi. *The Location of Culture*. London: Routledge, 1994.

Cabaret, Florence. "Classification in *The God of Small Things*." Durix, Carole and Jean-Pierre Durix, eds. *Reading Arundhati Roy's The God of Small Things*. Dijon, France: Editions Universitaires de Dijon, 2002, 75-90.

Coombes, Annie E. and Avtar Brah. "Introduction: the conundrum of 'mixing'." *Hybridity and Its Discontents: politics, science, culture*. Ed. Avtar Brah and Annie E. Coombes. London: Routledge, 2000, 1-15.

Friedman, Susan Stanford. "Paranoia, Pollution, and Sexuality: Affiliations between E.M. Forster's *A Passage to India* and Arundhati Roy's *The God of Small Things*." *Geomodernisms: Race, Modernism, Modernity*. Ed. Laura Doyle and Laura Winkiel. Bloomington, IN: Indiana UP, 2005, 245-61.

Moore-Gilbert, Bart. *Postcolonial Theory: Contexts, Practices, Politics*. London: Verso, 2000.

Roy, Arundhati. *The God of Small Things*. New York: Harper Perennial, 1997.

Sharpe, Jenny. *Allegories of Empire: The Figure of Woman in the Colonial Text*. Minneapolis: U of Minneapolis P, 1993.

13

The Regional Novel and Aravind Adiga's *The White Tiger*

Arpa Ghosh

In 1981, Salman Rushdie won the Booker of Bookers for his *Midnight's Children*,[1] a text frequently cited as a classic case of 'writing back to the centre'. Rushdie's achievement is his successful departure from the rooted, centred, regional focus of the traditional Indo-anglian novel as written by the trinity of R.K. Narayan, Mulk Raj Anand and Raja Rao. Living in Britain, and writing about pre-partition Kashmir, Rushdie sets *Midnight's Children* in a mindscape elliptically linked to reality. His self-conscious, mock-heroic, deeply sarcastic style constantly draws attention to the despair and nihilism ingrained in his fiction in a way that is new in Indo-anglian writing. Formally and stylistically, Rushdie's book incorporates certain tenets of postcolonial and postmodern fiction writing as practiced by authors belonging to countries with a long, violent history of colonialism; authors like Gabriel Garcia Marquez, Ben Okri, Wole Soyinka, A.S. Byatt, John Fowles and J.M. Coetzee. The fiction of these authors is characterized by a certain timeless, modernist, existential, allegorical narrative with circular time rhythms that ensures a larger world audience, and superior critical acclaim. The ideological configurations of colonialism are analyzed and unearthed in these fictions. Reflexivity and experimentation with form with rather than straightforward narration and chronicling of history are the salient features of this school of writing. These writers question the very indices and texture of reality.

Working alongside these authors is a parallel set of authors who are much more rooted and focused in native, regional cultures. Their approach is that of the regional novelist, the *bhasha sahityik*. It is not as if these writers totally eschew postcolonial and postmodernist strategies. But formally, they are more traditional, largely relying on classic realism and naturalism as narrative forms to convey their vision of life. Novelists like Andre Brink, Alan Paton, Mario Vargas Llosa, Margaret Drabble, Angus Wilson, Orhan Pamuk and Bessie Head are less experimental and mocking in their representation of reality. Nor do they prioritize modernist narratives over classic realist narratives. Their negotiation with realism as a narrative strategy is tortured. They recognize the pitfalls of false, metonymic representation of interregnums; confusing, nightmarish time periods of tremendous conflict between rival power structures. But even when these novelists question outer reality and its political and ideological ramifications, in fine the injustice of it all; even when they are clearly disillusioned and disheartened by the hopelessness of the situation, they retain their belief and confidence in outer reality. In effect, somewhere deep down these writers believe in reparation and political amelioration.

Aravind Adiga, just two books old[2], subscribes to the school of the rooted, centred Indo-Anglian novelist who is interested in improving reality instead of questioning it. Traditionally, Adiga is closer to the trinity of Narayan-Anand-Rao than to the more distinctly pocopomo ethos of Salman Rushdie. In Adiga's writing we find a global Indian racked and ridden by corruption. But it is an India we immediately recognize and identify with. The central consciousness, by and large in both his texts, is the down-trodden, urban and rural landless poor tottering under the pressures of traditional tortures like casteism and poverty as well as comparatively new problems of terrorism and sedition.

The rooted Indo-anglian novelist operating largely within the parameters of classic realism and writing about native culture, native economy and native politics raises the question of his choice of language. To an extent Indo-anglian novelists like Mulk Raj Anand and Aravind Adiga encroach upon the space of the *bhasha sahityik* (regional novelist), often drawing from the same fund of regional experience. The question posed is why should novelists like Anand and Adiga not write in an Indian regional language? Often, a novelist writing in English yet choosing a regional, topographically and culturally mapped subject is suspected of encouraging and fostering the English-regional language divide that is part of the Indian colonial hangover. Aficionados of *bhasha sahitya* feel that such Indo-anglian writers are different from *bhasha* novelists only so far as they enjoy the patronage of international publishing houses, a global market, and the 'superior' cultural status that comes with big money and big publicity. In fact, compared to the meticulous and exhaustive representation of the regional novelist's subject (a subject that has enveloped him from childhood, and of which he has a thorough knowledge), the Indo-anglian writer's grappling with the same subject is often viewed as watery, facile and less grounded.

Many years ago, in his preface to *Kanthapura*, Raja replied to the above charges after his own fashion:

> The telling has not been easy. One has to convey in a language that is not one's own the spirit that is one's own. One has to convey the various shades and omissions of a certain thought-movement that looks maltreated in an alien language. I use the word 'alien', yet English is not really an alien language to us. It is the language of our intellectual make-up—like Sanskrit and Persian was before—but not of our emotional make-up. We are all instinctively bilingual, many of us writing in our own language and in English. We cannot write like the English. We should not. We cannot write only as Indians. We have grown to look on the large world as part of us. Our method of expression therefore has to be a dialect which will someday prove to be as distinctive and colourful as the Irish or the American. Time alone will justify it.

> After language the next problem is that of style. The tempo of Indian life must be infused into our English expression, even as the tempo of American or Irish life has gone into the making of theirs. We, in India, think quickly, we talk quickly, and when we move we move quickly. There must be something in the sun of India that makes us rush and tumble and run on. And our paths are paths interminable. The Mahabharata has 214,778 verses and the Ramayana 48,000. Puranas there are endless and innumerable. We have neither punctuation nor the treacherous 'at' and 'ons' to bother us—we tell one interminable tale. Episode follows episode, and when our thoughts stop our breath stops, and we move on to another thought. This was and still is the ordinary style of our storytelling. I have tried to follow it myself....[3]

It is a longish quote, but articulate and cogent in its justification of the Indo-anglian writer's choice of English as medium of expression. The quote also pleads for the author's freedom of choice in subject-matter. Increasingly, literature is becoming ghettoized. Authors rarely venture beyond their known realm of lived experience. Jane Austen's advice (in one of her letters) to her niece to stay back in her village when her characters go a-visiting London and wait for their return before resuming her story since London is unknown territory is now being followed by novelists as never before. Now, Bengali Americans write about Bengali Americans, gays about gays, and blacks about blacks. Though written in 1970, Raja Rao's eloquent plea to exercise the writer's autonomy holds good even in these modern times, when the grand narrative of the classic realist text is all but dead from the critics' persistent questioning of the author's right to venture into territories not his own. When writers like Mulk Raj Anand and now Aravind Adiga, emerge, once in a while, to boldly step out of class and status barriers and write books about the dispossessed from the point of view of the dispossessed, the experience is at once refreshing and discomfiting. *Coolie, The Untouchable*, and *The White Tiger* are not grand narratives, but they give us a worm's view of India in a moment of historical, cultural and economic change.

What is it about *The Untouchable, Coolie*, and *The White Tiger* that sets the reader's teeth on edge? 'The reader' meaning the middle class and upper middle-class 'English medium' reader of Indian writing in English, for this is the only readership that Anand and Adiga will ever get. No coolie or latrine-cleaner has even heard of Mulk Raj Anand, and only time will tell how many drivers and servants read *The White Tiger* as they linger outside malls and five-star hotels waiting for their masters to finish their shady business.

We are not raising the unfair, clichéd question of an educated author from a privileged, wealthy class (Ph.D from Cambridge—Anand; salutatorian graduate from Columbia University, New York—Adiga) choosing to write about the dispossessed. Male authors, have written intimately about women, (Geoffrey Chaucer, Leo Tolstoy, Bankimchandra Chattopadhay, Gustave Flaubert, to touch the tip of the iceberg), and have been appreciated for their insight. For example, that the early twentieth century Bengali novelist Saratchandra Chattopadhay understood the female psyche better than the poor little woman herself was a widely held view even a couple of generations ago.

Obviously, writers like Anand and Adiga leave no stone unturned in the way of research and background work. There is no glossing over and no simplifying an unfair, appallingly exploitative Indian society that all but kills its poor and needy. The problem lies in the way the novels are received rather than in the intention of the writer.

Portraying the dispossessed and deprived of India—the menial labourer, the slum-dweller, the refugee—is a rarely-questioned, time-worn practice of regional literature (Bhasha Sahitya). Authors from privileged, educated backgrounds have always written about the poor and the lowly. An author like Mahasweta Devi has made her career writing about the exploited tribal people of India. Her short stories *Daupadi* and *Stannadayini* (Breast-giver) are powerful and hard-hitting. In his novel *Shei Shomoy* (Those Days) Sunil Gangopadhay devotes an entire sub-section to the portrayal of life in the servant quarters of the Shingha palace; their hierarchies, exploitations, power equations and politics, ascent to and descent from the seat of power and influence, above all, the raw deal that women servants get for their hard labour. *Shei Shomoy* (1985) is about early nineteenth century Bengal. Closer to our times is Sunil Gangopadhay's *Purbo Pashchim* (East West) (1988) dealing with the partition and its aftermath in seventies Bengal, in which novel we encounter the character of Harit Mondal, an erstwhile East Bengalee potter reduced to a beggar-refugee in the wake of the Partition. Harit's downslope to dispossession, beggary, starvation, separation from dear ones is accompanied by flashes of intellect and leadership qualities that can be compared with the energy and life-force of Balram Halwai the small-fry hero of Adiga's *The White Tiger*. Other examples are Shirshendu Mukhopadhayay's novels *Manabjamin* (The Human Earth) and *Parthib* (Worldly Concerns); poignant country-city exposes where unjust and inequitable distribution of wealth and the crushing disadvantage of the countryside compared to the city are focused upon, and Samaresh Mazumdar's *Kalbela* (The Hour of Doom) (1984) with its devastating portrayal of Kolkata slum life.

All these writers are warmly honoured for their prescience and skill in recreating the life of the underprivileged. But do these writers, many of them privileged city-dwellers and all of them learned and knowledgeable, not take upon themselves the task of speaking on behalf of the illiterate subaltern? Without a doubt they do, but since their medium of expression is a regional language like Bengali, a language they share with their untaught subjects, their sleight-of-hand goes unnoticed. Their art is seamless, the scissors-and-paste indiscernible.

Writing about the poor, the first problem that writers like Mulk Raj Anand and Aravind Adiga negotiate with is the discrepancy between the language they choose as a medium for their art (English in India is an elitist language) and their subject-matter that is deeply rooted in the soil of India and is the seclusion of the poor and underprivileged from opportunity and happiness. The scope of interaction, between diverse cultures, religions, provincial and national beliefs and customs, the mainstay of Indian writing in English, is very limited, almost non-existent under the circumstances. The poor live in a claustrophobic world; a window-less attic. To represent this world the novelist has to adopt a rigorous and relentless naturalistic style. Mulk Raj Anand and Aravind Adiga actually make a spirited foray into the literary prefecture of the regional novelist when, against all language odds, they boldly engage in a serious discourse of the poor.

The strategies Adiga uses in *The White Tiger* are, one, use of the beast fable or bestiary, and two, a hard-headed naturalistic hammering of unpleasant, obnoxious and crudely real details of the lives of the rural and urban poor. The use of beast images like 'mongoose', 'country mouse', 'stork' dehumanizes fictional subjects while giving them flat humour comedy outlines. 'Vitiligo-lips' draws attention to a disfigurement squeezing the subject (a fellow driver) dry of all its humane qualities reducing it to a single deforming mark. The impression that the Indian poor live according to the law of the jungle is emphasized thus.

Painstaking naturalistic details are darkened rather than lightened by a Jonsonian humour[4] Adiga's style in *The White Tiger* is closest to that of Ben Jonson's Humour comedy that dehumanizes its villainous subjects in order to lash out at the vices and malpractices that have riddled society. In keeping with his satirical style, Adiga constantly alludes to topical details like a drunken rich man's irresponsible driving that mows down a pavement dweller, stuffing suitcases and briefcases with cash to bribe corrupt politicians, the rich housewife's vacuous and aimless sauntering in the numerous malls of Gurgaon. These details substantiate the naturalistic texture of the urban setting of the novel. *The White Tiger* is a study of a gallery of rogues and spent forces unrelieved by a single morally upright character.

A novelist like Adiga is bound to face the problem of readership. The exploiters and torturers of the poor, Ashoke Sir, Pinky Madam and the Mongoose, rather than the poor themselves, comprise the readership of such a novel. It is this hard, ironic fact that makes the position of novelists like Adiga and Anand before him, shaky and dubious in the eyes of the serious critic.

Both writers however have emerged triumphant in their difficult and dogged mission, though the nature of triumph differs. Mulk Raj Anand's success lies in his Zola-like severe, pared naturalistic narrative style combined with the testy social humour of Dickens. Portraying Munoo, the fifteen-year-old menial servant and rickshaw puller of *Coolie* (1936)[5] Anand painstakingly charts Munoo's trajectory from ruddy innocence to disillusion and painful untimely death, relentlessly piling on gruesome details about disease, living conditions, dearth of food, pain of excessive physical labour, and harshness of punishment, exploitation and torture. At the same time, with Dickensian broad strokes he recreates the ground reality of India in the last years of British regime; the winter capital of Simla and the upwardly mobile metropolis of Bombay, along with a surfeit of colonial city caricatures as viewed through the eyes of Munoo, a representative of the poor locked away from the privileges of his own country. Munoo's eyes are the eyes of a child who learns a bitter lesson from the university of life. Munoo's impression of his ambience is self-alienating, larger-than-life and nightmarish.

What is *The White Tiger* all about? The simplest answer is it is a thriller, a very pacy read with a zestful, unrepentant criminal as its central consciousness. The first person narrative maintains a huge, insurmountable distance between author and protagonist. In no way can the protagonist Balram Halwai be related to the non-resident Indian, superior education flaunting author Aravind Adiga.

Coming almost seventy years after Mulk Raj Anand, Aravind Adiga (2008) has the advantage of having a more malleable English language at his disposal. His Balram Halwai, like Anand's Munoo is a child of nature, a social underdog used and abused by the rich whom he initially trusts with naive confidence. But unlike Munoo's story, Balram's tale has a fantasy-picaresque element.

Balram is a 'successful' student of the school of life. Tutored by his employers in the art of deceit and unconscionable criminal practices, Balram outwits them finally and in one bold stroke enters their class and status grabbing for himself the allowances and benefits that are cruelly denied to the poor and needy. In spite of the fantasy ending *The White Tiger* belongs to the genre of the underprivileged-subject novel like Anand's *Coolie* and *The Untouchable*, and these novels go a long way in incorporating English into the regional life of the Indian nation. At the same time the fantasy ending of *The White Tiger* undermines its sober, hard-hitting narrative thrust. The structure and theme of the novel are at variance with each other. The framework is that of an intriguing, half-humorous thriller with a structural concealment in the end that sustains the reader's interest. The theme is the inhuman, unjust deprivation and deceiving of the poor so that petty, noxious interests of the rich and the powerful of India can be served. Anand and Adiga show how in the absence of genuine role models poor servants blindly imitate their dishonest masters, and in this way draw attention to the need for educating the poor in India. A passage from Anand's 1935 novel *The Untouchable*:

> And he had soon become possessed with an overwhelming desire to live their life. He had been told they were sahibs, superior people. He had felt that to put on their clothes made one sahib too. So he tried to copy them as well as he could in the exigencies of his peculiarly Indian circumstances. (*Untouchable*, 1935)[6]

Disconcertingly, this phenomenon is repeated in Adiga's novel written almost seventy years later. When Balram absent-mindedly scratches his groin while washing ginger in Pinky Madam's kitchen, she screams at him:

> You're so filthy! Look at you, look at your teeth, look at your clothes! There's red *paan* all over your teeth, and there are red spots on your shirt. It's disgusting! (*WT* 146)

Balram takes serious notice of Pinky Madam's objections. His response:

> Why had my father never told me not to scratch my groin? Why had my father never taught me to brush my teeth in milky foam? Why had he raised me to live like an animal? Why do all the poor live amid such filth, such ugliness?
>
> Brush, brush, spit.
>
> Brush, brush, spit.
>
> If only a man could spit his past out so easily. (*WT* 151)

It is disconcerting that things have changed so little for the Indian poor in the space of so many years. Anand's and Adiga's novels are therefore significant historical documents charting untold, concealed history: "One fact about India is that you can take almost anything you hear about the country from the prime minister and turn it upside down and then you will have the truth about that thing" (*WT* 15).

Anand's *Coolie* has an omniscient narrative. Munoo is given very few lines. This adds to the reliability of the narrative as often the poor feel but have no voice to express their feelings. Balram Halwai, in contrast is an articulate speaker and *The White Tiger* is a very person narrative. The point of ambiguity is his reliability as narrator. Some of his statements (like the one quoted above) are so audacious and outrageous, that the reader is confused as to their veracity and honesty of purpose. In the absence of the harlequin, chimerical, and persuasive persona of Balram Halwai, *The White Tiger* would have been reduced to paralyzing morbidity, a limitation that often plagues serious political authors like Mulk Raj Anand and Mahasweta Devi. But the wit, humour, suspense, and excitement of Balram's narrative dilute the earnestness of the issue, widening the distance between the privileged, high-society novelist and his underprivileged, grass-root theme. It might seem Adiga raises the issue of economic and social injustice only to mock and trivialize it at the end.

Though radically different in their world vision, Anand and Adiga toil towards genuinely absorbing the Indo-anglian novel into *Bhasha Sahitya*. It would be interesting to gauge the reaction of underprivileged Indian readers to these novels that engage in an unrelieved portrait of the hapless poor who can only redeem their situation by slipping into criminal activities. Unfortunately, such an underprivileged reader, capable of comprehending the simple, colloquial, emotive Indian English of Anand and Adiga is yet to exist, and savour his mirror image reflected so uniquely in *Coolie* (then) and *The White Tiger* (now).

Notes and References

1. Salman Rushdie, *Midnight's Children*, first published by Knopf, 1980.
2. Aravind Adiga, *The White Tiger*, Noida: HarperCollins, 2008. All quotations are taken from this edition. Between the Assassinations, London: Picador, 2008.
3. Raja Rao, *Kanthapura*, Delhi: Orient Paperbacks, 20th printing 2004. 1st published 1970.
4. Ben Jonson was a sixteenth century English comic playwright who popularized the classic Humour comedy on English stage. He was famous for his dark, trenchant humour that accompanied his searing portrayal of urban corruption in his plays. His famous comedies are *Volpone*, *Alchemist*, and *Epicione*, or the *Silent Woman*.
5. Mulk Raj Anand, *Coolie*, South Asia Books, 1936.
6. http://www.kirjasto.sci.fi/anand.htm 12.15 pm, April 2, 2009.

14

The Subaltern Speaks: A Critical Reading of *The White Tiger*

Vandana Datta

When Arundhati Roy's book *The God of Small Things* won the Booker Prize it signified a major shift in the preoccupation of the Indian English writers. It decidedly was not the first passionate love story that defied all social norms. It was a landmark novel in that it drew the Indian English novel from the middle class drawing rooms out into the slums. And since then this trend has caught on. With the movie *Slumdog Millionaire* winning the Oscar it has been resounded unequivocally that the era of the underdog has arrived. And the Booker going to Aravind Adiga's *The White Tiger* makes it clear that the subaltern not only speaks, he acts as well, holding the reins in his hands.

Every age has its own centre and its own margins—that is to say, they are flexible and are defined according to the social configurations of the time. In the caste ridden society of India the upper classes had been at the helm of affairs for a long time. It's only in the twentieth century—a little before independence—that concern for the lower classes manifested in concrete terms. No wonder this concern found a reflection in literature too. Among the Indian English writers Mulk Raj Anand was probably the first to make an untouchable the protagonist of his novel. But though *Untouchable* is a study of Bakha's mind and psyche it offers a vague conclusion. Bakha is unable to take his own decisions and accepts the solution that is offered to him. Velutha in *The God of Small Things* moves a step further—he loves an upper class woman and establishes an intimate relationship with her. But he too is unable to fight the system. About two decades back Shanta Rameshwar Rao's *Children of God* had also made the same statement that for some children of God there is no escape from the social structure. The protagonist of *Slumdog Millionaire* is a loveable chap, both innocent and intelligent. But he is a child of his circumstances, his success depends on too many chances. Adiga's novel *The White Tiger* makes a breakthrough in this matter—his protagonist is a rare phenomenon like the white tiger, a determined person who plans out each and every move. He not only escapes the clutches of the system but also weaves a success story for himself.

The story is in the form of a letter to the Chinese Premier His Excellency Wen Jiabao written over the course of seven nights in the light of a chandelier, the light all the time being chopped up by the fan. Told in the first person it reveals accurate powers of observation coupled with a fine sense of humour. This is a story of the development of a half-baked fellow from a remote Indian village into a self-taught entrepreneur. It is the story of today's India, an India that belongs not just to the upper strata of society but to the people who have come up from the lowest rungs. The truth about India or about Bangalore, the hub of entrepreneurship is 'me' (4). The story of Bangalore is the story of the underdog. The metamorphosis of Balram Halwai into Ashok Sharma is the story of 'how entrepreneurship is born, nurtured, and developed in this, the glorious twenty-first century of man' (6).

This metamorphosis is worked out in the novel in two stages. There are two escapes that the hero is required to make in order to come on his own. The first is from the trap of Darkness and the second from the Rooster Coop. It is indeed ironical that the Gangetic plains, the earliest seat of civilization, 'a third of the country, a fertile place, full of rice fields and wheat fields' is today the least developed place in the country, that the river that earlier brought illumination today brings disease and death, that the land of emancipation is today the land of Darkness. While the rest of India flourishes in light this area remains shrouded in Darkness. And it is to this land of Darkness that the protagonist of *The White Tiger* belongs. Munna or Balram Halwai is not fortunate enough to have a regular schooling. Much against the wishes of his father who dreamt of a bright future for him, he is taken out of school by his grandmother and put to work in a teashop so that he could earn and help sustain the family. But right from the beginning Balram has it in him to try and improve his station in society. After much pleading he is allowed to learn driving. He gets the job of a chauffeur at the place of a big landlord of the village who hires him for his son Ashok and daughter-in-law Pinky who have recently returned from the States. His dream chance comes when he moves along with his masters to Delhi.

And in this moving to Delhi Balram makes his escape from the land of Darkness. He also manages to get away from the clutches of his family. He has seen his father kill himself trying to meet the demands of the family. He also realizes that his elder brother Kishan has now taken the place of their father. He himself refuses to sacrifice his personal growth to the needs of the family. The family to him is the all-devouring trap that eats up alive the way it did to his father and now will do to Kishan:

> There was red, curried bone and flesh in front of me—and it seemed to me that they had served me flesh from Kishan's own body on that plate.... They were eating him alive in there! They would do the same thing to him that they did to Father—scoop him out from the inside and leave him weak and helpless.... (85-86)

He himself decides to get away from the trap of the family. He had stopped sending money much earlier. Now he cuts himself off as he declares: "I'm never going back there" (89). However, the ties are finally snapped much later in the story.

Escape from the second trap, from the Rooster Coop, is central to the novel. This is how Balram describes the Rooster Coop: "Never before have had so few owed so much to so many, Mr. Jiabao. A handful of men in this country have trained the remaining 99.9 per cent—as strong, as talented, as intelligent in every way—to exist in perpetual servitude; servitude so strong that you can put the key of his emancipation in a man's hands and he will throw it back at you with a curse" (175-76). They are all trapped like the chicken in the Rooster Coop: "Hundreds of pale hens and brightly coloured roosters, stuffed tightly into wire-mesh cages, packed as tightly as worms in a belly, pecking each other and shitting on each other, jostling just for breathing space; the whole cage giving off a horrible stench—the stench of a terrified, feathered flesh. On the wooden desk above this coop sits a grinning young butcher, showing off the flesh and organs of a recently chopped up chicken, still oleaginous with a coating of dark blood. The roosters in the coop smell the blood from above. They see the organs of their brothers lying around them. They know they're next. Yet they do not rebel. They do not try to get out of the coop.

> The very same thing is done with human beings in this country. (173-74)

And they too do not rebel, do not try to break out of the coop. For they know that if they try such a thing their family will be destroyed. It would take 'a freak, a pervert of nature...a White Tiger' (177) to do such a thing.

And indeed it is the White Tiger who has the guts to do such a thing. When after killing his master Mr. Ashok, Balram disappears with the red bag full of cash he knows full well that back in the village his family would be interrogated, tortured and destroyed. But to him his personal success is far more important. Getting out of the clutches of this system is far more important than the well-being of his kith and kin. He does not go back to his village. Instead, he heads for Bangalore and after lying low for sometime he starts his own business, 'White Tiger Drivers', a taxi service for call centres. Needless to add that he is a successful entrepreneur. And today he owns twenty-six Toyota Qualises, a macintosh laptop and a flat with a chandelier in his room, the chandelier being symbolical of his achievement that he can live in style like his old masters.

Balram attributes his success to his ability to dream big. Never satisfied with his station in life he always thinks of ways to move up. Today he runs a taxi-service but he knows that in a few years time he would like to take the next, leap may be into real estate. Years ago when he worked in the teashop he decided to become a driver. After working as a driver for sometime he begins detesting his position of a servant and desires to be on his own, be a man. And for this it was essential for him to murder his employer.

Not that Balram is a man with no moral compunctions. The fact is that moral or immoral, right or wrong is not the issue here. This is how the whole social system functions—Mr. Ashok was a decent person but had no scruples about sacrificing the life of Balram for the offence that his wife Pinky had committed. Balram had been told to take the responsibility of the accident on himself and bear the consequences. It's another matter that the whole thing went unreported and nothing was required to be done. But this incident proves an eye-opener for Balram—that there can be no love lost between employer and servant, that he is a small fry in a large network and will be demolished to the last bit if he even thought as much to refuse or rebel. This incident also intensifies Balram's desire to break out of this network, this rooster coop. Whatever price was to be paid for freedom—whether it was the life of his master or the lives of the members of his family—it was worth it. In moving out of the middle-class drawing rooms this novel also moves out of the middle-class value system. From a moral world it moves out into an amoral one where success alone matters. Becoming an entrepreneur, finding his place in Bangalore, the hub of entrepreneurship is also not a straight course:

> My country is the kind where it pays to play it both ways: the Indian entrepreneur has to be straight and crooked, mocking and believing, sly and sincere, at the same time. (8-9)

So while he is sincere and committed towards work he also takes recourse to bribing the police officials in order to establish himself in his business.

This is not to conclude that this novel encourages slyness and cunning and manipulation. What is right is right and what is wrong will always be wrong. What this novel presents is the mess in which our country is today where even to achieve the right things one has to adopt wrong ways. Adiga holds up a mirror to us—the reflection is ugly and brings home the truth of what we have made of ourselves.

Some very interesting and thought-provoking comments on the present day scenario in our country lie scattered all over the novel. To begin with, this is how the difference between India and China has been described: "...you Chinese are far ahead of us in every respect, except that you don't have entrepreneurs. And our nation, though it has no drinking water, electricity, sewage system, public transportation, sense of hygiene, discipline, courtesy, or punctuality, does have entrepreneurs. Thousands and thousands of them, especially in the field of technology. And these entrepreneurs—we entrepreneurs—have set up all these outsourcing companies that virtually run America now" (4). And again, "...we may not have sewage, drinking water, and Olympic gold medals, but we do have democracy" (96). There are prophetic statements about the future: "...the future of the world lies with the yellow man and the brown man now that our erstwhile master, the white-skinned man, has wasted himself..." (5-6). And this is what a man from the 'Darkness' has to say about the 'other' parts of the country: "I've seen twelve elections—five general, five state, two local—and someone else has voted for me twelve times. I've heard that people in the other India get to vote for themselves—isn't that something?" (100). Besides being a sarcastic comment on the pathetic condition of democracy in our country it also shows how relative and flexible a term 'other' is.

To conclude, *The White Tiger* is the story of the success of a village fellow in breaking away from the traditional caste structure and making it big as an entrepreneur in a modern city. But this success comes at a heavy price. The movement from the Darkness (village) into the Light (Delhi), ironically enough, signifies the beginning of the darker side of the story—

the story of 'a sweet, innocent village fool' corrupted into a city fellow 'full of debauchery, depravity and wickedness' (197). This happens because the rules of the game are determined not by any moral code but by sheer strength. It is a jungle law where might is right. Adiga talks about the caste structured India as 'a clean, well-kept, orderly zoo. Everyone in his place, everyone happy. Goldsmiths here. Cowherds here. Landlords there. The man called a Halwai made sweets. The man called a cowherd tended cows. The untouchable cleaned faeces. Landlords were kind to their serfs. Women covered their heads with a veil and turned their eyes to the ground when talking to strange men' (63). But today this 'zoo law' has been replaced by 'jungle law': "...the cages had been let open; and the animals had attacked and ripped each other apart.... Those that were the most ferocious, the hungriest, had eaten everyone else up, and grown big bellies. That was all that counted now, the size of your belly. It didn't matter whether you were a woman, or a Muslim, or an untouchable: anyone with a belly could rise up.... To sum up—in the old days there were one thousand castes and destinies in India. These days, there are just two castes: Men with Big Bellies, and Men with Small Bellies. And only two destinies: eat—or get eaten up" (64). That is to say, there are only two classes: the exploiter and the exploited. Such is human nature that whosoever is in a position to exploit does exploit. The big fish always feeds upon the smaller fish. Highly disappointing though but it is true that our world today is ruled by this law of the jungle and not by any sane human rationale. The tiger then—the white tiger—is bound to emerge as the winner.

Works Cited

Aravind Adiga. *The White Tiger*. India: Harper Collins, 2008. (All extracts quoted from this novel are from this edition.)

Mulk Raj Anand. *Untouchable*. London: Jonathan Cape, 1939.

Arundhati Roy. *The God of Small Things*. New Delhi: IndiaInk, 1997.

Shanta Rameshwar Rao. *Children of God*. Calcutta: Disha Books, 1978.

Edward Said. *Orientalism*. United States: Vintage Books, 1978.

Gayatri Chakravarty Spivak. 'Can the Subaltern Speak?' in *Norton Anthology of Theory and Criticism*. New York: W.W. Norton & Co., 2001.

15

Colliding Scapes of Cultures: A Reading of *The Inheritance of Loss*

Purnendu Chatterjee

Kiran Desai's Man Booker Prize 2006 winning novel, *The Inheritance of Loss* that lends to polyphonic discourses reflects the double operations of colonization and globalization. This paper seeks to explore the interface of Western and Indian cultures—brought out through the convergence of the tormented colonial past and an indeterminately positioned multicultural/multiethnic, globalized present—and the impact of cultural collisions on the characters in the novel. The cultural interface is created by the hiatus between the "independent self-concept" of the West and the "interdependent self-concept" (Markus and Kitayama, 1991) of the East. In doing so, the paper endeavours to present a model showing an inverse co-relation between the intellectual and ethical components of the migrants' characters where intellectual progress of the migrant leads to erosion of native moral values, and *vice versa*. Moreover, the paper will posit that the colliding cultures not only create "metonymies of presences" (Homi Bhabha, 1983) and the "not quite" and "in-between" (Elleke Boehmer, 2005), but also provide regenerative experience to the writer who is creatively rooted in her land of adoption and in recollections of her land of birth.

One of the commonalities between colonization and globalization, in spite of all the differences in essences and modes of operations, is that both involve collisions of cultures. In the processes of colonization and globalization, the domain of occidental cultures intersects the domain of native cultures.

Culture includes a wide range of concreteness and abstraction: from language to livelihood, from rituals and myths to arts and values and from codes of relationship to polity. Culture, therefore, is a social construct. It is, as Durkheim and Berger suggest, the source of more-or-less spontaneous actions and reactions of people and their mode of dealing with objective reality and subjective formations. Therefore, culture and its corollary, cultural identity are optional and variable. However, when freedom of an individual is jeopardized the optional character of culture and cultural identity remains a theoretical concept that cannot be put into practice. This state of pseudo optionality that amounts, in fact, to unoptionality creates a state, as Roop Rekha Verma suggests, of "transcendental choice-freeze" or "choice-closure" (1994).

This "transcendental choice-freeze", however, rarely happens and what mostly occurs in case of cultural collisions is what Durkheim, as translated by W.D. Halls, terms "objective facticity" (1982). The term "objective facticity" refers to the notion that social facts mould and shape an individual. However, "objective facticity" does not cause "transcendental choice-freeze" because what is objectivated or factified is a matter of human creation and human choice and the objectivation does not cancel either the alterability or alterity of the option. This "objective facticity" leads to creation of "mimic men" (Homi Bhabha, 1983) and precipitates "fractures of cultures" (Walter D. Mignolo, 1998).

Colonization created a kind of inaccurate doubling of the colonized as a reflection of the colonizers. As Stuart Hall suggests, important to its maintaining of power is the West's ability to "make us [non-whites] see and experience ourselves as Other" (2003). This often resulted in, what Homi Bhabha terms, "metonymy of presence" (1983). The "metonymy of presence" refers to the mimicry by the colonized of the colonizers. Bhabha elucidates his concept of the "metonymy of presence":

> Those inappropriate signifiers of colonial discourse—the difference between being English and being Anglicized; the identity between stereotypes which, through repetition, also become different; the discriminatory identities constructed across traditional cultural norms and classification, the Simian Black, the Lying Asiatic—all these are metonymies of presence.

The coloured colonized in their desperate bid to imitate the white colonizers become impoverished specimens of humanity who are almost the same as the colonial masters, but not the same, in Bhabha's words "almost the same but not white" (1983). These mimic men, living within the interfaces of two cultures, develop split identities. They hate to imitate, but cannot help imitating. This flawed mimetic effort obviously results in the creation of frustrated men who cannot come to terms with themselves as well as with the society.

Globalization celebrates, as Frederic Jameson (1998) argues, a "postmodern celebration of difference and differentiation" by placing almost all the cultures of the world in contact with one another. The contact, however, is not always direct. Often, it acts at a distance, as Held and McGrew point out,

> ...whereby the actions of social agents in one locale can come to have significant consequences for 'distant others'. (2003)

The "distant others" are, of course, the people of the "third world" who come under the influence of the culture of the "first world". The immigrants feel the direct influences of globalization. Globalization, as C. Vijayasree (1996) suggests, increased immigration and this resulted in intensification of the feelings of alienation and loss. The immigrants in their attempt to come to terms with a foreign culture in a foreign land become fractured images of life. Salman Rushdie brilliantly brings out the predicament of the immigrants:

> Human beings [immigrants] do not perceive things whole; we are not Gods but wounded creatures, cracked lenses, capable only of fractured perceptions. (1991)

Postcolonial literatures address the globalization issue in terms of the power relations, which flourish as a legacy of western imperialism. In doing so, "the mimicry of the postcolonial subject" destabilize or subvert the colonial discourse by establishing "an area of political and cultural uncertainty in the structure of imperial dominance" (Ashcroft, et al.). Diaspora writers, characterized by a constant shifting of subject position in terms of geography as well as ontology, rupture the placid postcolonial life within a colonial space and thereby disrupt the world of colonial space.

Commenting on Kiran Desai's *The Inheritance of Loss*, John Sutherland, the author of *Stephen Spender: The Authorized Biography* (2004) and the Chairman of Man Booker Judges, 2008 aptly pointed out:

> Desai's novel registers the multicultural reverberations of the new millennium with the sensitive instrumentality of fiction.

The "multicultural reverberations" produced by the dual operations of colonization and globalization creates a mosaic that spreads through the web of the novel.

In *The Inheritance of Loss* almost all the characters, in different ways, breathe dissimilar cultures from the mass in Kalimpong. The anglicized Sai learns at an early age that "cake was better than ladoos" (33), converses with the cook in a "shallow mix" of English and Hindi and prefers to lunch at Lets B. Veg. Culturally she does not match with Gyan who is more interested in celebrating Guru Nanak's birthday, Durga Puja or the Tibetan New Year than Christmas that interests Sai. Desai depicts the cultural collision between Gyan and Sai when a frustrated Gyan explodes:

> You are like slaves, that's what you are, running after the West, embarrassing yourself. (163)

This cultural collision sinks deep and finally breaks down Sai's love affair with Gyan.

Lola, Noni and Mrs. Sen refer to the Nepalis as Neps, agree that the Neps breed as fast as Muslims do and are the root cause of all the troubles in the hills. Mrs. Sen, Lola and Noni continue a decadent existence holding desperately to the first world that refuses to acknowledge such slips of humanity. In spite of being minor characters in the novel, they help the author in driving home the phenomenon of postcolonial neurosis. Mrs. Sen in weaving a sweater, that she never completes, for Rajiv Gandhi—her weaving lacks the vitality of Madame Defarge's knitting in Dickens' 'A Tale of Two Cities'—is stuck in time. She appears to be a close kin, sans ghastliness, of Miss Havisham in Dickens' *Great Expectations*. She vainly prides herself on her daughter for she works with the CNN and becomes a rival to the two sisters, Lola and Noni, because Lola's daughter works with the BBC. However, not all these first world associations can save them from being ruthlessly treated by the Gorkhaland activists. They are pathetic characters, haplessly and helplessly stranded in a time that is out of joints.

The character of the cook, Panna Lal, is also that of a culturally marginalized. He has to surrender pathetically to the Gorkhaland activists. He prides on the fact that his father served a white-skin and his son is in America. Thus, the bedraggled life of the cook comes under the influence of colonization and globalization. However, he does not share any cultural affiliation with Jemubhai.

The central male character in the novel, Jemubhai Patel, finds himself languishing on the interface of English and Indian cultures. Educated at Bishop Cotton School and having developed a profound veneration for the portrait of Queen Victoria that stood at the school's entrance, Jemubhai had grown fond of the colonial masters. Such was his proclivity for the English life that he married for going to England a woman who brought him dowry, disregarding the possibility of a happy conjugal life at home. Jemubhai's attempt to internalize the culture of the colonizers is not rooted in a transcendental choice-freeze. He had the vast and glorious Indian culture ready at hand. He could easily have used it as frame of reference to exercise his option of proudly carrying abroad his unmasked brown skin. Jemubhai, however, attempted to internalize uncritically the culture of the Britishers. This resulted in the creation of a dangerous inauthentic identity. Jemubhai realises that in trying to learn a foreign way of life he had become the mimic man, but he would not acknowledge it. When, after retiring from his job, he met his friend Bose who scathingly criticised the British, he decided to remain silent. He would not acknowledge that his exalted concept of the British had bitten the dust.

> He wouldn't tumble his pride to melodrama at the end of his life and he knew the danger of confession—it would cancel any hope of dignity forever. (208)

Therefore, he decided to buy Cho Oyu, a house made by a Scotsman and tucked away in the northeastern Himalayas. He felt that the location of the house would give him a shelter where he could hide not only from the eyes of his fellow men, but also from himself.

> The judge [Jemubhai] could live here, in this shell, this skull, with the solace of being a foreigner in his own country, for this time he would not learn a new language. (29)

Alienation, as Richard Schacht (1970) following Marx suggests, has dual aspects: alienation from others and self-alienation. Obviously, Jemubhai is not only alienated from himself, but also he is culturally alienated from the native people. He can hardly speak the tongue of the common people of Kalimpong and, therefore, does not develop any psychic and cultural relation with the mass. He hated his wife and developed a "misanthropy and cynicism" over the years. As he climbed the ladder of material success, his soul plummeted to new depths.

Desai, in the novel, seems to set up an inverse co-relation between the material success that the characters strike and their ethical aspects. Materially, the most successful character in the novel is the Judge and his creator suggests that he is an "ogre". Biju ends up as, materially, the poorest character in the novel and his love for his father reflects that his heart is in the right place. Characters like Harish-Harry, Gaurish-Gary and Dhansukh-Danny—how succinctly Desai anglicizes their names to reveal their existence on the interface of occidental-oriental cultures, just as she does with Lalitha (Lola) and Namitha (Noni)—pull of a barely decent living but try to uphold their Indianness. They do not become ogres. Harish-Harry, the owner of Gandhi Café, hates his white customers—he wants to break their necks—who are his bread and butter. His daughter, however, is Americanized and her independent-self concept is heavily criticized by her parents' interdependent self-concept. A similar conflict takes place between the anglicized Sai's independent-self concept and Gyan's interdependent-self concept. Gyan feels burdened by history, "family demands and the built-up debt of centuries," (157) while Sai is occupied with National Geographic and is not burdened by the demands of interdependence. The similarity between Harish-daughter and Gyan-Sai conflicts, though not in degree but in kind, reveals, as Tejinder Kaur points out, commonalities of experience of:

> ...the legal and illegal diaspora communities and individuals in America as well as by the people from other states, regions and communities from India residing in Kalimpong. (2007)

Biju's rat like life in America, shifting from one restaurant to another, reveals that he belongs to the "shadow class," just like his friend Saeed who is also an illegal "third-world" immigrant from Zanzibar into America. Biju is hardly able to make both ends meet in a world that strictly maintains the "first world"-"third world" power balance. Biju suffers under the onus of the first world life, yet he has enough strength of character to hold up an individual identity. Biju pedaled down the proud streets of America, carrying food to the different houses from Freddy's Wok. He trembled in the cold, is torn by his worries about his father and only finds peace in humming old Hindi film songs.

In singing the film songs, Biju shows enough strength of character to uphold the modern and integral part of India's culture. Biju's decision to return to India, in spite of the lure of lucre that had forced the "metonymies of presence" to be tied to a degrading life in the first world, is an indicator of his strength of character. On board, Biju's pledge to relinquish the life of America and begin anew an Indian life speaks volumes of firmness.

> In the mirror of this bathroom, Biju saluted himself.... Now, he promised himself, he would forget the insight, begin anew. He would buy a taxi.... And he'd build a house with solid walls, a roof that wouldn't fly off every season. Biju played the scene of meeting his father.... They'd sit out in the evenings, drink chhang, tell jokes. (286)

Biju's salute is symbolic: it is a salute to his vigour of character that has helped him break the shackles of the first-world's cultural regime. The salute not only implies that in spite of all his poverty and humiliation received at the hands of the "first-world" Biju's soul has not "plummeted to new depths", but also he has the sympathy of his creator.

Kiran Desai is ingeniously rooted in America, but still holds on to her Indian citizenship. Residing in America, she visits India frequently. Straddling across different geographical and cultural domains, Desai has been able to reap a rich harvest of creative vigour. As C. Vijayasree pithily notes:

> This experience of inhabiting two geographical and cultural spaces simultaneously is wrought with subtle and involuted tensions.... Such tension, however, has proved to be an active source of creative energy. (1996)

Desai's sensibility conceives the pattern of life in which she feels no alienation but sustains her native Indian heritage. In an interview, she confessed:

> I realize that I see everything through the lens of being Indian. It's not something that has gone away—it's something that has become stronger.

In the middle of all the collisions and intersections of cultures and its varying impacts on the characters in *The Inheritance of Loss*, Biju comes closest to his creator. As Desai does in life, Biju does towards the end of the novel: both follow the truth that Lord Rama delivered to his brother Laksmana when both were awed by the pomp and show of Ravana's Lanka:

> Api Swarnama yi Lanka na may Lakshmana rochathi
> Janani Janambhumische swarga dapi gariyasi.

Which translates to—"Dear Lakshmana, may be Lanka is truly golden and resembles heaven but the mother and the motherland are more sacred than heaven." This is Desai's *raison d'être*, her ultimate, in the novel.

Works Cited

Ashcroft, Griffiths and Tiffin. *The Empire Writes Back* (London and New York: Routledge, 1989, 2003).

Bhabha, Homi K. "Of Mimicry and Man: The Ambivalence of Colonial Discourse," *Modern Literary Theory: A Reader*, 4th Edition, eds. Philip Rice and Patricia Waugh (New York: Arnold, 1996), 380-87.

Boehmer, Elleke. *Colonial and Postcolonial Literature* (Oxford: OUP, 1995).

Desai, Kiran. *The Inheritance of Loss* (New Delhi: Penguin Books, 2006).

Durkheim, Emile. *Rules of Sociological Method*. Trans. W.D. Halls (UK: Amazon, 1982).

Hall, Stuart. "Cultural Identity and Diaspora", *Theorizing Diaspora: A Reader*, eds. Jana Evans Braziel and Anita Mannur (Malden [MA]: Blackwell Publishing, 2003), 233-46.

Held, David and Anthony McGrew. "The Great Globalization Debate: An Introduction", *The Global Transformations Reader: An Introduction to the Globalization Debate*, 2nd Edition, eds. David Held and Anthony McGrew (Cambridge: Polity Press, 2003), 1-50.

Jameson, Fredric. "Notes on Globalization as a Philosophic Issue", *The Cultures of Globalization*, eds. Fredric Jameson and Masso Miyoshi (Durham: Duke University Press, 1998), 54-77.

Kaur, Tejinder. "Problematizing Issues about Home, Homeland, Diaspora and Belongingness in Transnational and National Lands: A Study of Karan Desai's *The Inheritance of Loss*." Quoted in Reena Mitra, "Anatomising Immigrant Lives: Kiran Desai's *The Inheritance of Loss*", *Critical Responses to Kiran Desai*, eds. Sunita Sinha and Bryan Reynolds (New Delhi: Atlantic Publishers and Distributors, 2009), 86-98.

Markus, H. and Kitayama, S. "Culture and the Self: Implications for Cognition, Emotion, and Motivation" (1991), referred in *Social Psychology*, eds. Robert A. Baron, Donn Byrne and Nyla R. Branscombe (Delhi: Dorling Kindersley [India], 2008).

Mignolo, Walter D. "Globalization, Civilization Processes, and the Relocation of Languages and Culture", *The Cultures of Globalization*, eds. Fredric Jameson and Masso Miyoshi (Durham: Duke University Press, 1998), 32-53.

Rushdie, Salman. *Imaginary Homelands* (London: Granta Books, 1991).

Schacht, Richard. *Alienation* (Garden City: Doubleday, 1970).

Sutherland, John. Quoted in "Introduction", *Critical Responses to Kiran Desai*, eds. Sunita Sinha and Bryan Reynolds (New Delhi: Atlantic Publishers and Distributors, 2009), xv-xxx.

Valmiki. *Ramayana*, 6th Kanda, http://www.mihironline.com/2009/08/janani-janmabhoomischa-swargadapi.html

Vijayasree, C. "The Politics and Poetics of Expatriation: The Indian Version(s)", *Interrogating Post-Colonialism: Theory, Text and Context*, eds. Harish Trivedi and Meenakshi Mukherjee (Simla: Indian Institute of Advanced Study, 1996), 221.

Wikipedia/Kiran Desai.

16

Narrating History, Rethinking Nation: A Re-reading of Rushdie's *Midnight's Children*[1]

Arindam Das

The more History attempts to transcend its own rootedness in historicity and the greater the efforts it makes to attain...the sphere of universality, the more clearly it bears the marks of its historical birth, and the more evidently there appears through it the history of which it is itself a part, inversely the more it accepts its relativity...then the more it tends to the slenderness of narrative. —Foucault (1970, 371)

History,...—indeed the world, the universe, and all human life, and so too, every institution under which we live—is in a constant state of evolution. The world and everything in it is being created and re-created even as I speak, each hour, each day, each week, going through the unending process of birth and rebirth which has made us all. India has been born and reborn scores of time and it will be reborn again. India is forever; and India is forever being made. —Tharoor (245, 1989)

...the epistemological assumptions of history nevertheless continue to operate powerfully to order postcolonial reality, the resistance to these takes various

> forms, a prominent one of which is the problematizing of the boundary between literature and history. —Ashcroft (99, 2001)

Derrida's critiques the logocentrism of history: 'if the word "history" did not carry with it the theme of the final repression of difference, we could say that differences alone could be "historical" through and through from the start' (Derrida quoted by Young, 1993, 65). Moreover Derrida in his *Of Grammatology* (1976) connects the process of representation or re-writing with history: 'Historicity itself is tied to the possibility of writing. Before being the object of a history—of a historical science—writing opens the field of history—of historical becoming' (1976, 4). True to this deconstructive post-modern tradition and true to a manner most Lyotard like, Rushdie in his *Midnight's Children* (1981) dismantles the structures of universal truths and 'grand narratives' such as History and Nation and in the process shows the slipperiness and gaps of such absolute identities. My paper proposes to show the ways through which Rushdie achieves such subversions and appropriations, stripping bare the hitherto unchallenged conventions and traditions in his *Midnight's Children*.

The novel starts with a prologue by Saleem Sinai its protagonist:

> I was born in the city of Bombay...once upon a time. No, that won't do, there's no getting away from the date: I was born in Doctor Narlikar's Nursing Home on August 15th, 1947. And the time? The time matters, too. Well then: at night. No, it's important to be more.... On the stroke of midnight, as a matter of fact. Clock-hands joined palms in respectful greeting as I came. Oh, spell it out, spell it out: at the precise instant of India's arrival at independence, I tumbled forth into the world. *There were gaps.* And, outside the window, fireworks and crowds. A few seconds later, my father broke his big toe; but his accident was a mere trifle when set beside what had befallen me in that benighted moment, because thanks to the occult tyrannies of those blandly saluting

> clocks I had been mysteriously handcuffed to history, my destinies indissolubly chained to those of my country. (1995, 9) [self emphasis added]

It is these 'gaps' and fissures within the real historical process of a nation's evolvement that are filled in by the recollections and memories of the narrator Saleem. In *Imaginary Homelands* (1992) Rushdie discusses the writing of *Midnight's Children* and how he 'went to some trouble to get things wrong' (1992, 23). This purposely getting things 'wrong', is but to reinstate that such a 'wrong' is but another undocumented 'right' which co-exists along with the absolute documented 'Right', challenging the absolute's very foundation. Memory serves for Rushdie the fountainhead for such subversive counter realities. Recapitulating about *Midnight's Children*, Rushdie says: 'Writing my book in North London, looking out through my window on to a city scene totally unlike the ones I was imagining on to paper, I was constantly plagued by this problem, until I felt obliged to face it in the text, to make clear that...what I was actually doing was a novel of memory and about memory' (Rushdie, 1992, 10). Such erroneous narrations of memory create a contra reality, within the novel, whose validity is beyond the vouching of recorded and standard and customary History of a Nation:

> Reality is a question of perspective [...]. Re-reading my work, I have discovered an error in chronology. The assassination of Mahatma Gandhi occurs, in these pages, on the wrong date. But I cannot say, now, what the actual sequence of events might have been; in my India, Gandhi will continue to die at the wrong time. (1995, 198)

Thus goes one of the many memory-makings of Saleem Sinai—individualistic and regardless of true history, recreating the death of Gandhi. Rightly does Michael Reder observes that "When Rushdie speaks of 'memory,' he is speaking not of cultural memory or national consciousness but of individual memory, [...] the history in *Midnight's Children* is seen through the eyes of an individual: it is not the dominant, official 'History' but a history that is personalized and therefore given life, significance, and meaning" (1999, 226). Similarly Martine Hennard Dutheil in *Origin and Originality in Rushdie's Fiction* (1999), points to the central idea of *Midnight's Children* as 'the power of fiction' to capture—and invent 'a new reality' (1999, 10). But it is not merely in the death of Gandhi but from the pre-independent colonial India to India post-emergency that Saleem re-reads history and re-makes India.

In re-formulating 'history' to 'his story' Saleem is not without misgivings of him not being trusted. Catherine Cundy observes that Saleem is afraid that his stories might 'disintegrate into tiny, unreconstructable pieces. He is obliged by the internal compulsion of his own story to reach a certain point in history and the narrative, while his omniscience allows him to meddle with and distort both' (1996, 29). At times Saleem questions himself, 'discrediting the belief that truth is one and absolute, and holding that it is instead multiple, overlapping, conflicting' (Gorra, 1997, 121). Below mentioned is an instance of such a doubt raised at the inappropriate date of Gandhi's death:

> Does one error invalidate the entire fabric? Am I so far gone, in my desperate need of meaning, that I'm prepared to distort everything—to re-write the whole history of my times purely in order to place myself in a central role? Today, in my confusion, I can't judge. I'll have to leave it to others. (1995, 166)

But a whole cavalcade of critics and readers of *Midnight's Children* have appraised such subjective and biographic assessment of History and Nation in the most positive manner.

If modern theorists of nation theory like Benedict Anderson (1983; 1991) perceives of a nation as a homogeneous 'imagined political community', then Rushdie through his novel narrates that very space in a sense most Bhabhaesque to unravel its heterogeneity. Homi Bhabha defines this event in the following terms: 'Counter-narratives of the nation that continually evoke and erase its totalizing boundaries—both actual and conceptual—disturb those ideological manoeuvres through which imagined communities are given essentialist identities' (1994: 149). Thus it is the Nation's attempt towards this standardization and normalization which is subverted and appropriated by Rushdie through the multitudinous heterogeneous narratives within it. Rushdie thereby critiques all that which went to the making of an India, the Nation, as is evident through its standard historical estimations, especially language and secularity.

Narrating 'Language'

Syed Amanuddin in 'The Novels of Salman Rushdie: Mediated Reality as Fantasy' (1989: 44) suggests that *Midnight's Children* is about the act of writing itself, thereby asserting the significance of writing and language. If English for the British had been an ideological apparatus for creating a homogenizing rubric called India, then it is the very same which is appropriated by Rushdie in *Midnight's Children*. Alastair Pennycook forwards his view about the use of English in postcolonial settings:

> When we start to investigate the uses of English in colonial and postcolonial societies, then, it becomes important to acknowledge its importance not only as the language of imperialism but also as one of the key languages of resistance. English and the European languages were indeed the languages of the oppressors, the languages of cultural penetration, the languages of political and economic manipulation, threatening local languages, cultures and knowledges, and changing forever certain ways of life. But they were also the languages of political opposition and of founding new ways of enunciating the struggle for independence. (1994, 262)

It is here that Rushdie 'chutnifies' English and dislocates the language in its syntactic and syntagmatic structures. Rushdie in his attempt to write back to the 'standard English' disrupts it to the core. A particular character in *Midnight's Children* is called 'The Rani of Cooch Naheen', whose portrait gradually fades away to ultimately reveal a blank canvas. A discerning translation of the word 'Cooch Naheen' in Hindi reveals it to mean 'just nothing' and thus no wonder her painting fades away. Such insertion of Indianness into the customary code of English subverts the language.

Moreover the very genre of Novel is refashioned by Rushdie in his *Midnight's Children* by extending the memory of the subjective self to that of a nation's. Here I would like to concur with Frederick Jameson who says that the novel, an offspring of Western capitalism is born out of the radical split between private and public; however, in the Third World the novel resolves this division necessarily by taking the form of 'national allegories,' 'where the telling of the individual story and the individual experience cannot but ultimately involve the whole labourious telling of the experience of the collectivity itself' (1986, 85). Rushdie disrupts the very structure of a standard concept of novel. It is here to be mentioned that reading of texts, such as novels, in a standard secular language were thought by Anderson to be among various factors binding an imagined community to a Nation. Further the heteroglossic commingling of various genres: magic realism, journalistic documentation, poetic imageries, comic-epic mode, detailing of visual art forms all fuse to form something very fresh in *Midnight's Children*.

The other way of showing a discontinuity in the uniform language model for independent India is revealed through the 'Maratha language movement' episode of the novel. Saleem crashes into the marches of the movement and when the protagonist's linguistic acumen is tested, he replies in broken Gujarati: '*Soo che? Saru chee! / Danda le ke maru chee.*'

This is taken up by the marchers as their slogan and clashes with the Gujarati language marchers resulting in 15 deaths and 300 injuries. This in a result makes the erstwhile Government of India pass the State Reorganization Commission by Nehru in 1953. The committee submitted the report in 1955 and the recommendations led to the formation of Indian states on linguistic basis. Saleem passes his observation: 'In this way I became directly responsible for triggering off the violence which ended with the partition of the state of Bombay, as a result of which the city became the capital of Maharashtra—so at last I was on the winning side' (1995, 191-92). This particular incident thereby points to the fissures present within the project of an unvarying nation making. Thus the paradigmatic whole of a nation space is made disjunctive and fragmentary.

Narrating 'Secularism'

Benedict Anderson has suggested that in the process of formation of a modern nation traditional religious belief wanes and national narratives come to satisfy the desire for origins, continuity, and eternity (1991, 11). But as postcolonial nation India, as Partha Chatterjee would suggest in *Nationalist Thought and the Colonial World: A Derivative Discourse?* (1986), takes recourse to the inner spiritual world in its aspiration towards a national discourse. Chatterjee reminds that 'the superiority of West lies in the materiality of its culture, exemplified by its science, technology and love of progress. But the East is superior in the spiritual aspect of culture' (1986, 51). For Chatterjee India's modernism could never be a western 'derivative discourse'. He replies to the Andersonian model of nation:

> I have one central objection to Anderson's argument. If nationalisms in the rest of the world have to choose their imagined community from certain 'modular' forms already made available to them by Europe and the Americas, what do they have left to imagine? History, it would seem, has decreed that we in the postcolonial world shall only be perpetual consumers of modernity. Europe and the Americas, the only true subjects of history, have thought out on our behalf not only the script of colonial enlightment and exploitation, but also that of our anti-colonial resistance and postcolonial misery. Even our imaginations must remain forever colonized. (1993, 5)

In a lecture—*Our Modernity*—delivered by Chatterjee during a lecture tour in Africa in 1996 organized by SEPHIS and CODESRIA the theorist takes up cudgels with the Orient's received modalities of Western Modernity:

> My subject is 'modernity,' but more specifically, 'our' modernity. In making the distinction I am trying to point out that there might be modernities that are not ours, or, to put it another way, that there are certain peculiarities about our modernity. It could be the case that what others think of as modern, we have found unacceptable, whereas what we have cherished as valuable elements of our modernity, others do not consider to be modern at all. (1997, 3)

Of these cherished elements are a countries traditions, beliefs, culture, and religion. Even in Rushdie's *Midnight's Children* the Nehruvian Western modern secular national model for India is subverted and appropriated by Saleem's dismantling recollections. I would like to point here the image of the *tetrapod* in the novel that was associated with modern land reclamation. Dr. Narlikar a modern day doyen in the field of science is shown in the novel to place one symbolic *tetrapod* on the sea-wall 'as a kind of icon pointing to the future' (1995, 176). But a later visit to the same place by the scientist makes him baffled with the fact that

> a group of beggar-woman had clustered around the tetrapod and were performing the rite of puja. They had lighted oil-lamps at the base of the object; one of them have painted the OM-symbol on its upraised tip; they were chanting prayers as they gave the tetrapod a thorough and a worshipful wash. *Technological miracle had been transformed into Shivalingam....* (*Ibid.*) [Self emphasis added]

Thus Western secular modernism is narrated. Further Dr. Narlikar is killed by the Gujarati language marchers in their antagonism towards Marathi speakers which links the two aforementioned nation making ideologies and points towards their insufficiency and inappropriateness in a post-colonial nation. Josna Rege might criticize Rushdie and suggests that '[d]espite its conceptual freshness and vitality, *Midnight's Children* remains very emotionally committed to the narrative of the nation' (1997, 366) and that the novel 'romanticizes the Congress Party ideal of "unity in diversity"' (1997, 360)—or, alternatively, insist that Rushdie is disillusioned not with the nation *per se* but with the corruption of the postcolonial nation, because those who came to lead it were, as Timothy Brennan puts it, 'sell-outs and power brokers' (1989, 27). Yet my reading is far removed from such straitjacket reductionist criticism of Rushdie.

Here it should be reminded that the spiritualism talked about in the above section is not any kind of unity in religious belief structure of the nation, but rather is fragmented through and through. The schism occurs due to the multifarious religious sects that remain indissoluble within any single constitution of faith. Nehru much before he became the Prime Minister of India in an article 'The Psychology of Indian Nationalism' wrote 'India' has always shared a common and continuous history: 'even in the remote past there has always been a fundamental unity to India—a unity of common faith and culture. India was Bharata, the holy land of the *Hindus*' (1927, 219) [self emphasis added]. With a Derridian turn one might unravel how a going to be leader of India makes a statement of secularism which privileges the majority community's concern. It is such hypocrite secularism in the discourse of building independent India that *Midnight's Children* brings to the fore. When the Muslim Saleem, at whose birth Nehru writes a letter ['the Prime Minister wrote me a letter' (1995, 119)], contemplate in becoming the receptacle of destiny and purpose for the sake of nation gets subverted by his Hindu doppelganger Shiva who gives a reality-check to Saleem about the materialism of a self-centric nation:

> What purpose, man? What thing in the whole sister-sleeping world got reason, yara? For what reason you're rich and I'm poor? Where's the reason in starving, man? God knows how many millions of damn fools living in this country, man, and you think there's a purpose! Man, I'll tell you—you got to get what you can, do what you can with it, and then you got to die. (1995, 220)

Thus the contentious Hindu Muslim divides and the class conflicts, two ever unresolved issues of the nation, upsets the promises of the unified meta-narrative of modern secular nation.

It is perhaps this failed project of nation building and the unfaltering presence of heterogeneous fluid narratives that ultimately compels Saleem to come to a realization. Georg Lukacs in *The Theory of the Novel: A Historico-Philosophical Essay on the Forms of Great Epic Literature* (1971) makes an insightful mulling, an observation in line with the Rushdian disenchantment in *Midnight's Children*:

> And so, by a strange and melancholy paradox, the moment of failure is the moment of value; the comprehending and experiencing of life's refusals is the source from which the fullness of life seems to flow. What is depicted [in the novel] is the total absence of any fulfillment of meaning, yet the work contains the rich and rounded fullness of a true totality of life. (1971, 126)

With the declaration of Emergency by Indira Gandhi the disillusionment with nation comes to a full circle for Saleem. The midnight promises to its children make a crash landing and the false optimism of Saleem crushed. The 'One empty jar' (1995, 461) at the end in which no fragment of history could be stuffed by Saleem is still kept open for revision:

> The promise of revision should be constant and endless; don't think I'm satisfied with what I've done! ...yes, I should revise and revise, improve and improve; but there is neither the time nor the energy. (1995, 460-61)

The improperly imagined nation of Saleem is also the yet to be fully imagined one. If critics like Brennan and her ilk have criticized Rushdie for being internationalist and cosmopolitan in his outlook in the novel and a failure in ascribing any positive value to nation, then the precise reason lies in the fact that a failed 'national longing for form' (359) makes the postmodern migrant writer consider the possibilities of post-nationalism as the novel's undercurrent.

Note

1. My article at places is indebted to the views expressed in the following articles:
   (i) Su, John J. "Epic of Failure: Disappointment as Utopian Fantasy in *'Midnight's Children'.*" *Twentieth Century Literature (Rushdie)*, Vol. 47, No. 4. Hofstra University, Winter, 2001, 545-68. Web.08/03/2009. http://www.jstor.org/stable/3175993.
   (ii) Mannur, Anita. "'Back' Translation in a Postcolonial Indian Context: Language Construction in the Works of Shashi Tharoor and Salman Rushdie." *Journal of Postcolonial Writing*. 01 January, 1998. Web. 07/02/2009. http://www.informaworld.com/smpp/title~content=t713735330.
   (iii) Watson, David. "Borderline Fiction: Writing the Nation in Salman Rushdie's *Midnight's Children. Journal of Literary Studies*. 01 June 1998. Web. 09/02/2009. http://www.informaworld.com/smpp/title~content=t777285707.
   (iv) Heffernan, Teresa. "Apocalyptic Narratives: The Nation in Salman Rushdie's *'Midnight's Children'.*" *Twentieth Century Literature (Literature and Apocalypse)*, Vol. 46, No. 4, Hofstra University, Winter 2000, 470-91. Web. 15/03/09. http://www.jstor.org/stable/827843.
   (v) Needham, Anuradha Dingwaney. "The Politics of Post-Colonial Identity in Salman Rushdie". *The Massachusetts Review*, Vol. 29, No. 4, Winter, 1988/1989, 609-24. Web. 10/02/09. http://www.jstor.org/stable/25090032.

Works Cited

Amanuddin, Sayed. *The Novels of Salman Rushdie: Mediated Reality as Fantasy*. World Literature Today 46, 1989, 42-45.

Anderson, Benedict. *Imagined Communities: Reflections on the Origin and Spread of Nationalism*. Revised Ed. London and New York: Verso, 1991 [1983].

Ashcroft, Bill. *Post-colonial Transformation*. London: Routledge, 2001.

Bhabha, Homi. *The Location of Culture*. London: Routledge, 1994.

Brennan, Timothy. *Salman Rushdie and the Third World: Myths of the Nation*. London: Macmillan, 1989.

Chatterjee, Partha. *Nationalist Thought and the Colonial World: A Derivative Discourse?* Delhi: Oxford University Press, 1986.

——. *The Nation and Its Fragments: Studies in Colonial and Postcolonial Histories*. Princeton: Princeton University Press, 1993.

——. *Our Modernity*. Rotterdam/Dakar: SEPHIS and CODESRIA, 1997.

Cundy, Catherine. *Salman Rushdie*. Manchester: Manchester UP, 1996.

Derrida, Jacques. *Of Grammatology*. London: Johns Hopkins University Press, 1976.

Dutheil, Martine Hennard. "Origin and Originality in Rushdie's Fiction." *Looking for Origins in 'Midnight's Children' and 'Shame'*. Bern: Peter Lang, 1999, 1-34.

Foucault, M. *The Order of Things*. London: Tavistock Publications, 1970.

Gorra, Michael. *After Empire*. Chicago: The U of Chicago P, 1977.

Jameson, Fredric. "Third-World Literature in the Era of Multinational Capitalism." *Social Text* 15 (1986): 65-88.

Lukács, Georg. *The Theory of the Novel: A Historico-Philosophical Essay on the Forms of Great Epic Literature*. Trans. Anna Bostock. Cambridge: MIT P, 1971.

Nehru, Jawahar Lal. "The Psychology of Indian Nationalism." *The Review of Nations*. 1927, 177-228.

Pennycook, Alastair. *The Cultural Politics of English as an International Language*. London: Longman, 1994.

Reder, Michael. "Rewriting History and Identity: The Reinvention of Myth, Epic, and Allegory in Salman Rushdie's *Midnight's Children*." *Critical Essays on Salman Rushdie*. Ed. M. Keith Booker. New York: G.K. Hall & Co., 1999, 225-49.

Rege, Josna E. "Victim into Protagonist? *Midnight's Children* and the Post-Rushdie National Narratives of the Eighties". *Studies in the Novel* 29.3, 1997, 342-75.

Rushdie, Salman. *Imaginary Homelands: Essays and Criticism 1981-1991*. New York: Granta, 1992. *Midnight's Children*. London: Vintage, 1995 (1st published in 1981).

Tharoor, Shashi. *The Great Indian Novel*. New York: Arcade, 1989.

Young, Robert. *White Mythologies*. London: Routledge, 1993.

17

Possibilities of the Metaphorical in Salman Rushdie's *Midnight's Children*

Reena Mitra

"Art" as Kakutani observes, "does have a way of imitating life and writers have always been skeptical or incapable of unilaterally separating, the two".[1] Salman Rushdie, too, in writing *Midnight's Children* that bagged the Booker McConnell Prize for fiction in 1981, seems wittingly disinclined to dissever the two. He started, as Zola believed every literary artist did, "from the true facts which are our indestructible basis" but to show "the mechanism of these facts",[2] he had to modify them and resort largely to the metaphorical as well. It is in this specific orientation given to facts that his distinctive genius lies. By his own admission it is in *Midnight's Children* that he discovers his "true voice"[3] and is able to give direction to his inner urges and compulsions.

In an article in defence of his controversial novel, *The Satanic Verses*, Rushdie has made his aesthetic predilections very clear when he says, "Do not ask your writers to create 'typical' or 'representative' fictions. Such books are almost invariably dead books."[4] The novels that he really cares for are "those which attempt radical reformulations of language, form and ideas, those which attempt to do what the 'novel' seems to insist upon: to see the world anew".[5] And, this novel world-view, if it provides implications and inferences that are worth mulling over, fulfils one of the important functions of literature. *Midnight's Children* is a representative novel which foregrounds issues at a slant in a manner that evokes fervent and animated response. This obliquity, significantly, is sustained principally through the use of metaphor.

Midnight's Children is a literary response to a series of real-life situations that have been cleverly fictionalized through allusions, disguised as well as direct, to the country's recent as well as relatively distant past. The novel has an epic sweep[6] covering about six decades in the history of the Indian subcontinent. Book One covers the time from the Jallianwala Bagh incident in April, 1919, to the birth of the protagonist, Saleem, on August 15, 1947; Book Two extends up to the end of the Indo-Pakistan war in September 1965; and, Book Three envelops the period up to the end of the Emergency in March, 1977, encompassing the Bangladesh war as well.

At the fictional level, *Midnight's Children* depicts the events and experiences in the lives of three generations of the Sinai family. The account begins with their days in Srinagar and follows their passage through Amritsar, Agra and Bombay to Karachi where Saleem alone returns hidden in the basket of Parvati, the witch,[7] only to experience the tremors of the Emergency that had been clamped in India. At the semantic level, the novel, making profuse use of the non-literal and the figurative, is far more complex and has intriguing social and political reverberations.

The very first sentence of *Midnight's Children* is clearly illustrative of the intention and design of the novelist. The tale is decidedly meant to be at once an autobiography and a narrative, an account of facts and a yarn spun out of imagination, a blend of truth and fiction. "I was born in the city of Bombay[8]...clearly sets the tone for an autobiography but the latter half of the sentence—"once upon a time"—shifts the reader's attention and focus, and leaves him baffled as he makes a futile attempt to approximate fiction while facts make a clamouring and insistent bid for attention. He is mystified as to how "once upon a time" (1) can be a natural sequel to what goes before. And yet, the two are confidently set against each other as a revelatory beginning to "so dense a commingling of the improbable and the mundane!" (2).

The novelist in the work under study is punctilious not about the observance of chronology but about the metaphorical content of the book. There is a frequent forward or backward shift in time that makes it difficult to trace the proper sequence of events in the life of the protagonist. What the publisher's blurb says of Rushdie's book *The Satanic Verses*, one can say of *Midnight's Children*, too "...the past and the future chase each other furiously".[9] The narrator in the latter novel somersaults from the present into the past only to return to the present and then to embark upon the future. He feels that it is incumbent upon him "to write the future as I have written the past" (462) and for this he turns to the facility and potential of the mode of fantasy and the possibilities of the allegorical.

The element of fantasy in the novel is introduced in such a matter-of-fact way that the reader swallows it almost unquestioningly though he is aware of the fact that this is one of those extra-historical factors in the novel that lend it interest rather than authenticity. Yet, the two contrastive elements of the magical and the real shade off into each-other very naturally, the former, representative and metaphorical in nature, bringing into relief the historical truth the writer sets out to explore and fix. The reciprocity of the magical and the fantastic thus is essentially strategic in nature in the sense that it becomes a fictional mode of projecting reality and offers the real in terms of the fanciful and the bizarre.

Certain observations made by Rushdie in the course of the novel under consideration reveal his attitude to reality and bring home the message that the novelist's truth is different from that of the historian. Rushdie's narrator, in trying to bring out the nature of fictional reality, significantly states, "Reality can have metaphorical content that does not make it less real" (200). Clearly, then, Rushdie's treatment of history is in conformity with his idea of the metaphorical and of "illusory fictional reality"[10], which, while recording historical truth does not insist upon a total transcription of reality.

Midnight's Children are themselves metaphorically conceived in that they can be made to represent many things. The author himself refers to their symbolic character and draws the reader's attention to their representative aspect.

> They can be seen as the last throw of everything antiquated and retrogressive in our myth-ridden nation, whose defeat was entirely desirable in the context of a modernizing twentieth century economy; or as the true hope of freedom which is now forever extinguished; but what they must not become is the bizarre creation of a rambling diseased mind.... (200)

It is this "quality of visionary insights"[11] created by Rushdie's use of metaphors and symbols that lends distinction to his work.

Apart from the metaphorical value that the Midnight's Children have, each one of them has also been endowed with certain magical traits:

> What made the events noteworthy was the nature of these children every one of whom was, through some freak of biology or perhaps owing to some preternatural power of the moment or just conceivably by sheer coincidence, endowed with features, talents and faculties which can only be described as miraculous. (195)

The ascribing of supernatural qualities to these children is the author's means of lending validity to his protagonist's omniscience. Saleem's power of telepathy and the voices speaking inside his head enable him to provide the missing links in the narrative and to maintain the continuity of the story for "most of what matters in our lives takes place in our absence..." (19). Besides, even "memory cracks beyond hope of reassembly" (384). There are "fadings" and "gaps" and hence it is "necessary to improvise on occasion" (384)—"the trick is to fill in the gaps" (427).

The providing of miraculous powers to the children born on the midnight of Independence is emblematic of their involvement in the mythic past of India and significantly, this stance also enables the novelist to expatiate upon the superhuman traits of the mythic Hindu heroes by comparing his "midnight's children" with these prodigies; for example,

> ...to Shiva the hour had given the gifts of war (of Ram who could draw the undrawable bow; of Arjuna and Bhima, the ancient prowess of Kurus and Pandavas united unstoppably in him!).... (200)

As for Saleem, he himself refers to his magical traits, his "miraculous nature, which involved me beyond all mitigation in the myth life of India" (244). So, Saleem, Shiva and the other "midnight's children" are inextricably linked with the mythic-historical past of the nation as well as its present and future and embroiled in every way in the fate of the country, this involvement having been designed by the author to allow an understanding of the individual's life in terms of the historical forces. The characteristic juxtaposition of the two contrastive elements of fantasy and reality has been so skilfully effected in the narrative that one is left not with a sense of incongruity but with the consciousness of a comprehensive general design in which the magical and the real complement each other in foregrounding the historical truth in the context of the life of the individual. Thus, in the novel, the plying of the fantastic in tandem with the metaphorical offers the real in terms of the fanciful and the figurative. The symbolic Lifafa Das, the peep-show man demonstratively tries to capture "the whole of reality" (75) in his box as his creator did in his novel. As Rushdie himself establishes, "the original motivation was to write about my childhood home, Bombay at the time when I was growing up there...."[12] Later, however, this motivation took on larger implications and the work came to be a literary exploration of "the memory of a society in political and social decline".[13]

Rushdie, fully aware of the art of the novelist as historian avoids piling up facts and making his work only a mirror of the times. His is not a mere conventional, chronological narration of history but a metaphorical depiction that lends his work a forward linear movement in the account that traces the history of the protagonist and his "twin", the nation, from the pre-Independence days, through the attainment of

Independence to the recent times. The telescoping of time and the condensation of space is noteworthy besides, the metaphorical certainly does not detract from the impact of the novel. Rather, it adds a major dimension to it.

That the novel is autobiographical in content is evident from what Salman-Saleem says in the course of the story-telling: "...I reach the end of my long-winded autobiography; in words and pickles I have immortalized my memories" (459). Saleem, at the time of narration is working in a pickle factory and once again, the metaphorical steps in when he says that in writing this saga he hopes that

> ...one-day, perhaps the world may taste the pickle of history. They may be too strong for some palates, their smell may be over-powering, tears may rise to the eyes; I hope nevertheless that it will be possible to say of them that they possess the authentic taste of truth. (461)

The metaphor continuing, he clarifies his stand further and warns us against unsuspecting faith in his version of factuality —"distortions are inevitable in both methods (i.e. words and pickles). We must live, I am afraid, with the shadows of imperfection" (459). So, one must be wary, says the narrator for an autobiography is not totally reliable, authentic history. What is important, however, is "what the author can manage to persuade his audience to believe..." (270).

Briefly, what happens to Saleem is metaphorically what happens to the nation. In the novel, Saleem's life is the microcosm that affects and reflects the macrocosmic life of the state and reverberates with the impact of the happenings that plague the latter. Saleem is born at midnight on August 15, 1947, the very moment at which India attained her Independence. He is one of the thousand and one Midnight's Children who are also "the children of the time; fathered...by history" (118). The experiences of the child symbolize the experiences of the nation. The child and the nation go through parallel experiences of the pangs of birth, the caprices of childhood, the traumas of adolescence and the uncertainties of adulthood and their state of inter-relatedness cannot be contested.

One notable advantage of implicating history in one's fate and metaphorically getting intricately involved in the course of events in the life of the nation is evident. Proximity to an event tends to cause a loss of perspective. Rushdie's use of history in an attempt to understand his own life may be seen as an appropriate distancing device. As he explains in the novel, "Reality is a question of perspective; the further you get from the past, the more concrete and plausible it seems" (165).

Saleem's life, which is the novel, is sketched in metaphoric relation to the life of the nation. Aroused into analysis by the contents of the Prime Minister's letter, written to him at the time of his birth—"Your life will be, in a sense the mirror of our own" (238)—Saleem is set thinking "How, in what terms, may the career of an individual be said to impinge on the fate of a nation?" (238). And then, after strained thought comes the enlightenment and the "modes-of-connection" (238) are established:

> I must answer in adverbs and hyphens: I was linked to history both literally and metaphorically, both actively and passively, in what our (admirably modern) scientists might term 'modes-of-connection' composed of dualistically combined configurations of the two pairs of opposed adverbs given above. This is why hyphens are necessary: actively-literally, passively-metaphorically, actively-metaphorically and passively-literally, I was inextricably enlivened with my world. (238)

Confining ourselves to the metaphorical, the "passively-metaphorical" mode-of-connection included all socio-political trends and events which merely by their existence affected Saleem metaphorically; for example, in the reference to "The Fisherman's Pointing Finger" lay the latent connection between the child-nation's efforts to acquire adulthood and Saleem's own gigantic attempts at growing up. The "actively-metaphorical" referred to encompassed all those occasions on which "things done by or to me were mirrored in the macrocosm of public affairs" (238) and Saleem's individual existence was symbolical of the nation's state at that point of time. The mutilation of Saleem's little finger had let out spurts of blood; history, too, was marked by a similar maiming and a bloody violence had erupted.

Metaphors in *Midnight's Children*, if rightly interpreted, often provide a key to an understanding of the novel and the reality it projects. A prominent and sustained metaphor in the work used in relation to the similar lives of Saleem and the nation is that of the "chutnification of history" (459)—the pickling of time. A brief reference to this metaphor has already been made earlier in this work but for a clearer perspective on it and a better understanding of its implications one needs to go into a closer analysis of the parallel implied. The symbolic significance of the pickling process is that it preserves time and experience—private as well as public—and makes them available to the generations to come. The taste of the pickles may be "too strong" (461) for some and their smell "overpowering" for others, but they do, undeniably, preserve the taste of truth.

The requirements for "chutnification" are obviously raw materials—fruits, vegetables, fish, vinegar, spices. But also, clear penetrating eyes which can gauge the true quality of the vegetables, and a "discerning" (460) nose that can decide "what-must-be-pickled, its humours and messages and emotions..." (460). At Braganza Pickles are prepared not only Mary's recipes but also Saleem's "special blends" (460) which include "memories, dreams, ideas" (460) and which are for mass consumption: "Thirty jars stand upon a shelf, waiting to be unleashed upon the amnesiac nation" (460). In other words, "the past in reinterpreted and articulated for those who wish to taste 'the pickles' version of history" (460).

> There are, of course, because of 'the spice bases' the inevitable distortions of the pickling process. To pickle is to give immortality, after all..., a certain alteration, a slight intensification of taste, is a small matter, surely? The art is to change the flavour in degree, but not in kind; and above all...to give it shape and form—that is to say, meaning. (461)

This is Rushdie's aesthetic credo expressed in an easily understandable domestic image. The externals are of no consequence; what matters is the spirit of the thing.

Saleem refers to his tale as "memory's truth,"[14] (211) and what differentiates this truth from any other kind of truth is that

> memory has its own special kind. It selects, eliminates, alters, exaggerates, minimizes, glorifies, and vilifies also; but in the end it creates its own reality, its heterogenous but usually coherent version of events; and no sane human being ever trusts someone else's version more than his own. (211)

"Memory's truth" is highly selective and sets the limits of its own reality.

Rushdie's "chutnification" may be seen as an attempt to blend and mix ideas and events, individual life and public life in such a way as to give life a sense of continuity in the future that he has a longing for, and that he probably feared as lost on the memorable midnight. This explains his reference to his son and his son's son carrying on the process begun by him. We normally look back for a sense of continuity but he has brought the past into the present in order to extend his desire for a sense of continuity into the future. For him the past is not over but continues to make itself felt through its impact. So, it becomes a function of his life in the present. No wonder the boundaries are blurred not only between past and present but also between fact and fiction, imagination and reality. Rushdie dreams his desire into reality—the reality which consists of his life and his country's. The desire for immortality as well as that for continuity are parallel desires, both of which Rushdie cherishes and expresses forcefully.[15]

Another important metaphor in the novel that does not fail to draw one's attention is that of the perforated cloth through which Saleem's grandfather, Dr. Aadam Aziz, once examined as a patient his grandmother, Naseem, before he married her. The implication is that a narrative is a perforated sheet that conceals the whole, revealing only parts which appear in the nature of "trailers"[16] to arouse our curiosity.

Fantasy in *Midnight's Children* is the chosen mode of the author to enable himself to explore the possibilities of the metaphorical in a singular and unconventional manner. It, besides being a form of reality, also serves to add spice to the narrative and to provide relief from the strain of trying to comprehend the truth in terms of the factual. It energetically exploits the comic in character, situation and language providing the novel a strikingly fresh and absorbing dimension. Rushdie in *Midnight's Children* devises what Kundera visualizes as "a new art of novelistic counterpoint (which can blend philosophy, narrative and dream into one music);...."[17]

Rushdie's fantasizing mixed with first person narrative is a kind of modernistic device to stress the fictive nature of his fiction as also to accommodate fantasy to fact to represent or re-enact better those aspects of reality that have been poignantly experienced by him and would not be easily captured in words, which, in a categorically realistic novel, never fail. For Rushdie, the fantastic and the metaphorical alone can provide a compelling mode of communication whereby fiction emerges as a mode of reality, the reality of the author's self caught in a complex interplay with historical reality.

References

1. Michiko Kakutani, "Do Facts and Fiction Mix?", *New York Times Book Review*, Jan. 27, 1980.
2. Emile Zola, *Du Roman Experimental*, Chapter I, Le Roman Experimental (1880) transl. Belle M. Sherman (New York, 1893); quoted in Miriam Allott, "The Novel as a Portrait of Life", *Novelists on the Novel* (London: Routledge and Kegan Paul, 1965), 70.
3. "Raj Reversal", *Sunday*, Dec. 4-10, 1988, 30.
4. "In Good Faith", *Sunday*, Feb. 25-Mar. 3, 1990, 90—Rushdie's defence of *The Satanic Verses*.
5. Salman Rushdie, "Not Guilty!" *Sunday*, Feb. 8-14, 1990, 27.
6. Dr. Alistair Niven, "Indian Writing in English: Past and Present", Sahitya Akademi International Seminar, *Indian Literature in English and English Translation*, Feb. 25-28, 1986, India

International Centre, New Delhi—"...he (Rushdie) has brought back into English fiction a sense of the panoramic...."

7. In an interview, Rushdie himself tells us that he is convinced of the existence of the supernatural world. 'Network East', BBC-2, Sept. 24, 1988.
8. Salman Rushdie, *Midnight's Children* (London: Picador, 1982). All quotes hereupon cited are from the same edition of the book with page numbers given in brackets.
9. An extract from the cover-blurb of Rushdie's *The Satanic Verses* (London: Viking, 1988).
10. R.S. Pathak, "History and the Individual in the Novels of Rushdie", *Three Contemporary Novelists*, ed. R.K. Dhawan (New Delhi: Classical Publishing Company, 1985), 217.
11. Rita Joshi, "Fantasy as Reality: The Art of Salman Rushdie", *The Sunday Observer*, April 12, 1987.
12. "'Midnight's Children': Memories Recesses", *Northern Indian Patrika*, Sunday, Jan. 16, 1983, 1.
13. "Raj Reversal", *Sunday*, 29.
14. Rushdie, when interviewed by the BBC, referred to *Midnight's Children* as "a novel of memory",—'Network East', BBC-2, September 24, 1988. Again, in "*Midnight's Children*: Memory's Recesses", his interview was published in the *Northern India Patrika*, January 16, 1983, Rushdie speaks of the novel "as being about memory as well as being a novel of memory". He further explains, "It is about the way memory operates when you recall your life."
15. Cf. Carlos Fuentes, "Modern Literature Conference: The Politics of Experience", *The Centennial Review*, Vol. XXX, No. 2, Spring 86, 135: "It is important to realize that we remember in the present, that memory is a celebration of the present. It is in the present that we remember and we desire which are two things that come together in writing—memory and yearning. Wanting. Trying to identify with something."
16. Nancy E. Batty, "The Art of Suspense: Rushdie's 1001 (Midnights)", *Ariel*, Vol. 18, Number 3, July 1987, The University of Calagary Press, 61.
17. Milan Kundera, *The Art of the Novel*, transl. Linder Asher; (London: Faber and Faber, 1988); quoted in *Times Literary Supplement*, June 24-30, 1988.

18

Ecofeminism in Arundhati Roy's *The God of Small Things*, and the Meenachal River as an Encyclopedia of Race, Class and Culture in the Novel

Joyashri Choudhury

The image of life as a flowing river is found in both early western and oriental philosophy. Related to this image is the notion of life as a river that flows while it appears not to; when we step into it the river will have changed from what it was before, although it appears to be the same. T.S. Eliot has said, "The River itself has no beginning or end. In the beginning it is not yet the river, in its end, it is no longer the river. What we call the headwaters is only a selection from among the innumerable sources which flow together to compose it. At what point in its course, does the Mississippi become what the Mississippi means?"

Rivers can serve as symbols of identity, not only of one's own personality but of a nation as well. Sri Aurobindo also talked in a similar vein, "The work of the poet depends not only on himself and his age but on the mentality of the nation to which he belongs and the spiritual, intellectual, aesthetic tradition and environment which it creates for him." This is so very true of Arundhati Roy. *The God of Small Things*, lucidly reflects the mentality of that particular part of Kerala,

Ayemenem, to which she belongs and where she spent the greater part of her childhood. She picks up the Meenachal River from her childhood days. Most of the locales of *The God of Small Things*, are derived from this actual town and surroundings. The story jumps from one locale to another in typical fashion invented by the author. The Meenachal River assumes gigantic proportions in the book, moulding and shaping the lives of almost all the characters in the book. Roy herself has said, "To me, I couldn't think of a better location for a book about human beings."

"The river has taught me to listen, you will learn from it, too. The river knows everything, one can learn everything from it. You have already learned from the river that it is good to strive downwards, to sink, to seek the depths," wrote Herman Hesse (1877-1962) in the allegorical novel in 1922. The many-voiced song of the river echoed softly for Siddharta. Roy's Meenachal also reflects many pictures in the flowing water. The river's voice was full of frothy mirth and happiness for the children Estha, Rahel and Sophie Mol. And it sang with yearning and sadness, for Ammu and Velutha, as it flowed towards its chartered journey down the bosom of the earth.

Place Attachment: A place can get itself attached in our subconscious mind in a most forceful way. The physical space of a river has always succeeded in leaving an indelible impression on most of the world renowned poets and authors. And Arundhati Roy is no exception. The Meenachal River gets firmly etched on the canvas of the novel, flowing in and out of the lives of the characters depicted in the novel.

The concept of place attachment is complex and multifaceted. Scholars from diverse backgrounds such as family studies, psychology, geography, social ecology and gerontology have proposed various frameworks for understanding the phenomena (Low and Altman, 1992).

Attachment is the process of turning physical space into a place endowed with either individual or collective meanings. As Low (1992) writes, place attachment is "the symbolic relationship formed by people giving culturally shared emotional affective meanings to a particular space or piece of land that provides the basis for the individual's and group's understanding of and relationship to the environment." Low (1992) had illustrated how place attachments involve shared cultural meanings and actions that derive from socio-political, historical, and cultural events associated with place. And the place specified here is the river.

> I was born upon thy bank, river
> My blood flows in thy stream,
> And thou meanderest forever
> At the bottom of my dream,

wrote Henry David Thoreau (*Journals* 1906). He further goes on to say that rivers must have been the guides which conducted the footsteps of the first travellers. They are the constant lure, when they flow by our doors, to distant enterprise and adventure, and by a natural impulse, the dwellers on their banks will at length accompany their currents to the lowlands of the globe, or explore at their invitation the interiors of continents.

In "The River of Rivers in Connecticut," Wallace Stevens had put all he had into praising the American river. In doing this, he was doing for his landscape what Wordsworth had done in Tintern Abbey in praising the English river Wye. Arundhati Roy, similarly, sets her novel, *The God of Small Things*, in a Kerala village known as Ayemenem. She brings alive this village of Kerala where she herself spent her childhood days and succeeds in bringing alive before us the idyllic locale of the River Meenachal.

The kind of landscape we grow up in, lives in us forever, wrote the novelist, Arundhati Roy. The rural environment was important for her. "I don't think it's true of people who've grown up in cities so much, you may love building but I don't think you can love it the way that you love a tree or a river or the colour of the earth, it's a different kind of love. I'm not a very well read person but I don't imagine that that kind of gut love for the earth can be replaced by the open landscape. It's a much cleverer person who grows up in the city, savvy and much smarter in many ways. If you spent your very early childhood catching fish and just learning to be quiet, the landscape just seeps into you. Even now, I go back to Kerala and it makes me want to cry if something happens to that place", says the writer Arundhati Roy. It's no wonder then that Roy, being a woman, could not resist the temptation and the pull of her heart to be voiceferous in her contention of the environmental degradation of the River Meenachal. She delves deep into the heart of Meenachal and pinpoints its environmental degradation. The novelist Roy's pet subject on her love of nature and the environment makes a deep impression in the novel.

An Eco-conscious Novelist

Eco-conscious as the novelist is, her concern for the environment finds an adequate expression in *The God of Small Things*. Jason Cawley, one of the five Booker judges writes, "Roy's achievement...is never to forget about small things in life, insects and flowers, wind and water, the outcaste and despised." The novel lays bare how our environment is being subjected to decay and destruction and points out the reasons that lie behind it.

Estha and Rahel dreamt of the river in their childhood. They had reason to do so:

> It was warm, The water. Grey green. Like rippled silk. With fish in it. With the sky and trees in it. And at night, the broken yellow moon in it.

The placid river with a boat in which Rahel and her twin brother sailed "so old a boat that it had taken root. Almost." They become part of the surroundings which crowd with its numerous beings and objects teeming and alive—the mesmerizing River Meenachal with its fish and the broken yellow moon in it. Arundhati Roy magnificently shows the river as an inseparable component in the lives of the characters, Chako, Ammu, Pappachi, Velutha and others where they grew and learned the priceless lessons of life. "Here they learned to work. To watch. To think thoughts and not voice them." The twins ply the old boat and carry it when on land through chumps of nettles.

Likewise, the twins arrival at Velutha's hut is described in all the details. They come inside the hut, put down their small boat that "smelled of fish curry and wood smoke". The twins tell Kuttappen, Velutha's disabled brother that the boat needed repairing. The boat is brought inside and examined by Kuttappen who also warns the children about the river, the Meenachal. Some prophetic words come from him. "Really a wild thing.... I can hear her at night-rushing past with moonlight, always in a hurry. You must be careful of her."

What is Ecofeminism and how does it bond with Mother Nature?

In Kenya, women of the Green Belt movement bond together to plant millions of trees in degraded lands. In India, they join the Chipko (Tree-hugging) movement to preserve the precious fuel resources for their communities. In Sweden, feminists prepare jam from berries sprayed with herbicides to offer a taste to members of parliament—they refuse. In the United States, housewives organize local support to clean up hazardous waste sites. All actions are examples of a worldwide movement known by many as 'ecofeminism' dedicated to the continuation of life on earth.

Ecofeminism emerged in the 1970s at a time when consciousness of the connection between woman and nature increased. The term 'ecofeminism' was coined in 1977 by the French writer, Francoise d' Eaubonne, who called upon women to lead an ecological revolution to save the planet. During the 1980s cultural feminists in the United States injected new life into ecofeminism by arguing that both women and nature could be liberated together. Liberal, cultural, social and socialist feminism have all been connected with improving the relationship between humans and nature and each has contributed to an ecofeminist perspective in different ways.

Cultural ecofeminists hold that women are closer to nature than men because of their physiology and social roles. An ecofeminist vision by which nature is held in esteem as mother and goddess is a source of inspiration and empowerment to women. The ecofeminists goal is to restore the quality of the natural environment for people and other living and non-living inhabitants of the planet.

Samantha J. Callender asks what is it about the idea of women having some intimate connection with nature that is so appealing to people. For centuries, men have had the notion that women somehow have a special connection with nature.

According to many, some deep-rooted instinctive connection exists between women and that which is nature.

Arundhati Roy, the ecofeminist, is deeply concerned about the environment. She opposes the projects to build big dams in the Narmada Valley both on the considerations of the adverse effect it will have on the environment as well as the misery it will definitely bring to many. The Narmada Valley Development Project, she informs us, "will alter the ecology of the entire river basin of one of India's biggest rivers. For better or for worse, it will affect the lives of twenty-five million people who live in the valley. It will submerge and destroy 4000 square kilometers of natural deciduous forest. Its impact on the environment and the people living along the valley is already severe".

We cannot but appreciate her concern for the environment. This finds adequate expression in *The God of Small Things*. Roy takes up the river Meenachal and entwines all the big and small characters of the novel in its encircling bosom. As an object of beauty, Meenachal seemed a joy forever. When Rahel returned twenty-three years later, to her native place, the river "greeted her with a ghastly skull's smile, with holes where teeth had been and a limp hand raised from a hospital bed". Though it was June and raining, "the river was no more than a swollen drain now. A thin ribbon of thick water that lapped wearily at the mud banks on either side, sequinned with the occasional silver of a dead fish. It was choked with succulent weed, whose furred brown roots waved like thin tentacles under water. Bronze-winged lily trotters walked across it. Splay-footed, cautious". The river was no more than a "slow, slugging green ribbon lawn that ferried garbage to the sea" now. Estha too found that the river "smelled of shit, and pesticides bought with World Bank loans. Most of the fish had died. The ones that survived suffered from fin-rot and had broken out in boils."

At this point, we may well remember Benjamin Franklin's words, "In rivers and bad governments, the lightest things swim at the top." The river Meenachal is shown as a sufferer in the novel. The first third of the river was their friend. Before the Really Deep began. They knew the afternoon weed that flowed inwards from the backwaters of Komarakom. The Second third was where the Really Deep began. The third was shallow again. The water brown and murky.

In the chapter entitled, "God's Own Country," Roy narrates how years later, when Rahel returned to the Meenachal River, it greeted her with a ghastly skull's smile. And, ironically, we here have an inverse reaction. The river Meenachal had shrunk, whereas Rahel had grown.

Shit and pesticides are the two sources of pollution. As for the shit, children of the shanty hutments on the other side of the river defecating on the river bed may be responsible for it. The water of the river is used for washing clothes and pots too upstream and receives "unadulterated factory effluents" as well. Little wonder then that in summer, "the shit lifted off the river and hovered over Ayemenem". Such a disaster could have been avoided had people stopped short of demanding more from the river than it could give. But the blind pursuit of immediate gain, called the steroid syndrome by Arundhati Roy elsewhere in the novel, left no room for sane thought: "Down river, a salt water barrage had been built, in exchange for votes from the influential paddy-farmer lobby. The barrage regulated the inflow of salt water from the back waters that opened in the Arabian Sea. So now they had two harvests a year instead of one. More rice, for the price of a river." Thus we find that it is not wisdom or science that prevails but votes and lobbies that control them, and have the decisive voice in our society. The river suffers and we hear an 'ecofeminists' wrath in the description of the polluted river.

Arundhati Roy when asked the question of how she got involved in Narmada said, "I did grow upon the banks of a river and I did love a river very much and I actually was in Kerala, in Kojhikode. Some people, who live on the banks of the Chaliyar, came and asked me to go to the house of this activist Rehman, who had been fighting this for so long, and who had just died. And I did (visit his house).

"I came back and read about what was happening there. Suddenly this whole system was conjured up. I somehow felt that this struggle in the Narmada Valley was a symbol of this whole system that is at work and I wanted to make an alliance with it. I wanted not to play safe. I wanted to say I am on this side and I am not hedging my bets about it. And I know that it is a dangerous thing to do because you take a lot of flak. But if you are committed you have to do that. You have to step into the firing line."

We are Woman and Nature

Women have been associated with Nature from times immemorial. It is as if women have succeeded in crafting for themselves a language and a temperament which makes them echo in words or in actions the thumping spirit residing in the heart of Mother Nature.

'Man' and 'Environment' are two words that have invaded almost all spheres known to recorded history. Used in combination or in isolation, these two words ultimately focus our attention on nature and its components—be it land, water, air or the diversity of living forms. From an anthropomorphic viewpoint, man firmly believes that he is the ultimate force that manipulates the vagaries of nature. Historical events suggest that it is the other way round. Time and again nature has shown that its design and purpose are least understood by human being. Several of man's attempts to conquer natural processes have boomeranged, at times leading to irreversible and irreparable damage to nature. Man has been at the receiving end whenever he tried to dictate terms while dealing with nature. In the interest of human welfare, man has to understand his position in the scheme of nature and *vice versa.* By environment, we mean not only our immediate surrounding but also a variety of issues connected with human activity, productivity, basic living and its impact on natural resources, such as land, water, atmosphere, forests, dams, habitat, health, energy resources, wildlife, etc.

Like other animals man depends on environment and becomes an environmental factor with respect to other members in an ecosystem. Susan Griffen holds on to the idea that we are woman and nature; women have always been personified as the earth—the generous mother. These words have been echoed by Bourke Coekran who says that the earth is a generous mother; she will provide in plentiful abundance food and shelter for all her children if they will but cultivate her soil in justice and in peace.

Mother Nature is a common representation of nature that focuses on the life-giving and nurturing features of nature by embodying it in the form of the mother. Image of women representing mother earth, and Mother Nature are timeless. In prehistoric times, goddesses were worshipped for their association with fertility, fecundity and agricultural bounty. Priestesses held dominion over aspects of Incan, Assyrian, Babylonian, Slavonic, Roman, Greek and Indian religions in the millennia prior to the inception of patriarchal religion.

Almost all the myths on creation centre around women, be it the Olympian Creation Myth or the Greek Myth. It's no wonder then that Arundhati Roy, being a woman, creates a language of her own in the novel whereby, through the delineation of the different characters, she successfully voice her earnest concern for the environment and her deep, deep love of Nature is reflected again and again through the depiction of the Meenachal river.

Women and Nature bonds together wonderfully well. This bond of women and nature was highlighted is a comparative study of Kalidas's "Shakuntala" and Shakespeare's "The Tempest" in a piece of literary criticism by Rabindranath Tagore. Shakuntala is spiritually a part of the forest in which she grew up. If the setting is taken away it harms not merely the story-line. Shakuntala herself would remain incomplete without it. Shakuntala is integrally related to nature. In Shakuntala the woods and the trees maintain their individual identity, yet are spiritually entwined with the heart of man. Rabindranath Tagore writes that it is only possible for Sanskrit literature to give dumb nature so essential, so living, and so direct a role in a play. He goes on to say that it is possible to humanize nature. Such a spirit is to be seen in all our ancient literature. Sita's heart weeps for the forest even when she returns to the palace as queen. Her closest friends seem to her to be the dark streams and deer, rather than the teeming humanity around her. Roy's heart also weeps for the degradation she sees in the environment. In her novel, *The God of Small Things*, she gives idyllic descriptions of the village green and the river Meenachal:

> The nights are clear but suffered with sloth and sullen expectation. But by early June, the south-west monsoon breaks and there are three months of wind and water with short spells of sharp, glittering sunshine that thrilled children snatch to play with. The countryside turns an immodest green. Boundaries blur as tapioca fences take root and bloom. Brick walls turn mossgreen. Peppervines snake up electric poles. Wild creepers burst through laterate banks and spill across the flooded roots. Boats ply in the bazaars.

Nature is here fully alive. Roy unifies with nature in this novel. The feminist writer Janet Biehl says that ecofeminist laid claim to this connection with nature as part of being woman. Today many female nature writers and feminists lay claim to a connection of oneness with nature. In her poem, "Wild," Mary Donahoe becomes a creature of the wild, roaming the woods and communing with nature. Likewise, Roy's notions and thoughts about nature flits in and out of the novel. Her concern for the environment is explicitly seen in her portraiture of the river Meenachal flowing in and out of the lives of the numerous characters in the novel. No wonder, then, the novelist Arundhati Roy, answers to this tug in her heart and becomes distinctly environmentally conscious in the novel. She is uncommonly sensitive to the presence of a divine beauty in nature.

Place Character

K.E. Paulson introduces the concept of place character as a conceptual tool to understand how locality matters. Place character, she argues, is important to understand how qualities of place combine and influence local patterns in meaning and action. To understand this, we must cruise down Roy's Mighty Meenachal just as Mark Twain's most influential character was probably the Mississippi River itself, similarly we find the Mighty Meenachal becoming the most influential character in, *The God of Small Things*. Just like the Mississippi River, the changing lights and shadows of River Meenachal is beautifully drawn.

The call for sociology of local place has received considerable response within academe. Michal M. Bell discusses that places exist in our experiences of both our social sentiments and material interests, in our connections to the "ghosts" that reside in these places. Ghosts of places, Bell remind us are not just about our past geographical locations, history, memories of times long gone, they are also our connections to the materiality of our existence—social structures, power and inequality, difference and distinctiveness (Bell, 1977). Similarly, Roy's love for the rural environment of Kerala, her love of the tree, the river and the local place where she grew up, shapes and gives birth to her novel. And as echoed by her again and again, it is indeed quite true that the kind of landscape we grow up in, lies in us forever. River Meenachal is, therefore, sketched out beautifully by the novelist in the novel. Mark Twain wrote about the Mississippi that the face of the water becomes a wonderful book...(with) a new story to tell every day.

The Meenachal, the Novel's Major Symbol

Let us pause for a moment and refer to the emotional connection formed by one of the most famous of the American poets, Langston Hughes, to a physical location—here also a river, in the most famous of all the river poems, "The Negro Speaks of Rivers".

Langston Hughes' prefaces his poem by describing the moment he wrote it: on a train as a young man after seeing the Mississippi for the first time. He remembers being so moved that he wrote it on the only paper he had: the back of an envelope. Hughes' description of the river and its personal, social and historical significance has the quality of a transcendental revelation.

The poem further stresses that despite anyone's race, everyone is connected to each other. Every person has the common ancestry that originates with Adam and Eve. Although the original river has widely branched out, humanity can always be connected and traced back to the very first river. The first river is symbolic that all human beings are children of God. Roy's small things, helped and assisted by the river of life, which happens to be the river Meenachal in the novel, succeeds in cruising down the river and carves out a niche for themselves in the hostile environment they had confronted but nevertheless succeeded in their own little small ways.

As Michael M. Bell points out in his analysis of the picturesque village of Childerley, place remains as vital for securing tradition as for manifesting class conflicts. Place in Childerley, as it is 'Between the Rivers' remains the interpretative frame for people to examine their material conflicts and to interpret and negotiate their ethno-social identities. River Meenachal, likewise, having assumed the concept of place character, very soon becomes the encyclopedia of race, class and culture in Roy's *The God of Small Things.* Places and landscapes serve as evidence of the perseverance of subcultures and the most beautiful landscape of Ayemenem with river Meenachal flowing by, succeeds in preserving the culture of the community and gives specific identities to each of the characters portrayed in the novel. Omi and Wimsatt's (1980) theory holds good in this novel, for they have successfully exemplified that literature on landscape and social/ethnic identity suggests that places and landscapes serve as evidence of the perseverance of subcultures who have struggled to successfully retain their cultural identities.

Meenachal and the Hierarchical Structure of Power

Hierarchical structure of power and oppression at various levels in patriarchal societies are explored in the novel. Vellya Paapen feared for his younger son. An unwarranted assurance that was so unbecoming for a Paravan. Vellya Paapen's bickering made Velutha shun his home. He worked late. He caught fish in the river and cooked it on an open fire. He slept outdoors on the bank of the river. Velutha is born Paravan, son of a Paravan, "a community in Kerala, subjected to extreme ignominy through the ages". To escape the inhuman humiliations, Velutha's forefathers had embraced Christianity. But the Christians themselves had adopted, as a matter of natural form of adoption, the strict and unavoidable caste-system, thus the Paravans had only received the status of "untouchable Christian" with a separate church and priest.

But Velutha knew that the river Meenachal was as much his as it was to the other high-born people of Ayemenem. He belonged to the river Meenachal as much as it belonged to him. The water, the river—and the mud of the river belonged to him, as was the fish of the river. He knew of the power of the river and respected Meenachal. He could cook the best fish curry. Red fish curry cooked with black tamarind "The best fish curry", according to Estha, in the whole world.

And it was Velutha who made Rahel her luckiest ever fishing rod and taught Estha and her to fish in the river. Velutha, who seems to have been made bold by the spirit residing in Meenachal. He worked late. Did he behave like a Paravan? No, definitely not. He had that 'unwarranted assurance. In the way he walked. The way he held his head. The quiet way he offered suggestion without being asked. Or the quiet way in which he disregarded suggestions without appearing to rebel. River Meenachal's calm exterior and beneath a turbulent spirit—this same spirit is epitomized by the writer in Velutha's personality. The wild spirit of the river turns him into a river god to come and recklessly make love to an upper-class woman, Ammu. Velutha, seized by the spirit of the river, mocks at the demarcation of race and culture, sculpted out in Ayemenem, and through one sweep of his broad, athletic body he had traversed man-made demarcation and division. River Meenachal rise supreme. It is that natural agent that whips up powers in the eddies and, whirlpools of a man's emotive spirit. In contrast to the oppressive places on land, the river Meenachal, like the river Mississippi in "The Adventures of Huckleberry Finn," promises release. The tyranny of Ayemenem, its orthodox Syrian Christian traditions, the Marxist leanings, the Paravan man-made customs, makes the Meenachal mock the static, stultifying society on its banks. The great flowing Meenachal chalks out the elusive freedom to anyone who is brave enough to accept it. Far from distorting social reality, the novel maps the meandering sentiments, emotions of the neglected in society through mappings of the different bends of the river Meenachal.

Ammu's Saviour

For Ammu, there was only Ayemenem now. Ayemenem and the river Meenachal was her only savior—a front verandah and a back verandah. A hot river and a pickle factory. River Meenachal tells the story of Ayemenem, the people residing on its banks, the lives of the characters entwined amidst its abundance of water. River Meenachal was Ammu's companion. She spent hours on the river bank with her little plastic transistor shaped like a tangerine and had midnight swims. To ferry the boat across the river to love by night the man her children loved by day. Ammu knew the river as well as her children did and could have reached it blindfolded. She would hurry through the undergrowth and turn her walk into a run. She would arrive on the banks of the Meenachal breathless and sobbing for her rendezvous with her forbidden lover.

The locale of Meenachal river at night adds a different dimension to the sad tale of Velutha-Ammu love, its dark depths, its turbulent flow of water, its rugged banks they all add symbolic connotation to their foredoomed relation. Roy writes, "without admitting to each other or themselves, they linked their fates, their future". In spite of the extreme mortal wounds inflicted on them, the cruelties meted out and the closing of all the ways of release, their love triumphed over everything else. The bank of the Meenachal provides the backdrop for their love and a promise for tomorrow. But for these two socially marginalized beings, the future proved to be bleak and dangerous. The fluid, free-flowing movements of the river obliterates their future. Ammu was dead and Velutha's skull was fractured in three places—the sad result of their forbidden love. The novel focuses on several themes, but each intertwined with the Meenachal. A rural setting, with the village river flowing endlessly on its way and journey towards the sea. The Syrian Christian family, the rigid caste system prevalent in the village, nevertheless, fails to stop the love of Ammu and Velutha, the untouchable. But River Meenachal is immune to this cultural trap and the social overtures of the village. In fact, the river assumes a profound place in the narrative—a unique example of how a place can assume the features of a character. River Meenachal opens its arms to the two lovers, like Paolo and Francesca's illicit love.

The Children and the River

May in Ayemenem is a hot, brooding month. The days drag on. And the river gets small in size. It shrinks. But by June, the south-west monsoon breaks and then there are three months of wind and water. After Estha's return from his father, he readily embraced Meenachal as his comrade and one whose soothing touch was like an embrace from a dear and trusted friend. In the wind and rain, on the banks of the river, in the sudden thunder darkness of the day, Estha keeps walking. Estha had always been a quiet child. But his quietness makes silent communion with the soul of the river. And, therefore, Estha who seldom talked, took to walks down the banks of the river. Estha seemed not to mind the ugly, little changes in the river as long as he could walk on the river bank. He could neither feel the wetness of the sand or the sudden shudder of the cold puppy that had temporarily adopted him and squelched at his side. He walked past the old mangosteen tree and up to the edge of a laterite spur that jutted out into the river. The wet mud of the river under his shoes made rude, sticking sounds. And Estha remained pleasantly oblivious to the cold puppy shivering and to the goings on in the world, as long as he had Meenachal near him. The twins dreamt of the river in their dreams. The river was always 'theirs'. The coconut trees that bent into it and watched, with coconut eyes, the boats slide by. Upstream in the mornings. Downstream in the evenings. And the dull, sullen sound of the boatmen's bamboo poles as they thudded against the dark oiled boatwood.

The water of Meenachal was warm and grey green. Like rippled silk. In an almost poetic language, Roy writes that Meenachal had fish in it. With the sky and trees in it and at night, the broken yellow moon in it.

Most of their childhood adventures were facilitated by the river. Clandestine trips to the river were organised when they were children. One day, Estha, Rahel and Sophie Mol, dressed up in saris and imagined themselves to be Mrs. Pillai, Mrs. Eapen and Mrs. Rajagopalan and went to visit Velutha. Velutha, in his turn, talked to the children about the weather and about the river. It was as if Velutha wanted the children to know how important the river was and to value and respect it.

Death in the River

Mammachi and Baby Kochamma got news of a white child's body found floating down river where the Meenachal broadens as it approaches the backwaters. The body was of Sophie Mol.

Three children on the river bank Estha, Rahel, and Sophie Mol frolicking in the thick outgrowth on the river bank. They drag the boat over the wet ground, for all of them to climb in. Estha walked into the water with the boat, his legs moving in the manner Velutha had taught him to do. The rain-fed Meenachal deceived them, as in the dark, they couldn't see that they were in the wrong lane. The boat got into trouble. Both Estha and Rahel somehow scrambled out, muddy and wet only to discover that Sophie Mol was not with them. The boat had disappeared. The dark river, Meenachal, had just accepted the boat's offering. The river was dark and quiet. An absence rather than a presence, betraying no sign of how high and strong it really was. When the boat tipped over, Sophie Mol got sucked in. There was no storm-music, Roy writes, nor did any whirlpool spun up from the inky depths of the Meenachal. Neither did any shark supervise the tragedy. 'Just quiet handing over ceremony.' Meenachal accepting the offering of one small life.

The Freudian Death Instinct

Much of the novel *The God of Small Things*, has much in common with another American masterpiece that breathes the Mississippi River in and out, *The Adventures of Huckleberry Finn*. Like the river, Huck's narrative flows spontaneously and ever onward. Around each bend lie a possible new adventure, in the eddies a lyrical interlude. The twin's narrative also flows spontaneously around the river Meenachal. Three children on the river bank hatch up a plot. Like Jim and Huck in *The Adventures of Huckleberry Finn*, the twins and Sophie Mol climbed onto the boat and prepared to sail down the dark and quiet Meenachal. Like Huck's faked and staged death, Sophie Mol had convinced the twins that they would absent themselves from the grownups for a long enough time to arouse their remorse, the elders would search everywhere and just when they were sure that all three of them were dead, they would return home in triumph, valued, loved, and needed more than ever. But Sophie Mol was not to return evermore. River Meenachal accepted the offering—Sophie Mol's body, even though there were no whirlpool spun up from the inky depths of its bottom.

There is death here and sorrow. Meenachal could not have avoided this painful death.

The ideal symbol is the dark river itself, which is suggestive of the Freudian death instinct, the unconscious instinct in all living things to return to non-living state and thereby achieve permanent surcease from the pain of living. Sophie Mol unknowingly achieves this, even before she was old enough to experience the pain of living. But for Ammu, of course, death was what she was actually waiting for, right after her separation from her husband and the experiences of the hostile community back home. Meenachal is the mighty force of nature and offers escape for Ammu and Velutha from the blighting tyranny of the conceited society of Ayemenem. Meenachal erases man's inhumanity to man in one violent and ruthless stroke.

Every thing around Ayemenem revolved around the Meenachal River. As T.S. Eliot had written in "The Dry Salvages", the river is a "strong brown god", it is an archetypal symbol of the mystery of life and creation—birth. The Meenachal proves to be an agent of purification and of divine justice. The Meenachal was no longer visible from the house anymore, but a seashell always retains a sea-sense and likewise the Ayemenem house still possessed a river-sense. And long after we had finished reading the novel this river-sense pervades through our senses and the Meenachal gets firmly etched in our consciousness as an encyclopedia of race, class and culture in *The God of Small Things*.

Works Cited

Cassidy, G. Casay. *Langston Hughes—Voice Among Voices*.

CNN. *Cruising Twain's Mighty Mississippi*, January 18, 1977.

Das, Bijoy Kumar. *Twentieth Century Literary Criticism.*

Deb, Indrani. *Heteroglossia*, Vol. III, 2006. Translation from Bengali *The Tempest* and *Shakuntla* by Rabindranath Tagore.

Goodman, W.R. *A Manual of American Literature.*

Guerin, Wilfred L. et al., *A Handbook of Critical Approaches to Literature.*

Hutton, Susan. *Features*, online journal.

Joseph, Kurian and R. Nagendran. *Essentials of Environmental Studies.*

Kumar, Aravind. *A Textbook of Environmental Science.*

Rajimwale, Sharad. *The God of Small Things.*

Roy, Amitabh. *The God of Small Things*: A Novel of Social Commitment.

Shukla, Bhaskar A. *South Asian Women Writers.*

Vendler, Helen (ed.). *Voices and Visions.*

Internet Sources

1. http:/www. ecofeminism: html
2. http:/www. creationmyths: html.

Articles

1. A Consideration of Collective Memory in African American Attachment to Wildland Recreation Places—Cassendra Y. Johnson, University of Georgia and USDA Forest Service, Southern Forest Experiment Station, U.S.A.
2. Growing Old in Rural Communities: A Visual Methodology for studying place attachment—James J. Ponzetti, Jr.
3. In the Name of Development—The Story Between the Rivers—by Damayanti Banerjee, Doctoral Candidate, University of Wisconsin—Madison.
4. The Ghosts of Place—Theory and Society—Michael M. Bell, 1997.

19

'Re-Vision'—Creating a New Stream of Novel Writing: Arundhati Roy's *The God of Small Things*

Ishmeet Kaur Chaudhry

Indian writing in English embraces a complete milieu of a literary culture of India. This has evolved as a separate canon which encompasses the social, political and cultural aspects. Significant contributions have been made in this area by prolific writers from the pre-independence era till date. Indian English has also become an influential voice of the nation and an essential medium of communication. Indian authors have acclaimed a significant place amongst the International best sellers. They have also won a number of awards—Indian and International. One such post-modern writer who shares a prominent place in this region is Arundhati Roy. She was awarded the Booker Prize in 1997 for her debut novel *The God of Small Things*. Autobiographical in content, the novel is a story of every Indian. Pictured in Kerala, the novel features common concerns, probably relevant to all states of India, through a set of fraternal twins, 7 years old. The prominent facets that the novel captures are Caste-system, Communism and feminism.

Out of all others, what makes Roy unique and so the novel also, is the creative, poetic and the imaginative writing style. "The careless, reckless lines were mistaken for artistic confidence, though in truth, their creator was no artist" (Roy 17). These lines rightly speak of Roy's experience, not only in the entrance exam for architecture, but also, in novel writing. The same "artistic confidence" shows itself in her first novel. All lines, plot, episodes and techniques seem to be perfectly mastered but are for sure accidental. Also, the "careless, reckless lines" are about her life and incidents. The novel being autobiographical in content is about Roy and is based on her experience of life.

The God of Small Things has created a new trend in Indian writing in English. It is about various different subjects, both simple and complex: love, madness, sex, revolt, anguish, joy and social, cultural, political and psychological human concerns. The depth and high seriousness with which Roy treats these issues and emotions makes them important concerns for life. The element of satire, little humour and a touch of innocence adds to the rhythmic poetical language and quality of narrative. She not only portrays the ways of the world but also attacks and challenges the hypocrisy of society. Roy is known to be one of those who dare to break the rules.

This paper is an attempt to bring out the various aspects which Roy has revisited in the social and cultural context related to a small state of Kerala. She says "They all crossed into forbidden territory. They all tampered with the laws that lay down who should be loved and how much." Likewise, Roy crosses the "forbidden boundaries" enters into the "unknown territories", only to discover what lies in them. Yet these "unknown territories" seem to be familiar to an average Indian reader, as it is a story of India and her people. This paper aims at how Roy captures these oppressive forces and creates a new form in the Indian Women Writings. It captures experience of women with an eye of a woman and gives its woman a new voice. The paper also focuses on how the language and the conventional themes are twisted, reshaped and restructured into a new model.

The God of Small Things is a "re-vision" not of an old text, but of a universal experience depicted through the various women in the novel. As Adrienne Rich speaks of "re-vision" as an "act of looking back, of seeing with fresh eyes, of entering an old text from a new critical direction—is for women more than a chapter in cultural history: it is an act of survival" (Dead 35).

In the same vein, the narrative is also about "an act of survival" for all the women in general. More so, it is an historical inversion from the past to the present, a struggle of the modern women to unravel the past and adapt to the present. The struggle for existence and identity universally represented through Ammu, who strives to find her own space, but is condemned by the society. Another quest for seeking a self-identity is depicted through the two twins, which is a representation of the two aspects or the two separated selves of an individual, perhaps that of Roy, as the novels bears autobiographical references. The opening passages of the novel that depicts the identity of the twins as a joint entity, "Esthappen and Raphel thought of themselves together as Me, and separately, individually, as We or Us," (Roy 2), collides with the incestuous contact towards the close of the novel. Though this collision apparently seems to be destructive but is contemplative and reflective of a definitive search for identity. The incestuous love-making of the twins signifies a re-joining of the separated selves into back into one whole. In this connection Scott Trudel says:

> The twins love-making is a metaphor for their search for this fractured and traumatized joint identity in their adulthood, and it is a real, physical and emotional expression of their grief and longing. (4)

This is significant of a re-union. Also, the episode of this incestuous love-making appears in the last chapter of the novel as a flash back in the past. It seems to be cleverly patterned technique in the plot, by giving the novel a circular for. The novel starts with the twins and completes with the twins, finishing as a complete circle.

Ammu is shown to be a young widow neglected by almost everybody. She has no support in her life and looks up to Velutha who offers himself to her unconditionally. Velutha is a medium of escape from the turmoil and the suffering she faces in her life. He becomes a symbol of fulfillment for her. This relationship gains further significance when contrasted to Chacko's relationship with a lowly women. Ammu meets the contempt of the people around her who term her relationship as illicit, unethical, immoral and sinful, whereas Chacko's musing is the "Man's need". This highlights the bias of the society towards men. Chacko gets away with everything and Ammu pays for every 'sin' she commits. Roy attacks the hypocrisy of the Indian society where men are given prominence over women. She questions the old norms and highlights the oppressions of the patriarchal society carried on women.

The novel evolves as a new canon of women's writing wherein the nature of the male-dominated world and outlook on the issues related to female, are questioned, exposed and attacked. This also becomes a record of the suppressed female experience. It exposes the so-called mechanisms of patriarchy and a cultural mind-set based on such notions.

The position of the women folklore in India and the constant struggle of the women against their incessant exploitation, torture and struggle has been realistically depicted by Roy. The marginalized or the other the "untouchable" Velutha and Ammu's share a similar position that of being deprived, exploited and unacceptable.

Marginality is another theme dealt within the novel. Roy points out the distinction based on castes within the Indian society. The age-old discrimination is still prominent and has been the great impediment in the growth of the down-trodden. In this connection Trudell aptly says:

> Roy allows the reader an insight into the emotional basis behind the careful, planned brutality of those dedicated to Kerala's social code, such as the Touchable Policemen who believe that in beating Velutha to death they are enforcing the Love Laws and "inoculating a community against an outbreak". (2)

The contrast between the two sections of the society, the touchable and the untouchable, is depicted in the contrast between the Big God and the Small God. The Big God presides over the bigger aspects, incidents and happenings in the world, which are "vast, violent, circling, driving, ridiculous, insane, unfeasible, public turmoil of a nation". Whereas the Small God is "cozy and contained, private and limited" and resides amongst the people chained in the engrossing forces from which liberation is impossible. These forces do not let them understand and change. They further turn "resilient and truly indifferent" and take resort in mass movements. This is a time when the idea of democracy brings with it a social change in India. As a consequence it is a time of transition for people and also difficult for them to accept the change. The narrative points out the conflict and relevantly, relates it, to the cause of many problems. In the same vein Douglas Dupler suggests:

> The characters in Roy's novel exist in a culture of strict rules. There is a caste system and a class system that exert much force upon the characters. Conflict is created for individuals who can't adhere to these systems of social organization and control. Indeed the greatest conflict in the story, a love affair between Ammu and Velutha, is the result of individuals rebelling against the historical and cultural structures of caste and class; this is an affair between a Touchable and an Untouchable. (12)

Through this Roy brings a struggle between individuals and the class, where the individual seem to be struggling for his/her democratic rights, Ammu for her liberation from the traditional notions of feminist restrains and Velutha, from the discrimination based on class and creed.

Dupler also suggests that the narrative bears a colonial influence due to the presence of Margaret and also because of Chacko's education in England; Baby Kochamma's conversion into a Roman Catholic (13). It would not be appropriate to rate these influences as a result of colonial experience as Margaret's union and later divorce to Chacko is because of the reason of Chacko's education in England. Probably, England finds prominence in the novel because of the influence of Christianity in Kerala which is very old and bears a historical reference to the Syrian Christians and not because of the Britishers historical incursion. Rather, it is a post-colonial aspect when studying abroad has become common and an average Indian has an easy access into other countries.

More than this, the language and the style becomes classic and unique as Arundhati Roy delights in verbal innovation and stylistic tricks. She liberates narrative writing of the traditional patterns and form. Non-conformity to language rules is apparently visible. She joins words together according to her convenience and doesn't bother about capital or small letters or about spacing within the word such as when Ammu asks Rahel to "stoppit", Rahel "stoppitted". At times she uses joined words as "whatisit?", "whathappened?" In the same connection Joyce Hart quotes:

> ...but with one more distinctive characteristic added to the mix—Roy's poetic and imaginative writing style....
>
> One of the first elements of the author's writing that readers confront as they begin this novel is Roy's creative vocabulary—creative in the sense that she makes new words. (4-5)

Hart points out that this serves two purposes, one it serves to attract reader's attention and second, that it this technique describes the objects with much greater depth than most single adjectives and metaphors could possibly do. He says that such words "offer the reader vivid images through short expressive words" (5). This sort of verbal exuberance adds to Roy's originality.

The use of pun and irony is used intelligently to point-out at some sensitive social concerns. Evident from the episode when Ammu's goes to the police station and meet Inspector Thomas Mathew, he casually taps at Ammu's breasts. Roy highlights the action as casually as the attitude of the policeman:

> 'If I were you,' he said, 'I'd go home quietly.' Then he tapped her breasts with his baton. Gently. Tap, tap. As though he was choosing mangoes from a basket. Pointing out the ones threat he wanted packed and

> delivered. Inspector Thomas Mathew seemed to know whom he could pick on and whom he couldn't.
>
> Policemen have that instinct. (8)

Behind the policeman, were a red and a blue board on which described "POLICE" as Politeness, Obedience, Loyalty, Intelligence, Courtesy, and Efficiency. Ammu was called a *vesya*, by the inspector and the children asked the meaning of the term. Roy points out at the erogenous hunger of these strata of society. The art of her craft lies in the fact, that neither does she sermonize, nor is harsh, while dealing with such issues. She handles such cases very casually, sensitively and tactfully when she points at the objectionable things. Her writing tends towards abstraction and generalization as it aims for a detached and a 'scientific coolness' of tone. But, at the same time, she provokes the thought of the reader by reflecting such situations in reality.

Corresponding, a decline in the Marxist's values has been emphatically depicted. The various themes of discrimination and dominance of the male patriarchy are interwoven to bring out the rift between the rich (have) and the poor (have-not), the weak and powerful, and the touchable and the untouchable. The Marxist's values contrasts the actions of Comrade Pillai. When Velutha is arrested, the comrade disowns Velutha, who was a worker of Comrade's party. Inspector Mathew goes to arrest Velutha but before arresting he goes to confirm the truth behind the charges levied on him. The comrade, not only refuses to acknowledge him, but also doesn't refute the charges. This gives the inspector all the more reason to torture Velutha to death. Roy, this ways has effectively satirized politics and the political parties. The ideology becomes more theoretical and is a political confute in reality. She explains how people modern politics is suffused with dishonesty, falsehood and deception.

The story evolves out of an unconventional narrative style unlike the traditional narrative order. The plot works on a memory-lane rather than opening up sequentially. It is similar to the stream of consciousness technique. More so, the style is poetical and whimsical. Even a small action of blowing the nose is explained thus:

> Rahel summoned all her strength. *Please God, please make it come out.* From the soles of her feet, from the bottom of her heart, she blew into her mother's handkerchief. (133)

The force with which Rahel blows her nose has been presented with a unique and detailed seriousness. The perspective in the entire narrative at all stages of life, be that of childhood, adulthood or any other period is beautifully rendered with a creative amalgamation of inventiveness, independence, originality and wonder.

There is a great deal of realism within the novel. The depiction of South India is the real India, quite near to reality, and not that of a creative imagination. Her originality lies in portraying the cultural, political and the social trends through a lifetime creation of such characters who are a replica of their people. Roy's technique is unique also because she has employed what is called an "architectural method" probably, a term connected to her writing because she was educated as an architect. Roy claims that:

> I would start somewhere and I'd colour in a bit and then I would deeply stretch back and then stretch forward. It was like designing an intricate balanced structure. (Qtd. In Sinha *God* 15)

It seems that Roy employs a similar method in writing the novel. This technique brings with it a revolution and a birth of a new style of writing. The novel also "starts somewhere", is coloured a bit, then stretches back and moves forward and finally knits into a balanced structure.

The narrative is an amalgamation of many techniques of novel writing, more correctly novel and poetry writing. A few important things that are prominent in the novel are: realism woven into imagination, perspective, the point of view, the narrative and the stream of consciousness technique with a precision of architectural balance. The autobiographical content which reveals through the depiction of the two seven-year-old twins is a portrayal of the two-sides of Roy's own character. The last chapter of the novel reveals a love-making of the twins. The love-making is the reunion of the two divided selves of a single personality. The perspective and the point of view is depicted through actions, settings, events and characters as an integral part of the novel. Various characters in the novel have their own point of view and each of them through this represent an ideology in the true sense. Most of the musings and the observations within the novel deal with those of the twins—Rahel and Estha. They are a representation of the innocence of a child who features the details of events as they happen without adding their analysis or critical comments.

Their mother, Ammu's point of view is the ideological inversion from the traditional mindset into the modern. She also depicts a revolt from the age-old clichés of society. She also represents the dominated Indian woman who is a victim to the oppressions of the male-dominated society. Baby Kochamma and Uncle Chacko are representative of the rigid norms of society, who look at others skeptically.

In conclusion, it would be appropriate to point out, that Roy has not looked at various themes as a confrontation or rebellion against the hypocritical society, by attacking the problem of unapproachability and by questioning the position of women only. She creates a wave where the depiction of various socio-cultural aspects meet a satisfying end in union. This union is symbolic of integrity and harmony even in disorder. She also creates a style of writing by forsaking the conventions and rules of language. It seems that novel liberates itself and the whole tradition of novel writing from the shackle of rule and regulations. The theme, style, structure and the technique have a sense of freedom, it seems that Roy herself seeks liberation from the suffering in her past through the creation of this masterpiece. More so, novel also voices many underlying concerns to which society is a victim. This truly Indian piece sets a new trend in novel writing in India with the precision and perfection of such an artist whose "careless, reckless lines" actually bear an "artistic confidence".

Works Cited

Arundhati, Roy. *The God of Small Things*. India: Penguin Books, 1997.

Bhatt, Indira. *Arundhati Roy's The God of Small Things*. India: Creative Books, 1999.

Dhawan, R.K. *Arundhati Roy: The Novelist Extra-ordinary*. India: Prestige Pub., 1999.

Dodiya, Jaydip Singh. The Critical Studies of Arundhati Roy's *The God of Small Things*. (ed.) India: Altantic Pub., 1999.

Rich, Adrienne. "When We Dead Awaken: Writing as Re-vision". *On Lies, Secrets and Silence*. New York: W.W. Norton, 1979.

Sharma, R.S. *Arundhati Roy's The God of Small Things*, Critique and Commentary. India: Creative Books, 1998.

Sinha, R. *Arundhati Roy: The God of Small Things*. India: Educational Publishers, 2000.

Sunderan, K.V. *The God of Small Things: A Saga of Lost Dreams*. India: Atlantic Pub., 2000.

On-line Articles

Trudell, Scott. "Critical Essay on *The God of Small Things*" *Novels for Students*. Thomson Gale, 2006. http://www.answers.com /topic/the-god-of-small-things-criticism. 23rd Nov, 2009, 1-4.

Dupler, Douglas. "Critical Essay on *The God of Small Things*" Novels for Students. Thomson Gale, 2006. http://www. answers.com/topic/the-god-of-small-things-criticism. 23rd Nov. 2009, 12-16.

Hart, Joyce. "Critical Essay on *The God of Small Things*" *Novels for Students*. Thomson Gale, 2006. http://www.answers.com /topic/the-god-of-small-things-criticism. 23rd Nov., 2009, 5-8.

Contributors

Esterino Adami. University of Turin, Italy.

Jackie Haque. Senior Lecturer, Tarunnessa Memorial Medical College, Gazipur, Bangladesh.

Meenakshi Raman. Associate Professor of English and Communication, Group Leader, Languages and Management Group, BITS Pilani-Goa Campus, Zuari Nagar, Goa.

Erin Warde. Professor Menon, GIS in Post-Colonial Theory and Literature.

John Nkemngong Nkengasong and **Magdelene Atanga Mafor.** Department of English, University of Yaounde 1, Cameroon.

Diviani Chaudhuri. Department of Comparative Literature, State University of New York at Binghamton.

Alessandro Monti. The Department of Oriental Studies, University of Turin, Italy.

Anita Myles. Reader in English, D.D.U. Gorakhpur University, Uttar Pradesh.

Nishi Pulugurtha. Senior Lecturer, Department of English, Brahmanand Keshab Chandra College, Kolkata, West Bengal.

Garima Gupta. Lecturer, School of Languages, SMVDU, Katra, Jammu and Kashmir.

Prakash Chandra Pradhan. Department of English, B.H.U. Varanasi, Uttar Pradesh.

Christina Bertrand Firebaugh. Doctoral Student in English Literary, University of Denver, Denver, Colorado, U.S.A.

Arpa Ghosh. Senior Lecturer in English, Vivekanand College for Women, Barisha, Kolkata, West Bengal.

Vandana Datta. Department of English, College of Commerce, Patna, Bihar.

Purnendu Chatterjee. Research-scholar, Rabindra Bharati University and Assistant-Master, Hooghly Collegiate School, West Bengal.

Arindam Das. Lecturer in English, Department of Humanities, Heritage Institute of Technology, Kolkata, West Bengal.

Reena Mitra. Senior Reader, Department of English, Christ Church P.G. College, Kanpur, Uttar Pradesh.

Joyashri Choudhury. Lecturer, Department of English, Khagarijan College, Nagaon, Assam.

Ishmeet Kaur Chaudhry. Faculty in Comparative Literature in the School of Language, Literature and Culture Studies, Central University of Gujarat, Gandhi Nagar, Gujarat.